STOP THE INTRUDER™ | KNOWLEDGE IS THE BEST PROTECTION™

STOP THE INTRUDER™

Knowledge is the best protection!™

By K. David Benton

Gold Seal Productions, LLC ™
Atlanta, GA

STOP THE INTRUDER™ | KNOWLEDGE IS THE BEST PROTECTION™

STOP THE INTRUDER™
Published by
Gold Seal Productions, LLC™
2451 Cumberland Parkway, Suite 3496
Atlanta, GA 30339-6157
(866) 613-3653

Copyright © 2012 by Gold Seal Productions, LLC, Atlanta, Georgia.

No part of this publications may be reproduced, stored in a retrieval system or transmitted in any form or means except as permitted under Sections 107 or 108 of the 1976 US Copyright Act.

GOLD SEAL PRODUCTIONS MAKES NO REPRESENTATIONS OR WARRANTIES REGARDING THIS EBOOK, EDUCATIONAL MATERIALS, WEBSITE OR THERE CONTENTS. ALL INFORMATION IS PROVIDED FOR USE "AS IS." GOLD SEAL PRODUCTIONS DISCLAIMS ALL WARRANTIES, EXPRESS OR IMPLIED, INCLUDING WITHOUT LIMITATION THE IMPLIED WARRANTIES OF TITLE, NON-INFRINGEMENT, MERCHANTABILITY AND FITNESS FOR A PARTICULAR PURPOSE, WITH RESPECT TO THE WEB SITE, EDUCATIONAL MATERIALS AND ANY WEB SITE WITH WHICH IT IS LINKED. GOLD SEAL PRODUCTIONS ALSO MAKES NO REPRESENTATIONS OR WARRANTIES AS TO WHETHER THE INFORMATION ACCESSIBLE VIA THIS WEB SITE, OR ANY WEB SITE WITH WHICH IT IS LINKED, IS ACCURATE, COMPLETE, OR CURRENT.

Gold Seal Productions and its agents, employees, suppliers, and contractors shall in no event be liable for any claims, charges, and contractors damages, liabilities, losses, and expenses of whatever nature and howsoever arising, including, without limitation any compensatory, consequential, incidental, direct, indirect, special, punitive, or damages, loss of use, loss of data, loss caused by a computer or electronic virus, loss of income or profit, loss of or damage to property, claims of third parties, or other losses of any kind of character, even if Gold Seal Productions has been advised of the possibility of such damages or losses, arising out of or in connection with the use of this Web site, or any Web site with which it is linked. You assume total responsibility for establishing such procedures for data back up and virus checking, as you consider necessary.

It is your responsibility to evaluate the accuracy and completeness of all information, opinions, and other material in this book and website or any website with which it is linked. Price information is subject to change without notice.

All Rights Reserved, Copyright 2012

ISBN-10: 0985217502
ISBN-13: 978-0-9852175-0-1
LCCN: 2012946277 (Library of Congress Number)

STOP THE INTRUDER™ | KNOWLEDGE IS THE BEST PROTECTION™

Acknowledgements

I would like to thank my wonderful wife, Maria, without her encouragement and support, this would have never been possible.

I would also like to thank:

- Angela Turlington and Kristine Smith, who patiently edited this manuscript;
- Phillip Mahan, who worked countless hours on our marketing plan; and
- Dasha Perlin, who provided her illustrations and artistic touches.

STOP THE INTRUDER™ | KNOWLEDGE IS THE BEST PROTECTION™

Table of Contents

Description 8

The Facts 9

About the Author 10

Chapter 1 – Security Fundamentals 12

Security Myth

Four Elements of the Golden Triangle

Access

Cover

Escape

Opportunity

Chapter 2 - Defense in Depth 21

Zone Two - Inner Funneling Zone

Recap

Doors and Windows

Door Anatomy

Locks 101

Windows

Place lighting near windows

Communications

Protective Measures

Chapter 3 - Home Invasion Planning 46

Choice 1: Comply

Choice 2: Flee

Choice 3: Resist

Sound

Early Warning Systems

Man's Best Friend

Electronic Early Warning Systems

Alarms

Emergency Communication Plan

Communication Devices

Chapter 4 - Digital Valuables 59

Sensitive Data

Partition Encryption

Container Encryption

Chapter 5 - Emergency Disc 76

Security Containers

Inventory/Marking

Chapter 6 - Lethal Force 81

Firearms

Research

Locate a Firearms Range

Purchasing Decisions

Types of Home Protection Firearms

Shotgun

Legal Considerations

Self Defense

Conclusion 104

Appendix 1 - Emergency Contact List 106

Appendix 2 - First Aid Equipment 107

Appendix 3 - State Crime Analysis 108

Historical Information 159

Murder and Manslaughter 159

Historical Information 160

Forcible Rape 160

Historical Information 161

Robbery 161

Historical Information 162

Aggravated Assault 162

Historical Information 163

Burglary 163

Historical Information 164

Larceny-Theft 164

Historical Information 165

Burglary 165

Locksmiths by State 166

Crime Analysis 203

Robbery Location Analysis 204

Burglary Location Analysis 204

Larceny-Theft Location Analysis 205

Larceny Theft by Value 205

Regional Information 206

Interview with a Killer 207

Resource List - Alphabetical 273

References 307

Description

This training course reveals what you need to know to protect your home, family and property from the scoundrels who make their living ripping people off while utterly annihilating their sense of security.

By taking the necessary steps to protect your family and reduce the likelihood of a break-in or home invasion, you'll sleep better... and your insurance rates will likely drop, too, when you can prove what you've done to keep your premises secure and your loved ones safe.

STOP THE INTRUDER™ | KNOWLEDGE IS THE BEST PROTECTION™

The Facts

Security is most robust when established in a series of four security zones. This audio series describes each of these zones in detail and tells you, step by step, how to create them.

Next, we'll expose the methodology of criminals. When scouting out new victims, criminals search for four things that help them commit their crimes. These four elements form "the golden triangle". We'll fully explain each element and reveal how to use effective countermeasures against them.

Finally, we'll show you how to protect your privacy using data encryption, how to safeguard your computer with data backup, how to create an effective communication plan, and we'll share information for using lethal and nonlethal force.

About the Author

David Benton has been a security professional for almost two decades. Initially trained as a Counterintelligence Special Agent with the US Army, he worked in numerous operations performing security assessments and conducting investigations.

After leaving the Army, he worked for the Georgia Bureau of Investigation as a supervisor of its Computer Evidence Recovery Team. He is the author of two books and numerous articles. Benton received extensive training at the US Army Intelligence Center at Fort Huachuca, Federal Bureau of Investigation's Quantico Training Facility and has worked on a team that received an award from the Director of the Central Intelligence Agency.

In this ground-breaking training course, his background, skills and abilities are distilled into practical easy-to understand steps to give you the information you need to STOP THE INTRUDER!

STOP THE INTRUDER™ | KNOWLEDGE IS THE BEST PROTECTION™

Chapter 1
Security Fundamentals

STOP THE INTRUDER™ | KNOWLEDGE IS THE BEST PROTECTION™

Chapter 1 – Security Fundamentals

Your home is your castle. It contains memories, emotions, and treasures. You may consider it secure. But how would you feel to arrive home one day to find irreplaceable mementos of times past and loved ones gone ransacked, items passed down from generation to generation gone forever? Even if you rent your home and have nothing of significant sentimental or commercial resale value in the way of treasures, your rental is where you go to relax and unwind at the end of the day. It's your sanctuary; you probably consider it safe.

When an uninvited intruder makes his presence known (immediately as with a home invasion robbery or with the trail of tears and terror he leaves behind when you're not home) what you lose?in addition to any valuables you may have?and miss most is your sense of security. Everyone living with you becomes traumatized. Knowing that someone has violated your space hits you in the gut and in the heart.

STOP THE INTRUDER™ | KNOWLEDGE IS THE BEST PROTECTION™

The violation is compounded when the trespasser is a professional criminal and has gained unrestricted access to your personal effects and private information. And if he (or she) breaks in, you face the additional expense of immediately ordering emergency repairs (or making them yourself), including taking increased security measures to help ensure that you never face the nightmare again.

To truly understand the emotional impact of a break?in, imagine it; take a walk in the virtual nightmare of returning home and discovering a kicked?in front door. It's hanging haphazardly by a single hinge. Inside, everything is overturned; some of your belongings are broken. The jewelry handed down from your beloved grandparent is gone. Your electronic equipment is gone or lies in ruins. The family computer is gone, taking with it the only copy of the pictures you've taken of your kids growing, your wedding day and honeymoon, and more. Your intimate apparel has been handled, rifled, perhaps defiled, and is lying all over your bedroom.

Dread and anger enter your life with a vengeance; you can't shake the feelings. You've been violated. Your home has become the proving ground for a long-lasting, unshakeable nightmare.

> **EACH ADDITIONAL LAYER OF SECURITY PROVIDES AN ENVELOPE OF PROTECTION.**

This scenario happens every day in nearly every neighborhood across the United States. The hardest truth to take in is that, in many circumstances, the nightmare is avoidable.

The purpose of this series is to show you the principles and methods that will decrease the likelihood of this happening to you and your loved ones. The principles are straightforward, easy to understand and employ, and cost effective. You can apply the principals, with some slight modifications, in single-family homes, apartments, town homes, condos and mobile homes.

Security Myth

While achieving absolute security is elusive (even the Pentagon was breached on 9/11), it's possible to make your surroundings much more secure. Each additional layer of security provides an envelope of protection. This layering concept is called defense in depth. The layers enhance each other and provide additional benefits above and beyond any single application.

This "snowball security effect" can be significant. Just as tearing a single piece of paper by hand is a cinch; trying to tear apart an inch?thick stack becomes impossible. No professional burglar will waste the time trying; there are easier pickings next door or just down the street.

Routine use of a residence or property increases your security risk. The more you use your property (and/or invite others to use it), the harder it is to secure. Here's an example: you can make your computer 100% secure from the threat of viruses and malware. It's easy! Simply disconnect the computer from the Internet, unplug it from the power, and put it inside a fireproof, high-security safe! Your computer will never be infected by a virus or worm again.

In the same way, the more you use an item or your property, the greater the challenge it is to secure. The human factor is significant. The greatest potential risk to security is the human ability to move around. As humans interact with things, Murphy's Law enters the game. When more than one person is involved, security becomes more difficult. Add children and young adults and security becomes an even-greater challenge. Each of these challenges creates unique difficulties and opportunities.

Stopping an intruder isn't as simple as installing one type of lock or having a particular security system. Security is a mindset: embrace and integrate it into everyday life so you can rest easier knowing that potential breaches have been dealt with routinely while you're relaxed and in full control of your emotions. Education and vigilance, combined with interlocking security layers, can save you a bundle and ensure peace of mind. The layers work together and complement each other.

STOP THE INTRUDER™ | KNOWLEDGE IS THE BEST PROTECTION™

This session teaches the application of four specific layers of home security.

They are:

1. Outer deterrent zone

2. Inner funneling zone

3. Access control zone

4. Refuge

To understand home security defense, let's fully examine and understand what's involved. The two primary threats we'll address here are burglary and home invasion/robbery. Each of these presents specific challenges. The Federal Bureau of Investigation collects, analyzes and publishes a range of information about crimes via the Uniform Crime Reports (UCR) for use by public and private sectors.

A burglary occurs when someone unlawfully enters a residence or other structure for the purpose of committing a crime. The FBI reported (as part of the 2010 UCR) that a burglary occurs every 14.6 seconds. There were an estimated 2.1 million burglaries within
the United States in 2010. Burglary accounts for more than 23 percent of the total number of property crimes committed within the United States. An analysis revealed the following:

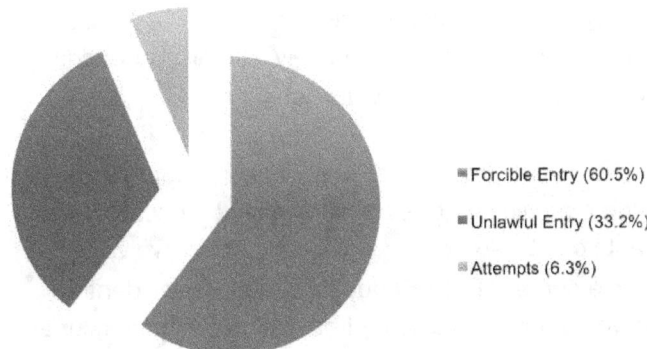

STOP THE INTRUDER™ | KNOWLEDGE IS THE BEST PROTECTION™

Forcible entry refers to the breaking of an access control point or device in a successful effort to gain entry. An unlawful entry occurs when someone enters an unauthorized area for illicit purposes but doesn't necessarily break or destroy an access control point. (An example of this would be entering a house through an unlocked door or window.)

According to the FBI's UCR, the average burglary costs the victim more than $2100. Individual residences aren't the only targets of criminals: commercial enterprises can also be victimized. To reduce the loss to their bottom line, many businesses aggressively invest money in security. Many have loss prevention programs aimed at reducing the risk of burglary, shoplifting and other common avenues of loss. This increased commercial security posture has caused many criminals to focus their efforts on residential communities and individual homes.

Criminals consider a private house a prime opportunity. Hard earned property and valuables are their targets. Statistics demonstrate that most residential burglaries happen during the day when homeowners and their dependents are at school or work. On average, burglaries increase during the summer months and are at their lowest historically in February. Based on arrest information, the average burglary is committed by a male, twenty-five years old or younger.

These criminals are looking for items that are easy to convert to cash, including jewelry, guns, watches, laptop computers, VCRs, video players, CDs, electronic game stations and other easy-to-carry high-dollar devices. The stolen goods can be sold online or through "fences" or pawnshops. The FBI's 2010 Uniform Crime Report noted that just over 18 percent of property crimes were cleared by arrest or other means. This means a residential burglar has an 82 percent chance of getting away with his or her crime! It's no small wonder why they keep their dirty day jobs!

The second crime is the home invasion or residential robbery. A home invasion occurs when a criminal enters a home while the occupants are present. These events can be extremely violent and may involve the commission of multiple crimes. The FBI doesn't separate residential robberies (also known as home invasions) from robberies that occur at other locations (e.g., in a vehicle or on a street corner) so it isn't possible to provide specific statistical information on these crimes. But make no mistake: home invasion crimes are among the most frightening and traumatic events when viewed from the victims' standpoint.

An example of a home invasion robbery occurred in Cheshire, Connecticut on July 23, 2007. Two men fled from a home which was engulfed in flames. After ramming a police car, the men were apprehended. In the front of the house lay 50 year old Dr. William A. Petit. He had been severely beaten. After the Fire Department extinguished the flames, the bodies of his wife, Jennifer Hawke-Petit, 48, and their daughters, Hayley, 17, and Michaela, 11, were found.

The police investigation revealed that the men had targeted Mrs. Petit and her daughter Michaela while they were grocery shopping. The men followed them home and returned later in the evening. They entered the home through an unlocked door and found Dr. Petit asleep on a couch. They viciously beat him. They moved upstairs where they subdued the ladies, then separated and tied them up in different bedrooms. Mrs. Petit and her youngest daughter were sexually assaulted before the house was set on fire. Both men were convicted of these crimes and are currently in prison.

DID YOU KNOW?

THE AVERAGE RESIDENTIAL BURGLARY RESULTS IN A LOSS OF OVER $ 2,000 PER OCCURRENCE.

(HOW MUCH COULD A PROFESSIONAL BURGLAR "EARN" BREAKING INTO YOUR HOME?)

To effectively prevent crimes, it's important to understand the elements required to commit a particular crime from the criminal's prospective. The criminal's perceived need is the driving factor for the commission of his or her crime. The purpose may be to obtain some money or property to exchange for drugs or to feed some other illicit habit. Although on rare occasions a crime may be committed to feed a criminal's family, this is generally not the driving factor. Robbery may simply be the most expedient manner for a criminal to generate income.

STOP THE INTRUDER™ | KNOWLEDGE IS THE BEST PROTECTION™

Crimes can be highly sophisticated (Oceans 11) or ridiculously simple. In either case, it's important to understand the elements in terms of "the golden triangle". To successfully repeat crimes, criminals master the various elements of the golden triangle; their failure to do so will likely result in swift arrest.

Four Elements of the Golden Triangle

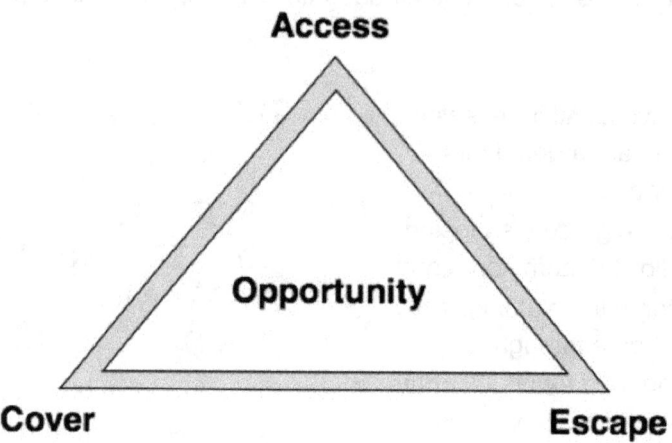

Access
A criminal must be able to physically obtain items to commit a residential burglary/robbery. Frequently this involves disabling an access control device (a lock or some other item).

Cover
A criminal must remain hidden to avoid detection. Any time a break-in is observed, emergency responders will likely be quickly notified. By using appropriate cover, a criminal ensures that he/she has the time it will take to fully exploit all of the items at a given location.

Escape
The criminal's ability to fulfill his driving need and leave the scene with the items he wants. If a criminal can't avoid swift capture, he or she is less likely to engage in the activity in particular locations.

STOP THE INTRUDER™ | KNOWLEDGE IS THE BEST PROTECTION™

Opportunity

A criminal is always seeking, or attempting to create, the right time to commit a crime. The opportunity may be a garage door inadvertently left open during the day or an unlocked window. These provide an optimal opportunity for a criminal to obtain their heart's desire.

The golden triangle also provides an effective blueprint for creating defense in depth strategies to stop the intruder. By carefully examining each of these elements, opportunities can be mitigated or altogether neutralized. By effectively combining countermeasures to each of these items, your residence can become a fortified castle.

Chapter 2
Defense in Depth

Chapter 2 - Defense in Depth

Securing your home is best done by creating a series of security layers. These layers create a synergy. This means by combining them together it creates a much greater effect than by adding one to another. If security could be numerically measured then a synergy is created by multiplying two numbers together instead of adding two numbers together.

$$\text{Regular - } 4 + 4 = 8.$$

$$\text{Synergy - } 4 \times 4 = 16$$

Zone One - Outer Deterrent Zone
This zone begins ten feet from the side of your residence and extends outward to approximately 100 feet, or to the edge of your property line (whichever comes first). This zone often has strangers passing through it at different times. In some urban areas your property line may be just steps away so specific modifications and countermeasures must be employed to effectively address the issue.

STOP THE INTRUDER™ | KNOWLEDGE IS THE BEST PROTECTION™

The purpose of the outer deterrent zone is two fold.

First, it should create an impression of the residence. The overriding message should be: this residence is very secure.

Criminals are constantly scouting new victims and opportunities. They are always looking for the next treasure trove. Your task: convey that your residence is not an easy target.

Second is the need to insure that there is no cover for a criminal within the outer deterrent zone. Cover is one of the primary elements of the golden triangle. Cover lets a criminal observe without drawing attention. Your task: remove all areas of concealment.

When the military creates a new operating position, the first thing it does is clear the area around the base. This lets the guard clearly observe the individuals and vehicles that come close. For criminals to successfully commit a burglary or home robbery, it is essential for them to gather as much information as possible. This lets them select the easiest, most lucrative targets. The process helps determine the following:

- ★ How many people live there?
- ★ Does this home have items that are easy to convert into cash?
- ★ What are the occupants' schedules?

Criminals need time to collect information like this. They can collect it in a variety of ways: by observing the residence, by picking up the resident's trash, or by intercepting the resident's mail. To accomplish this, the criminal may need to sit in a parked car on a side street or hide in the bushes.

Whenever you suspect someone of acting in these ways, contact your local law enforcement immediately.

Don't ever attempt to confront the suspect directly. Law enforcement personnel are trained to collect information and conduct themselves in a safe and secure manner.

Your goal is to stay safe. Physically confronting a suspect is a fool's errand.

STOP THE INTRUDER™ | KNOWLEDGE IS THE BEST PROTECTION™

Removing cover is fairly simple and straightforward. Your goal: make it easy to see everyone inside the outer deterrent zone. Remove items or employ countermeasures against unchangeable elements. Here are some suggestions.

Prune trees branches and shrubs regularly. No tree should provide a place for someone to hide. Remove all branches lower than eight feet. This is especially critical if any of the low-growing branches are load-bearing. A load-bearing branch is any branch that can support 50 lbs or more of dead weight before breaking. Remember: the average criminal's profile is a male under the age of twenty-five. Climbing into a tree is usually easy to accomplish at this age.

Keep your lawn neatly manicured. If your lawn is overgrown, your residence conveys "nobody's home". If your lawn isn't maintained, other general security issues are also likely to be overlooked.

Shrubs should be extremely dense and thorny. This makes hiding inside difficult and uncomfortable. Remove visual obstructions. If these are shrubs, keep them sufficiently trimmed. The deterrent zone must be void of hiding places. Everyone within this area should feel fully exposed; there should be no place to hide. The entire area should be closely inspected during the day and at night to ensure that all issues are appropriately addressed.

Nightfall can create unexpected areas of cover and concealment for criminals. Observing a vehicle's occupants is much easier in daylight; at night the challenge is greatly increased. The cover provided by nightfall can be mitigated by adding adequate lighting, one of the most inexpensive security options. Your night-time lighting is adequate when you can describe the color of a person's hair. (The many benefits of lighting will be discussed in greater detail in the next section.)

When cover is removed, the next step is to put into place a series of deterrents. A deterrent is anything that will discourage a criminal from targeting your residence.
Deterrents can be divided into two different categories:
- soft deterrents;
- hard deterrents.

A soft deterrent is informational in nature. Your task is to communicate to the criminal that the area is closely monitored. This doesn't require major modifications. A good example is an alarm monitoring sign. These signs should be placed so they can be easily observed from anywhere within the zone. The signs should also be easy to see by anyone walking on a sidewalk or driving by in a vehicle.

If you employ an alarm service, request signs from them. Alarm service signs offer the alarm company frees advertising while notifying potential criminals that your home is monitored. Even if you don't have an alarm service, you can purchase alarm service signs on the Internet; they may serve as a limited deterrent for amateur criminals. Sophisticated criminals will know which alarm companies are operating within their areas of operation. Professional criminals will also likely profile the alarm company's response time.

A hard deterrent is a physical barrier between a criminal and a residence. Hard deterrents include fencing and dense, thorny shrubbery. Homeowner's associations may restrict specific types of fencing and other hard deterrents. Decorative fencing and livestock fencing is generally not considered a hard deterrent. (Any barrier a criminal can step over or easily open is not a hard deterrent.) Conduct a thorough examination of any fencing prior to installation. Talk to your installer about the security options available on your project.

The number of individuals who don't provide a serious level of security within their homes because of a fear of being locked out is shocking. Some people even put a key on the exterior of their homes! The average burglary costs the victim over $2100. A locksmith isn't cheap, but the risk of placing a key outside your home for fear of a lockout far outweighs any potential benefits.

If lockout is of significant concern, you can use controls to provide safe emergency access to your home. But please note: an emergency key should be used for emergencies ONLY, never routinely. An observant criminal can watch a child walk over to a plant, move an object, and unlock a door, then replace the key. And be sure to keep any emergency key within the outer deterrent zone; don't store it any other area. Keep the key at least 10 feet away from the residence.

Criminals know that residence owners tend to hide keys close to the doors. If you use an emergency key, take appropriate security measures. Purchase a good key holder from any home retailer. A good example is a combination

STOP THE INTRUDER™ | KNOWLEDGE IS THE BEST PROTECTION™

key lock like the ones used by realtors. Your key holder should be locked to an immovable object: this prevents criminals from stealing the key locker and taking it to another location to extract the key. An emergency key can also be stored with trusted neighbor home or nearby relative.

STOP THE INTRUDER™ | KNOWLEDGE IS THE BEST PROTECTION™

Zone Two - Inner Funneling Zone

The inner funneling zone is the area between the outer deterrent zones and the physical exterior of the residence. The inner funneling zone forms a ten-foot ring around your home. While the outer deterrent zone may have people passing through it for various reasons, the inner funneling zone should not unless your residence is in an extremely dense urban environment. The purpose of the inner funneling zone is to channel visitors to the access control points. This zone is also designed to channel visitors away from areas of weaker security.

Use landscape to channel foot traffic. A good example: plant thick hedges to direct visitors to the locations you want them to be. Although it isn't difficult to force one's way through a row of hedges, directional hedges will guide trustworthy individuals. Also use hedges to discourage individuals from viewing and accessing windows. If possible, all entry-level windows should have a thick row of hedges along their exterior extending approximately four feet past the window in both directions. This prevents criminal from easily checking to see if the windows are vulnerable.

Here is a short list of hedges which are often used to enhance security.

- Berbers Darwinian
- Berbers frikartii Telstar
- Berberis, Green
- Berberis, Purple
- Berberis Stenophylla
- Blackthorn
- Buckthorn, Sea
- Gorse
- Holly
- Holly, Blue
- Holly, Golden Variegated
- Holly, Japenese
- Holly, Silver Hedgehog
- Holly, Silver Variegated
- Mixed 'Native Hedging' Collection
- Pyracantha, Golden Sun
- Pyracantha, Orange Glow
- Pyracantha, Red Column
- Quickthorn
- Robinia Pseudoacacia
- Rose, Dog
- Rose, Hansa
- Rose, Rugosa
- Rose, Rugosa Red
- Rose, Scotch
- Rose, Sweet Briar
- Rubus Cockburnianus

Keep your inner funneling zone completely free of trees and of load-bearing branches from adjacent trees in your outer security zone. Any trees within the inner funneling zone should be removed. Although they may provide an energy benefit (shielding your home from sunlight in the summertime) the security risk far outweighs any potential savings. Remember: being ripped off is expensive. A criminal can use trees to gain access to upper windows. (In general, second story windows are less secure than ground floor windows.)

As part of your general security inspection, make sure your lawn furniture and ladders are properly secured. A criminal carrying a ladder down the street would attract attention. He or she would really stand out while crossing the yards of several residences!
If a criminal can find an unsecured ladder in a backyard, it provides a great opportunity to access upper windows. A criminal may also gain access to an upstairs window by putting a chair on top of other patio furniture.
It's very easy to secure your patio furniture to the ground by digging a hole. Place a small steel plate at the bottom of the hole with an I bolt sticking from the plate to above ground. Fill the hole with concrete. Lawn furniture can also be chained to the ground. Both of these ideas are great alternatives, making outdoor furniture difficult to use for nefarious purposes.

Because the inner funneling zone forms a ring around a residence, it will likely include the exterior utility hook up. This is where your utilities connect to your residence from various utility and telecommunication providers (usually located near the rear corner of a residence). The exterior utility hookup spot presents a series of special and unique challenges for security-conscious homeowners: it must remain accessible by authorized personnel; and it provides a single point of failure for telecommunications. Even if your residence is using a VOIP I phone system, the Internet service provider must have access.

Telecommunications cables are usually easy to identify; they're close to the ground. Although it may not be permissible to enclose this area with a hard deterrent, it may be possible to encase the cabling within a metal conduit. This option prevents criminals from easily cutting the cables with a pocketknife. Local building ordinances and laws tightly control this area. Consult your local utility providers to create permissible solutions to this challenge.

Evening and nighttime hours present special challenges. While most residential burglaries occur during the day, information strongly suggests that

potential targets are scouted out at night. During the daytime, natural sunlight will often reflect off light?color objects and glass, causing glare and reflections, making it difficult to see inside a house. Because homes are lit from the inside at night, it's much easier to see inside after dark.
And darkness offers additional concealment opportunities for criminals. Adequate outdoor lighting is an effective countermeasure to these unique challenges.

The human eye adjusts to a wide range of variations. Light enters the eye through the pupil, striking the rods and cones in the rear of the eye. The pupil controls the amount of light entering the eye and is very sensitive. When it's light and bright outside, the pupil contracts to prevent too much light from entering. At night, the pupil dilates to allow additional light in; this is known as night vision.

There are two types of lighting: constant and activated. As the names imply, constant lighting is on all night long; activated lighting is triggered.

Constant lighting should be used adjacent to all ground-level access points. A fifteen-foot area should be well lit during nighttime hours at all times. These lights are usually controlled by an indoor switch or a photocell mounted outside the home. DO NOT leave exterior lights on during the day: criminals will assume you're not home! Some folks believe it's important to leave their exterior lights on 24/7 when they're traveling. Not so! Lights going on and off are an indication of occupancy to criminals and neighbors.

If you're going away at night or for extended periods of time, interior programmable switches provide the widest range of flexibility. They allow you to turn on the lights at a slightly different time on different days of the week. From an outside observer, lighting variations provide additional proof of occupancy. An additional advantage is automation, which insures that the homeowner doesn't need to remember to turn lights on/off. It's very important to automate as much of your security as possible.

How much light is necessary to provide adequate protection?

Light should be sufficient to provide full and complete visibly as is seen two hours prior to sunset. The easiest way to check the amount of light is to ask someone to stand at a distance outside in full daylight, as far away as possible to still be able to detect the his or her eye color; then return to the same spot about two hours after sunset and ask the subject to stand in the same spot. Nighttime lighting should be increased until the subject's eye color can be clearly seen at the same distance he or she was during broad daylight.

Activated lighting comes on when triggered. An example is a floodlight attached to a motion detector. This lighting may be used to supplement constant lighting. Activated lighting is particularly useful if there is an especially dark area on the exterior of your residence which isn't frequented on a regular basis. If someone walks within range of the sensor, the light will turn on. Unfortunately, small animals or wind-whipped debris may activate this lighting, too.

Please Note: Accent lighting isn't the same as security lighting. Accent lighting is used to call attention to particular features around the residence. These lights generally shine directly on the side of a residence. While they provide some level of illumination, they are by no means comparable to security lighting. Security lighting should always face away from your residence. The goal: to remove the cover of darkness that provides access to a criminal.

Recap

Commonly used pathways should be well lit using constant lighting. This will prevent a criminal from hiding along pathways and ambushing you on your way into your home.

Infrequently used pathways should have (at minimum) activated lighting. It's best if the area is also illuminated with constant lighting. This application will depend on your unique circumstances and other factors.
There should be no dark areas along pathways leading to your residence.

Zone Three - Access Control Zone

Doors and Windows
In terms of security, most people think about doors and locks. It's true: these devices play major roles as access control points for your residence. But ensuring adequate protection requires a lot more than purchasing a lock and installing it.

Your doors are the gateway into your home. Since most residential burglaries occur when residents aren't at home, doors should be properly secured at all times. To prevent a home invasion, it's important to disengage your access control device only after you're completely confident that your visitor is not a threat. (Once disengaged, even the best lock provides zero protection.)

> EVERY LOCATION & CIRCUMSTANCE IS DIFFERENT. WHAT WORKS AT ONE HOME MAY NOT WORK AT ANOTHER.

When an unknown person approaches your home, ascertain their identity and purpose before allowing them access to your home. A peephole is recommended at all access points, mounted no higher than 58 inches. It should have a 160-degree view of the exterior. A peephole lets you see who's on the other side of the door. Peepholes are inexpensive and easy to install.

A closed circuit television camera is another way to observe who has come to call. The camera's greatest benefit is its ability to remotely view what's happening, providing an even greater level of safety. It's important to place the camera at such a height and location to provide a good overview of the front door area and a close up view of the visitor's identity.

In the case of a home invasion/robbery, a criminal may employ a ruse to get you to trust him or her and disengage your access control devices. Criminals have been known to wear a construction hard hat pretending to be from the local utility company. Uninformed homeowners may disengage all access control devices for these individuals only to be greeted with a weapon (and possibly worse) once they are inside their homes.

Anyone posing as a representative of a utility should be challenged. Identification documents should be examined remotely. Obtain their full name and employee identification number and make a quick telephone call to the company to make sure the individual is legitimate. This protocol is especially important when a child is at home. Children are taught to obey the instructions of adults, but they should always challenge the identity of strangers. And children should be taught never to reveal when an adult is not home; instead, they should say their parent is busy and can't come to the door (or the phone).

Door Anatomy

There are numerous doors available to homeowners in a wide variety of shapes and sizes. The most common is the single entry door, found in most homes across America. In a traditional frame home, these doors open to the inside. In most mobile homes, these doors open outward.

Another common door is the double door, essentially two doors that fold together and meet in the middle (also called a French door).

Another option is the sliding door. These doors glide along a track in the floor.

Single and double doors are usually held in place by three hinges and secured with a wide variety of locks. Single and double doors can be composed of metal, wood or composites and can be mounted with various opening mechanisms, ranging from the traditional knob to the more exotic.

Doorways are only as secure as the reinforcements in the framing. The best lock mounted on an unreinforced doorframe provides very little protection. To have adequate protection, the entire doorframe and hardware must be completely reinforced. This begins with securing the hardware to the doorframe with at least 8-inch screws. This ensures that the hardware is securely connected to the studs within the doorframe and wall. The doorframe must be reinforced to insure that the framing does not fail when stressed. To function properly, the best lock relies on the doorframe remaining intact.

Most locks come with a small striker plate attached to the doorframe. These strikers use a one or one and a half inch screw to connect them to the doorframe. The bad news: these strikers and screws are woefully inadequate when it comes to providing any level of protection.

The fastest door-breaching method is called a kick attack. The intruder simply kicks the doorknob or strikes it with a tool causing the door to open. The striker plate and wood absorb the total force. If this area is not reinforced, it can be breached in less than ten seconds.

Nor does the traditional striker provide sufficient surface area to dissipate any marginal level of force a determined criminal will provide. While a common striker can be slightly enhanced by using eight inch or longer screws, a security striker plate should be installed to provide an extra level of protection. The best security plates are eight to thirty inches long. These should also be secured with six or more screws in each plate using screws at least eight inches in length. The longer the security plate, the more evenly the force is applied across the door framing. Rule of thumb: the longer the striker, the more force that's necessary to cause it to fail. The security striker plate should be solid steel.

The door itself should be secured with a security striker plate. This plate is mounted directly on the door and should correspond to the doorframe striker plate. The same general rules and principles apply for the doorframe striker plate.

When the doorframe and door have been reinforced, the next component is the lock. The most common lock available is called the knob-and-key lock. This is a lock in the doorknob itself. The common unreinforced knob-and-key lock is little more than a nuisance to a criminal. Deadbolt locks provide a far higher level of security. When a knob-and-key lock is used in combination with a dead bolt, security increases. There is a wide variety of deadbolt locks on the market. They come in a range of finishes, shapes and sizes. (Please pay attention to the local building codes in your area. Some codes prohibit certain types of locks or devices.)

A deadbolt lock comes in a single or double keyway lock (more commonly referred to as being single-sided or double-sided deadbolts). A single-sided deadbolt uses a key on one side to disengage the lock on the other side. A double-sided deadbolt requires a key on both sides to disengage it. While a double-sided deadbolt does provide significantly more security, some fire codes don't allow them. The concern surrounds a double-sided deadbolt requiring a key to exit: the deadbolt might trap an occupant inside the house in the event of a fire. Contact a local building inspector to determine what is allowable in your area. Having said this, the double-sided dead bolt is the most secure. Decide for yourself the level of security you need for your residence.

Locks 101

Two organizations evaluate locks: the American National Standards Institute (ANSI) and Underwriters Laboratories (UL). Both organizations put access control devices through a rigorous series of tests to determine construction and quality.

The grading system is made more complicated because lock operation and lock security can be graded separately. This means it's possible for a lock to be a grade one with regard to the way it works and grade two with regard to how much security it provides, so it's important to pay attention to the packaging when you purchase locks.

Grade One
This lock is the highest level and provides the most security. These locks should be used on all external access control points.

Grade Two
This lock is designed for light security. This grade lock would be used for bathrooms.

Grade Three
This lock provides the lowest level of security and quality.

A double (or French) door is a challenge to secure. Since there are two moveable doors which fold together, the challenge is significant. The first step is to lock one of the doors into place. Do this by installing reinforcing bolts at the top and bottom of the door. This ensures that one door is providing a secure platform to secure the other door to. Standard door reinforcements should be applied to both doors, too. As with other doors, high security screws should be used throughout the door-framing reinforcement. If additional security is needed a security gate reinforcement can be installed on the outside of the door. This will provide an even greater level of security, as it would prevent someone from directly accessing the door.

A sliding door uses a different locking mechanism than a regular door. Sliding doors are not as vulnerable to force as other types of doors unless they're composed of glass. In this case, the glass should be of security grade (break-resistant). Sliding doors can also be prevented from opening by inserting a wooden or metal rod into the sliding track. This prevents them from moving along the track and keeps the door from opening. This security principle can also be applied to a standard door with a security rod. Brace a removable rod between the door and the floor or an adjacent wall. When these rods are in place, they keep the door shut. (A doorstop provides a small level of protection using the same principle.)

There is one product that provides almost no level of protection. This is the misnamed "security chain".

STOP THE INTRUDER™ | KNOWLEDGE IS THE BEST PROTECTION™

When a stranger rings a doorbell, some residents use a security chain to slightly open the door so they can talk to the visitor. These chains are grossly insufficient; one kick would break them. Your primary locks must remain engaged at all times for you to be secure. Never disengage them to greet an unknown individual.

Windows

Windows are frequently overlooked when it comes to security. The average residential window offers scant protection against break-ins. Most windows are held closed by a small inadequate latch.

Three primary security layers should be implemented to properly secure a window:

- Security Pins
- Protective Films
- Latched Screens

Security Pins

Security pins are solid steel or brass pins about the size of an adult's pinky. These pins are inexpensive and easy to install. Install a pin in the corner of each window across from the normal security latch. To install the pin, drill a small hole slightly larger than the security pin itself. When in place, the security pin keeps the window from being raised. Security pins come in a variety of sizes.

Some pins are countersunk into the window frame. This makes extracting them difficult without a special tool.

Protective Films

Although standard glass is vulnerable to breaking and entering, there are several products that significantly increase its resistance. Depending on the level of protection you need, there are coatings which can be applied directly to the glass. Glass coatings significantly reinforce standard glass, making it impact-resistant. In addition to increased security, these applications offer a higher degree of protection from flying debris during weather-related events. Replacing glass with a transparent composite provides the greatest protection. Depending on the type you install, it can render the window resistant to impacts up to and including small caliber bullets. As the level of protection increases there is a significant increase in price so weigh your considerations as the budget for your residential reinforcements is allocated.

Latched Screens

It's easy to overlook the benefits of keeping a window screen securely in place. While the screen itself cannot stop an intruder, it does provide an indication that the residence is being probed for vulnerabilities. And a screen prevents an intruder from pushing on the glass directly to determine if a window is properly locked; to do this, the intruder would have to cut the screen, leaving a clear indication that your home security is being tested.

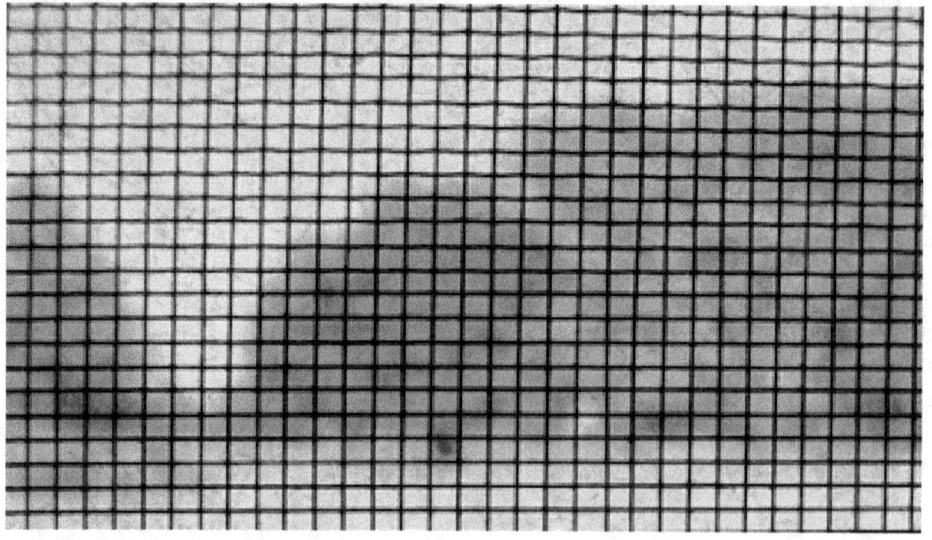

Garage Doors

If your residence has a garage, the vehicle should be parked inside it. When a garage is used for storage and your vehicle is parked outside then it is in a very vulnerable position.

Manual
If a manual garage door is being used, the door should be locked whenever the garage door is closed. It should stay closed except while allowing your vehicle to enter or leave. It does not matter if you have the best locks in the world, if your garage door is open.

Automatic
If you're using an automatic garage door opener, make sure it has a rolling combination; this prevents criminals from opening your garage door remotely. This is standard on most newer garage doors. The garage door should also have an anti-lift guard; this feature automatically secures the garage door in the event someone attempts to use a car jack to raise the garage door by force.

STOP THE INTRUDER™ | KNOWLEDGE IS THE BEST PROTECTION™

Zone Four - Interior

Your home is a sanctuary, your refuge from the outside world. This is the place where you should be safe from the outside world. Employ the following items to increase your security posture at home.

Limit the amount of information that can be obtained about the occupants of your home. As noted earlier, during daylight hours it's difficult to see clearly inside a home because the interior is often in shadow. At night, the situation is reversed because there is more light inside the house than out, which makes obtaining information about its occupants far easier. Put effective countermeasures in place to mitigate against unwanted snooping and intrusion. Control indoor lighting at night
Don't fill the interior of your residence with light at night. Unless you're careful in this regard, someone outside your home can determine the number of valuables you own and their placement, and the number of occupants and each of their schedules.

Place lighting near windows

Placing your lighting near windows creates shadows inside your residence. Avoid allowing lights to silhouette you or your family members. By strategically placing lighting near the windows you cause the light to glare and reflect off the windows. Do this in combination with window sheers and blinds. Windows sheers disperse and reflect light. When sheers are combined with window blinds, security effects are increased.

And remember: whenever your eyes are in strong light, your pupils will contract making it very difficult to see people who may be outside your residence, moving in darkness.

Elements of a Good Safe Room

Long before an intruder gains access to your residence, put a plan in place that details what each family member should do. Your residence should have at least two different places to shelter in place. Call these places your refuge or safe rooms. The purpose of these places is to provide a temporary secured area for family members to wait for emergency first responders.

Careful structural consideration should be given to the placement of your safe room/refuge. Take into account the location of the sleeping area of each of the regular occupants. Stairways or hallways should be considered. Minimize your proximity to exterior walls and windows.

Your safe room might be located within the master bedroom closet and should employ the same access control techniques as an exterior entryway. And your safe room wall should be reinforced. Carefully consider the threat and the response time of local law enforcement. The safe room should be constructed to provide sufficient protection against a determined intruder for double the time required for first responders to arrive. This can be increased or decreased depending on the threat (or lack thereof) as determined by you under the most extreme scenarios you can imagine.
There is a wide variety of options for providing additional safe room security.

There are three different types of reinforcement for safe rooms:

> ✱ Light reinforcement includes the application of multiple layers of plywood on the interior walls, floor and ceiling.
> ✱ Moderate reinforcement includes the application of ceramic plating, security fabric or metal plates.
> ✱ Heavy reinforcing includes the application of steel reinforced concrete.

Remember your safe room does not need to be anything more than a master bedroom closet, which has been reinforced.\

Each safe room/refuge should have following minimum attributes:

Communications

Your safe room should be designed to be a temporary waiting area for you and your loved ones until first responders arrive. Your needs will vary greatly from location to location and from person to person. Your waiting time may be from several minutes to several hours if your residence is in a remote location. It's vital to have several methods of communication in case notification of first responders must wait until you're inside your safe room. This might include a panic button which, upon activation, immediately contacts first responders. A cell phone is also critically important because the internal telephone system may be compromised by the criminals.

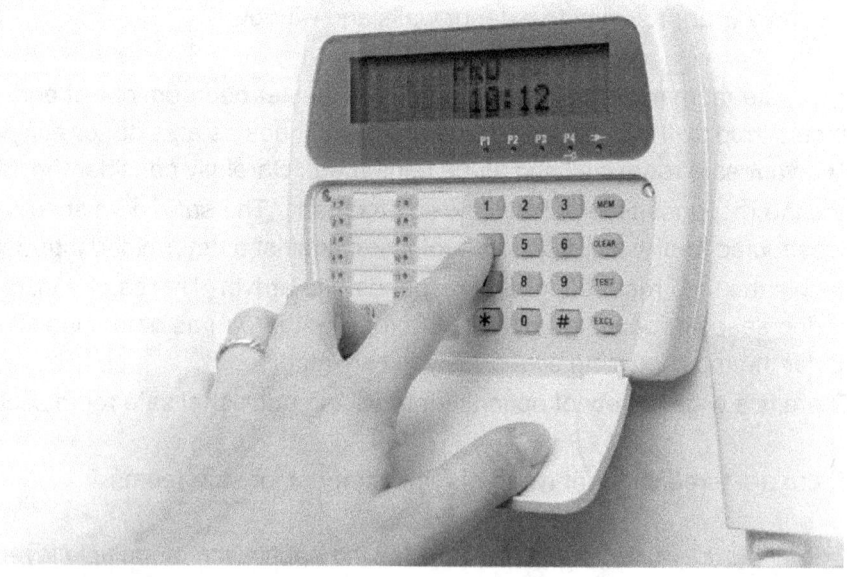

Lighting
Your safe room should have its own internal lighting. This is as simple as placing a battery-powered flashlight inside the room. Keep extra batteries in the same room and exchange the batteries on a regular schedule.

Water
Have extra water inside your safe room. If you're in the room longer than you expect, this is very helpful. It is generally not necessary to store food in your safe room. A person can survive weeks without food. Your safe room is generally not designed to be used for that length of time.

STOP THE INTRUDER™ | KNOWLEDGE IS THE BEST PROTECTION™

First Aid Kit

This can use useful if someone has become injured, while getting to the safe room. Here is a short list of useful items for this kit.

- Absorbent compress dressings (5 x 9 inches)
- Adhesive bandages (assorted sizes)
- Adhesive cloth tape (10 yards x 1 inch)
- Antibiotic ointment
- Antiseptic wipe packets
- Aspirin
- Blanket (space)
- Breathing barrier (with one-way valve)
- Instant cold compress
- Nonlatex gloves (size: large)
- Hydrocortisone ointment
- Scissors
- Roller bandage (3 inches wide)
- Roller bandage (4 inches wide)
- Sterile gauze pads (3 x 3 inches)
- Sterile gauze pads (4 x 4 inches)
- Oral thermometer (non-mercury/nonglass)
- Triangular bandages
- Tweezers
- Quick Clot

It is also important to have a good first aid manual. There are many of them available. There are a few good titles.

Title:	Everything First Aid Book: How to Handle Falls and Breaks, Choking, Cuts and Scrapes, Insect Bites and Rashes, Burns, Poisoning, and When to Call 911
Author:	Nadine Saubers
Paperback:	320 pages
Publisher:	Adams Media (March 1, 2008)
ISBN-10:	1598695053
ISBN-13:	978-1598695052
Dimensions:	4.4 x 0.8 x 7 inches

Title: The American Red Cross First Aid and Safety Handbook
Author: Kathleen A. Handal
Paperback: 384 pages
Publisher: Little, Brown and Company; 1 edition (May 27, 1992)
ISBN-10:   0316736465
ISBN-13:   978-0316736466
Dimensions: 7.8 x 0.9 x 9.2 inches

Title: The Essential Guide to Emergency Medical Procedures and First Aid, 5th Edition
Author: Paul S. Auerbach
Paperback: 535 pages
Publisher: Mosby; 5 edition (July 3, 2009)
ISBN-10:   0323068138
ISBN-13:   978-0323068130
Dimensions: 6 x 0.9 x 9 inches

Protective Measures

Have some type of defensive equipment inside the safe room.

Defensive equipment can include blankets, heavy coats, helmets, shields, loud sirens, and other items that deter others from harming you.

Offensive equipment can include hammers, golf clubs, saws, knives, guns and other items…but remember: if you lose control of offensive weapons, they can be used against you. The use of force will be covered in a later section.

Remember you do not have to built Fort Knox in order to protect your family. In most circumstances you will only need to delay the intruder until law enforcement arrives at your home.

STOP THE INTRUDER™ | KNOWLEDGE IS THE BEST PROTECTION™

Chapter 3
Home Invasion Planning

Chapter 3 - Home Invasion Planning

The Wilsons are a family of four. The father is John, 40 years old. Mary is his wife, 35 years old. They have two children, Jane and Krissy, both 10 years old. John is sitting in the living room watching the football game on a Sunday evening. Suddenly there's a loud noise at the front door. Walking to the front door, John sees two unsavory-looking characters. He stops. It's clear they're kicking in the door because he can see the doorframe failing and he hears wood breaking. It will be just a matter of seconds before the door fails. He knows the door hasn't been reinforced (something that's been on his Honey Do list for three weeks). One more kick and these maniacs will be inside the house.

What should John do?

What would you do?

No one wants this kind of thing to happen, but it occurs with frightening regularly. The choices John makes will have life?altering consequences. Even if the criminals leave, the trauma to his family will be significant.

In this situation, the first thirty seconds are most critical to the survival of John's family. He has to make a choice. What should he do? In a split second, there are only three choices to make. These are:

Comply

Flee

Resist

None of these options are optimal, yet he must choose. During a home invasion, the first 30 seconds are generally the most violent. This is easily one of the most life?altering events in John's life. Literally, John's choices will change the course of his family forever.

In his situation, there are generally no good options; there are only three bad ones. Long before this situation happened, John should have made his choice and developed a plan of action. Now he has just 3-5 seconds to create a plan.
But you have a little bit longer because (thank God!) this scenario hasn't actually happened to you yet!

Choice 1: Comply
Surrendering may be the only alternative in certain circumstances. This choice puts the resident at the mercy of the attacker. Physical limitations may make this the only viable alternative for certain individuals with disabilities. Whatever choice is made, it is absolutely critical that the victim in this scenario doesn't panic. The unfolding circumstances will likely be life-altering. Making poor choices while under siege will compound the risks and potential consequences. Remain as calm as possible!

Given this choice, it's very important to never agree to leave the current location. Studies indicate that when a victim is moved to a secondary site, the chances of surviving this type of incident decrease dramatically.

Choice 2: Flee

If someone is trying to breach the access control point, your number one objective is to stay safe. This includes getting away from the danger and to a safe place. Each resident should know at least two primary emergency routes for exiting the residence at all times. Each resident should know the location and routes to the safe room. A family meeting should be held quarterly to discuss emergency exit procedures. A code word should be established and agreed upon. When this word is shouted in the home, every family member should immediately exit the home via the nearest escape route. By selecting several predetermined routes and practicing the drill, you will help to ensure that your family members will react appropriately during an actual emergency.

It's also important to consider that someone may attempt to ambush your family members as they leave the home. This is why special consideration must be given on the exact escape routes out of the residence. Every location and circumstance is different. What works at one home may not work at another; this is ok. Just explore all the options and develop a workable plan together.

Choice 3: Resist

As anger over your situation develops, this may be your first, natural instinct. As your adrenaline surges your first thought may be to resist. It's very important to remain calm and think during this time. Criminals choose a specific residence for a reason. They may have been observing you for some time. The element of surprise provides the criminal a significant advantage. This can only be countered with careful and reasoned planning and drills.

In the military units are taught that there is only one way to get out of an ambush: attack. The concept is "violence of action". This means the defender must throw every ounce of energy into his defense. Your physical condition will play a large role in your decision.

Homeowners can respond with two different types of defenses. The first: deadly force, employing some sort of weapon (a firearm; a blunt weapon like a baseball bat; or an edged weapon like a knife). This may also be called lethal force. Lethal force weapons will be discussed in their own section.

The second alternative is called less-than-lethal. Less-than-lethal weapons attack one or more of our primary senses but don't inflict long-term harm. Sight, sound and smell are easily overwhelmed. Properly employed, these less-than-lethal alternatives can provide a significant response to an attempted home invasion.

Chemical Sprays can affect multiple senses simultaneously. Chemical irritants are available in most areas in the United States. The available sprays use one of three ingredients: Orthochlorobenzalmalonitrile, alphachloroacetaphenone or OleoresinCapsicum. Check with a local law enforcement official to determine which if these are allowable in your area.

Orthochlorobenzalmalonitrile (CS) is a micro-pulverized irritant. It rapidly affects the eyes, nose, skin and throat. CS spray can be toxic in high concentrations and to people with respiratory issues. It causes intense burning, watering of the eyes, choking and vomiting. It generally has little effects on animals. It isn't widely available to the public.

Alphachloroacetaphenone (CN) is an irritant; its crystals are suspended in liquid. This mixture is pressurized to create a vapor. Widely used 30 years ago, it is now obsolete. It was very common in military and police applications. This product is slow acting compared to others and may not be effective against an individual high on drugs or intoxicated.

STOP THE INTRUDER™ | KNOWLEDGE IS THE BEST PROTECTION™

Oleoresin Capsicum (OC) is an irritant extracted from chili peppers. Commonly called pepper spray, it is the most common option. Many people consider it to have the most pronounced effects. It can cause intense breathing difficulties, burning sensations, choking and nausea. The legal limit can be as high as 15% active ingredient within certain areas. The effects last up to 45 minutes. If one of the above isn't available, nonconventional sprays may be the only alternative in certain situations. A commercial chemical fire extinguisher may momentarily disorient an attacker. This may provide all of the advantage you need to get to safety.

Sound

Criminals detest anything that draws attention to them. (This is one of the components of the golden triangle: cover.) Loud sounds attract unwanted attention and makes escaping far more challenging. So it may be possible to repel an intruder by creating a significant ruckus. There are several readily available, reliable noise?makers. The first is a marine air horn. These are signaling devices used by commercial and recreational watercraft. They produce an enormous amount of sound. If someone is attempting to break into a residence, a series of loud bursts from this device will certainly attract a lot of attention. Marine air horns can be purchased at marinas and boating shops.

Another device is a simple referee's whistle. This device can be kept over a doorknob and picked up by any member of the home and used. Especially when used inside, this can create a significant noise footprint.
You may want to consider a wireless panic button with an exterior siren. This can attract a lot of attention.

Early Warning Systems

It is critically important to remain vigilant about the happenings in your local community and surrounding areas. Your residence is not an island unto itself. Your security can be influenced by many factors, any of which can change quickly when criminal elements move into new areas. An example: a local gang stakes out territory near you. This can cause a dramatic spike in criminal activity. When a military unit sets up a base of operations one of the initial systems it puts into place is a series of listening/observation posts. These serve to warn the commander of approaching danger. The principle is the same when it comes to your residence.

Man's Best Friend

A dog can be a great early warning device. Humans and dogs share three primary senses: sight, sound and smell. Humans generally process information from sight, then sound, then smell. Dogs process information from smell, then sight, then sound.

Animals can sense things far beyond the range of what is possible to our limited abilities. Depending on the breed, their sense of smell starts around

1,000 times better than ours and goes up to almost 1,000,000 times in some breeds.

Some people think a residence needs a big dog to deter a criminal. Not true! Yappy small breed dogs have deterred many criminals. And because dogs have far greater senses of smell, they can smell a criminal long before a human can sense something is wrong. Dogs are also territorial; they're not crazy about strangers. But if your dog "has never met a stranger" he or she will not raise the alarm when a criminal comes to call except perhaps to wag his or her tail. But even that is of value: you're alerted to the presence of an unanticipated caller.

To reap the full benefit of owning a dog, place "beware of dog" signs around your yard. This is often as disconcerting to criminals as an alarm company sign. Criminals know that a dog is likely to make a lot of noise if they try to enter the house. Criminals also know that dogs have sharp teeth. This may be just enough to get the criminal in your neighborhood to abandon your place to target another.

Electronic Early Warning Systems

As discussed earlier, it's very important for you to keep abreast of the happenings in your community. Google has created a great and easy way to do this. It's called Google Alerts.

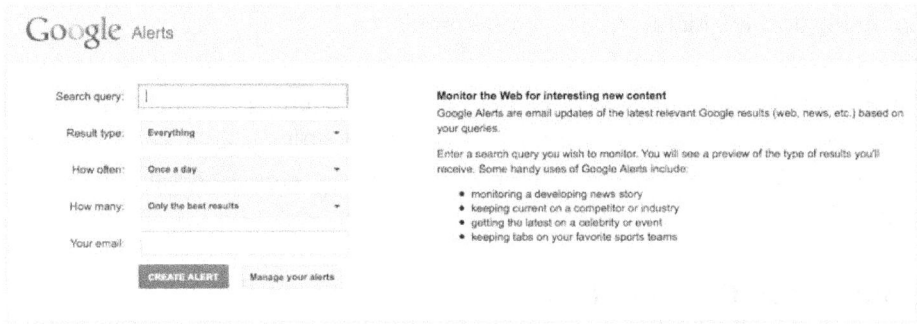

Google Alerts monitors the Internet for new content based on specific keywords that a user enters into the system. This content can be delivered daily, weekly or as it happens. Since Google alerts are free, you can set up as many as you need to ensure that the information you seek is relevant and current. So create a series of alerts and test them. Start the process by going to www.google.com/alerts. When the information is confirmed via email, you can begin the process.

Here are some examples for searches:
* "Your street name", city state
* Burglary, city, state
* Robbery, city, state

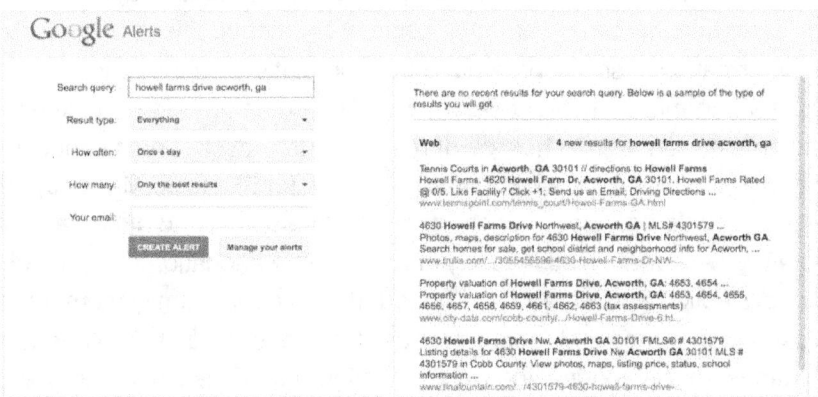

Manage your alerts within Google by creating a Google account.

Alarms

An alarm system can be a very important component in securing a residence. It's best to buy a high quality security system from a reputable company that will install, maintain and monitor it.

All doors and windows should be monitored with security contacts. These trigger the alarm in the event a door or window is opened. Interior motion or infrared sensors can supplement the contact points. Keep the alarm on at all times

Emergency Communication Plan

First responders (police, fire fighters, SWAT teams, etc.) are important keys to the successful conclusion of any emergency. Your ability to communicate with them in all circumstances is vital. Your challenge is making sure you can maintain reliable contact with them during a break-in or other emergency. In many situations it's vital to contact first responders at warp speed. The following sections provide valuable insights for establishing your communication plan.

Any model communication plan must include simplicity. The principle: "Keep It Simple, Silly" (KISS). An effective communication with first responders should be actionable with very little advance training because a babysitter, neighbor or guest may need to use the plan?lives depend on it.

Your first task: collect all essential information in one location and keep it there. To do this, use an emergency bottle. (The concept isn't original.) When information is scattered around the home, it's hard to relay the necessary information to first responders. The bottle (or other container) should be large enough to hold all of the vital information, and it should be waterproof. An olive/pickle bottle is a good size for this task. Make sure your emergency bottle has a permanent home so it's easy to find during an actual emergency. An ideal location is to put the bottle in a location that provides a level of protection and where it will be found by a guest, family member or first responder. Since first responders are trained to check the refrigerator for medications, this is an ideal location. A refrigerator is insulated and metal, which provides a level of protection for the contents. It's also large enough to locate even if the power goes out. Many homes have burned to the ground without disturbing the contents inside the refrigerator. This makes your refrigerator a prime location for your emergency bottle; but whichever location you choose, be sure you adhere to the above-named standards.

The appendix offers sample emergency information sheets which you can print and complete at your convenience (but the sooner the better!). It's very important to have an information sheet for everyone at your residence. Be sure the information is regularly updated; an outdated medication list can cause serious consequences. When you've completed the information sheets, roll them around a pencil (or similar-sized instrument) and place them inside the emergency bottle to keep the contents tightly compressed. Use a rubber band to secure the paper in place. A sample emergency sheet is included as Appendix 1.

Your emergency bottle should contain the following:
- ✓ The address, cross street and GPS coordinates of your location.
- ✓ Full names and identification information of each occupant of the residence.
- ✓ An updated, well-maintained medication and disease list.
- ✓ A primary and secondary direct dial emergency.

In the event of a widespread emergency, 911 may be overwhelmed with calls; direct dial numbers to first responders may not. These numbers are easy to get prior to an emergency event, but when power/Internet is lost, they become much harder to find. Here is a representative list of direct dial numbers to include: fire, sheriff, city police, room numbers, ambulance service, police, state patrol, nearest hospitals, your family physicians.

The entire contents should be placed inside your emergency bottle. Also include several moisture absorbers in the bottle to remove the water vapor that's trapped inside the container; doing this will preserve the contents for quite a long time. Moisture absorbers can be bought for medicine bottles. Place a label inside the bottle facing out. The words "emergency information" should be clearly visible to anyone reading the bottle. Finally, put a note on refrigerator door that reads "Emergency Information Inside."

STOP THE INTRUDER™ | KNOWLEDGE IS THE BEST PROTECTION™

Communication Devices

These days the vast majority of Americans have a cell phone. This technological marvel provides almost instant communication as long as the supporting infrastructure is in place.

The Federal Communications Commission requires that cell phone providers process 911 calls even if the phone doesn't have a plan with a particular carrier. As global positioning sensors and other technologies are incorporated into the modern cell phone, it's now possible in some cases to summon first responders without speaking. While privacy advocates voice legitimate concerns, these new technologies offer very real safety features.

Although the use of landlines (wired home phones) is on the decline, these instruments offer numerous advantages during an emergency situation. A traditional telephone draws its power from telephone wires (this is because in the early days of the telephone, many homes didn't have electricity), so even if your electricity goes out, a wired phone will still provide telephone service. (This applies to a traditional phone, which is directly attached to the wall with a cord. A cordless phone requires power at the base station to make the phone work.)

Even if you've chosen not to use a traditional phone service, your residence should still keep at least one wired phone line so you can dial 911 during any kind of emergency.

STOP THE INTRUDER™ | KNOWLEDGE IS THE BEST PROTECTION™

Some residents employ a citizen's band (CB) radio. CB's are widely used by professional drivers for communication. First responders monitor CB radios on specific channels. (Channel 16 is the emergency channel.) A special license isn't required to operate CB radios. These radios require a power source, but they can be a great communication link during emergencies. The major draw back of these radios is their lack of range.

Amateur Radio, which is often called HAM radio, provides a much longer range and options. However this form of communication requires a license and is more situated to contacting parties at great distances, then contacting local law enforcement/emergency responders.

Chapter 4
Digital Valuables

Chapter 4 - Digital Valuables

Most homes contain numerous treasures, many with irreplaceable sentimental value. An example: a Rolex watch passed down through the generations. This watch would be of great monetary value from a collector's point of view but it would have far greater sentimental to family members who regard it as a part of their history.

Most expensive items can be insured in case they're lost or stolen, but sentimental items can never be replaced by money: the loss of family treasures can cause their owners enormous emotional suffering. Many homeowners and their families are emotionally attached to the items in their homes. And with the advent of digital information, sentimental items may be digital files stored on a hard drive inside a computer. Many people keep one-of-a-kind, irreplaceable treasures and vital information on their computers. The value of these stored items far exceeds the value of the computer itself. Digital pictures (often stored solely in a home-based computer) have replaced film. Additionally these may be the only documentation of certain

STOP THE INTRUDER™ | KNOWLEDGE IS THE BEST PROTECTION™

events. One determined thief can steal decades of memories, loads of private information (tax returns, business ledgers, trade secrets, intellectual property, social security numbers, medical records, etc.) and everything else your computer holds. Next step: identity theft and a whole new world of trouble and heartache.

It's helpful to understand how data is stored on a computer so you know how to protect it. A computer system is made up of a series of components; each plays an important role in its routine operation. It is beyond the scope of this course to fully explain the nature and operation of a computer, but it's important to know that computer data is generally stored on a hard drive or on removable media. A hard drive is the rectangular metal cube mounted inside your computer.

The hard drive contains all the digital information you choose to store there. A computer can contain multiple hard drives: there is usually at least one, but there can more. The data stored on your hard drive isn't fragile: even if your computer goes though fire, as long as the hard drive itself remains intact there is a good chance your data can be recovered.

Inside a hard drive's metal cover is at least one ceramic plate. This plate spins at a high rate of speed. An arm moves across the plate. As the arm moves, electrical impulses are sent to the platter causing information to be inscribed on the plates. An electronic board controls the mechanical components on the bottom of the drive. This board is usually green.

STOP THE INTRUDER™ | KNOWLEDGE IS THE BEST PROTECTION™

Digital information can be divided into two categories:

❖Sensitive;
❖Routine.

Sensitive data contains information, which would cause harm or embarrassment to the user if the information were made available to the public.

The remaining data is called routine data. Even though routine data may not cause harm or embarrassment if revealed to others, losing it can be significant because even though the data is routine, it may be of great sentimental value and should be protected from theft and hardware failure. Sensitive data should be protected from unauthorized individuals via a process called encryption.

Routine data is protected through the data backup process, which involves making a copy of the data and storing it in another location.

Each operating system has it's own method of backing up data. The windows operating system is not exception. This program is accessed to highlighting the my computer icon. Click on the right click mouse button. The following information will be displayed. Once clicking on the properties button then select the tools tab to display the screen below.

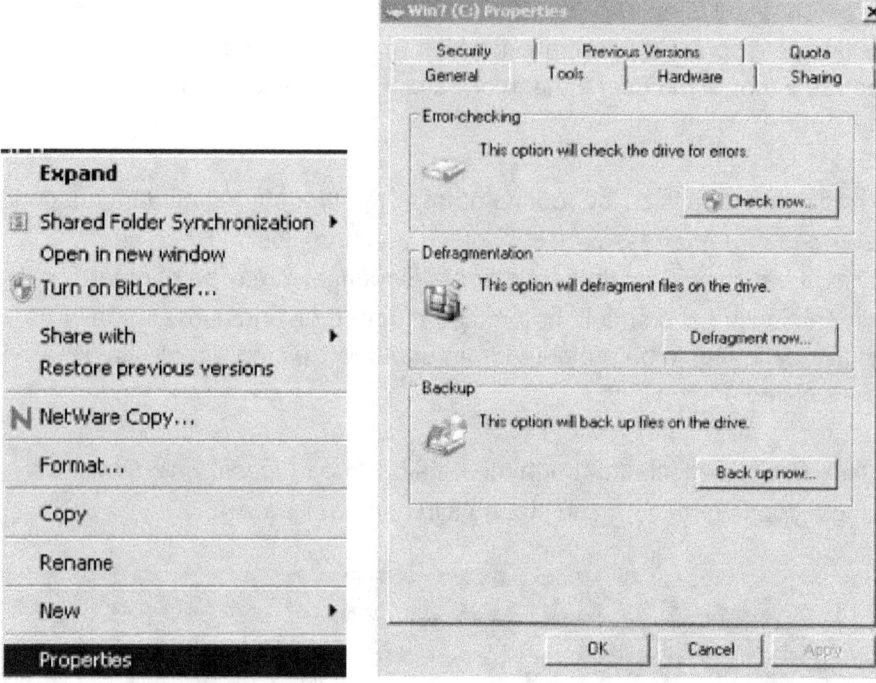

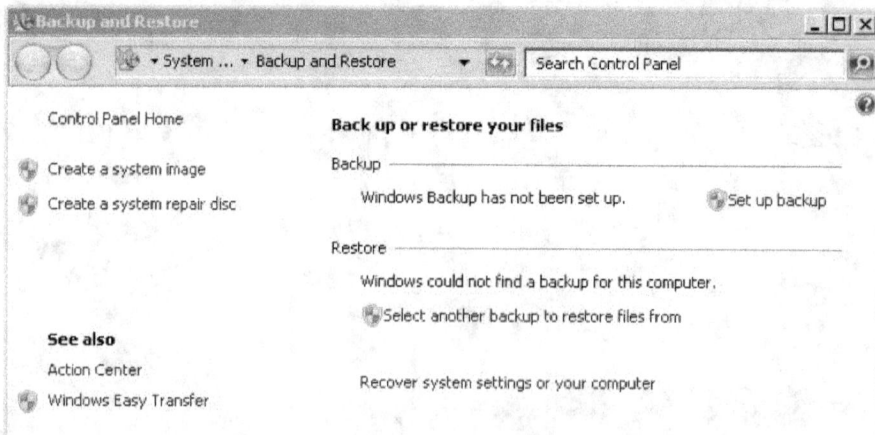

Click on the setup backup link. This will allow you to select the location of the backup. It is very important that the backup is stored on a separate hard drive or on a network share. If your data to be backed up and the backup file itself are stored on the same hard drive, this information will be lost in the result of the hard drive failure. The location is selected by click on the appropriate location. This will highlight the drive.

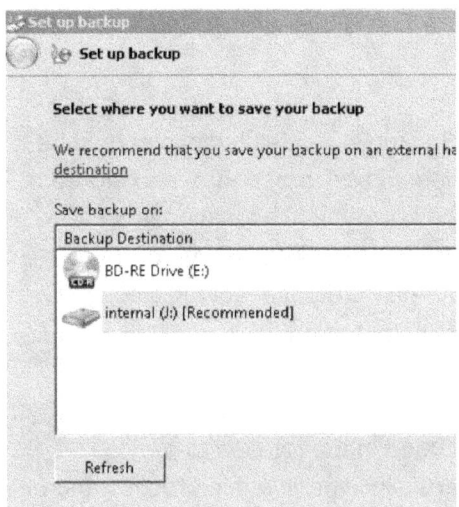

This concludes creating a data backup file with Windows 7.

The Macintosh operating system has a utility called Time Machine which is used for data backup. Connecting an external hard drive to the computer evokes this program. The operating system automatically prompts users to create backups.

There are also third parties utilities which can be used to back up data. These programs vary enormously in price and complexity. Third party programs may protect the data with encryption and let the user back up data to an external back up device (e.g., a tape drive).

Data backups should follow the rule of three: copies of the data should be backed up in three different locations. This rule applies to both Time Machine and the Windows backup utility. Having three different devices (e.g. three different external hard drives) is an example of this process. The primary backup device should be connecting to the computer system on a regular schedule while a backup of the data is created onto an external hard drive labeled "Backup A."

The second hard drive is labeled "Backup B." Backup B is stored in the residence safe most of the time. On a regular schedule, the hard drive labeled Backup A is rotated with Backup B. These drives should be rotated on a regular schedule. Doing so provides a reasonable degree of assurance that the most current data has been backed up within a reasonable period of time.

The third hard drive should be labeled "Backup C." A full backup should be created onto Backup C. This hard drive should be transported and stored at an offsite storage site. A safe, secure and cost effective location is a safe deposit box at the user's local financial institution. Once every quarter, a full backup should be created on Backup C. The hard drive labeled Backup C should then be transported and stored in the safe deposit box. This provides reasonable amount of protection.

Of course, additional hard drives can be used in the rotation to provide additional protection. It's important to carefully schedule this process and be sure the data backups are completed on a regular schedule. By rotating the hard drives in the manner described, you help ensure that even if a single hard drive fails, most of your data will be available via a backup. If you lose your computer and a backup hard drive, then the hard drive labeled B can be used to restore the data. In the event of a catastrophic event (e.g., a gas main explosion) you can still retrieve off site backup from the hard drive labeled C.

Sensitive Data

Sensitive data can cause substantial harm when it is revealed to unauthorized people. This data may include:
* Full Name
* Full Address
* Social Security Numbers
* Credit Card Numbers
* Tax Information

All sensitive information should be protected. Printed information should be stored in a high-security safe or inside a safe deposit box. For digital information, an encryption program should be used. Encryption programs vary wildly in process and application. Each encryption program uses its own security methodology. There are generally three approaches to securing digital information:

- Whole Disc Encryption
- Partition Encryption
- Container Encryption

Whole Disk Encryption

This process involves encrypting the contents of an entire hard drive. During the startup process, the computer prompts the user to enter a password or phrase. Using industry-recognized programs, this process offers the greatest protection for all of the data on a hard drive. A negative consequence of this type of encryption is that if a hard drive experiences a hardware failure it can render the data completely inaccessible even by data recovery specialists.

There are numerous version good commercial programs, which offer this level of protection. A google search reveals a large number of possible options for this sort of encryption.

Partition Encryption

In nontechnical terms, a partition is usually associated with a drive letter. A partition example would be the c drive on a hard drive. Securing this partition involves encrypting all of the information on the partition. This ensures that all information on a partition is secured.

This is the type encryption, which is used within Windows 7. It is known as Bit Locker.

Container Encryption

This is, in effect, like having an encrypted folder on a hard drive: anything placed within the folder is encrypted. When unopened, this folder is often seen by the operating system as a single file. When accessed, this folder may be connected to the operating system as another drive letter. This makes accessing the information simple and straightforward.

There are a number of very good encryption programs available on the Internet. Truecrypt is widely available and is free for personal use. It can be downloaded from www.truecypt.com

STOP THE INTRUDER™ | KNOWLEDGE IS THE BEST PROTECTION™

Truecrypt uses an encryption method called "on the fly"; this means the data is encrypted just before it is written to disk. The program supports at least four different encryption algorithms:

- AES
- Serpent
- Two Fish
- Cascades.

While all of these encryption schemes are good, AES is a great option. The U.S. Government developed AES (Advanced Encryption Standard). Truecrypt offers a wide variety of options; some are very advanced. The instructions provided will only cover the sensitive information within an encrypted container.

Once installed the program could be launched. This will bring up the below screen. In order to create the button, just click on the create volume button.

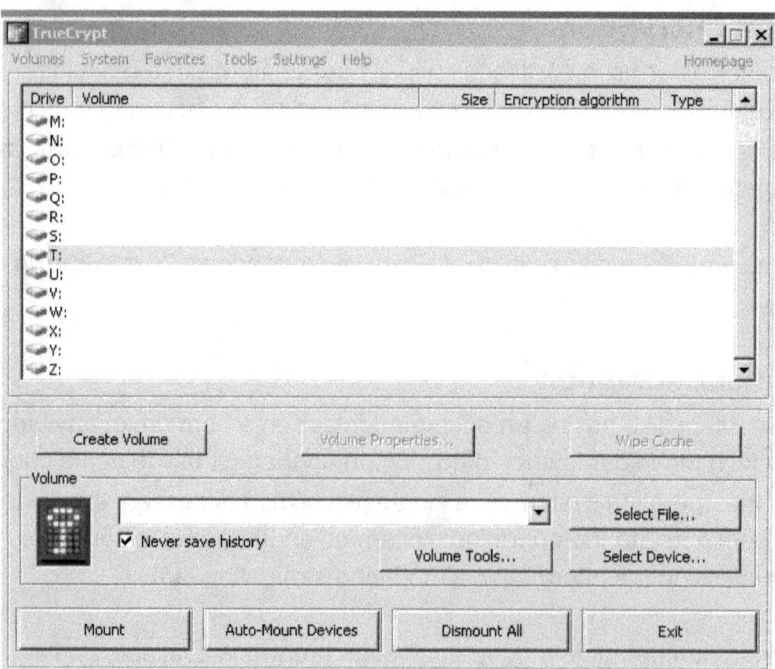

Once this is done, the following screen will be displayed.

www.StopTheIntruder.com

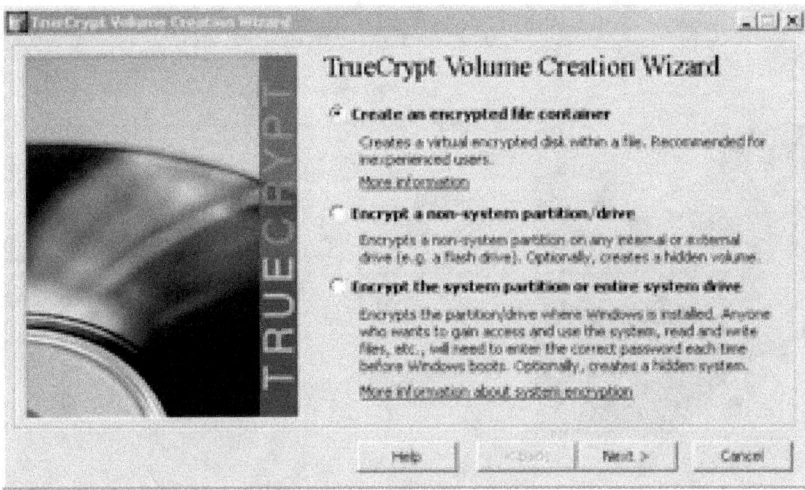

Users are given three choices:

☑ Create an encrypted file container. This process is used to create a Truecrypt file. Once this file is created, it appears like any other file on the hard drive, but it can only be opened using the Truecrypt program with the appropriate password.

☐ Encrypt a non-system partition/drive. This process is used to encrypt an entire drive letter. This may be used to encrypt a thumb drive or a drive that doesn't have the operating system located on it.

☐ Encrypt the system partition or the entire system drive. As indicated, this option is used to encrypt the volume, which is used to boot the computer system. This requires that users enter their Truecrypt passwords while their computer system is booting.

Highlight "create an encrypted file container", click on the next button, then ensure that the Standard Truecrypt Volume button is selected and click on the next button.

STOP THE INTRUDER™ | KNOWLEDGE IS THE BEST PROTECTION™

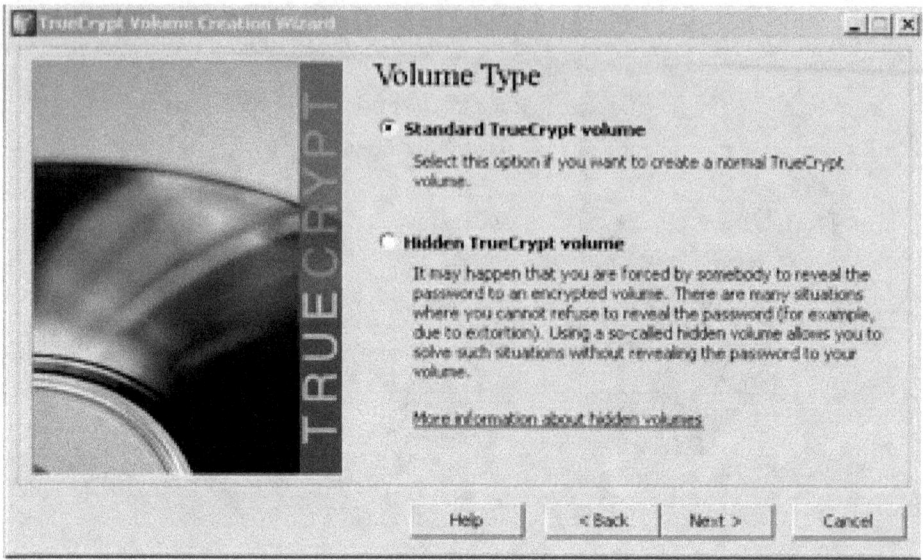

As the information in the box indicates, the Truecrypt file can be located anywhere on the system. It is a file just like any other file. Click on the select button and choose where the file should be created and the file name. After you've chosen the file name, it's helpful to give the file the extension of .tc. (This will identify the file to the operating system as a Truecrypt file but you're not required to give it this file extension.)

When complete, choose the next button.

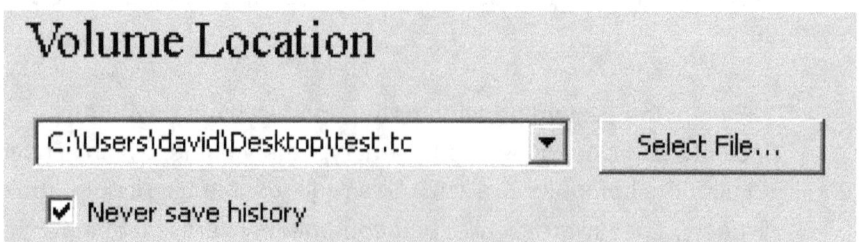

Truecrypt provides a series of options for encrypting the data. The default provides a high level of security. It is possible to change the encryption options. Simply select the preferred options and select the next button.

STOP THE INTRUDER™ | KNOWLEDGE IS THE BEST PROTECTION™

The next option is to choose the size of the container. It's important to choose a size that's slightly larger than the maximum size of the data you'll be storing. For example, if you have 400mb of data to be encrypted, create an encrypted container that is at least 500mb in size.

When your information is input, click on the next button.

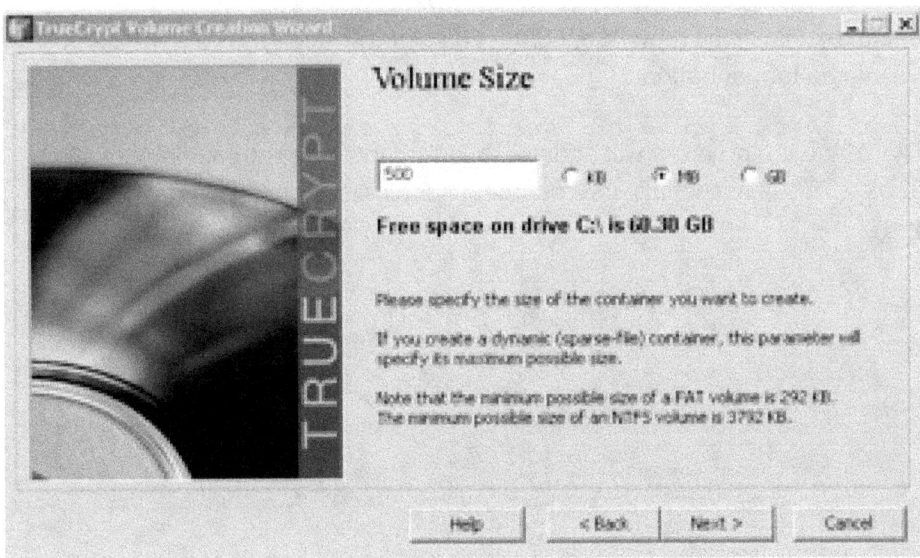

STOP THE INTRUDER™ | KNOWLEDGE IS THE BEST PROTECTION™

Input your password next. It's important to use a very good password. As the box indicates, it should include upper and lower case characters and some special characters. When you've input the information, choose the next button.

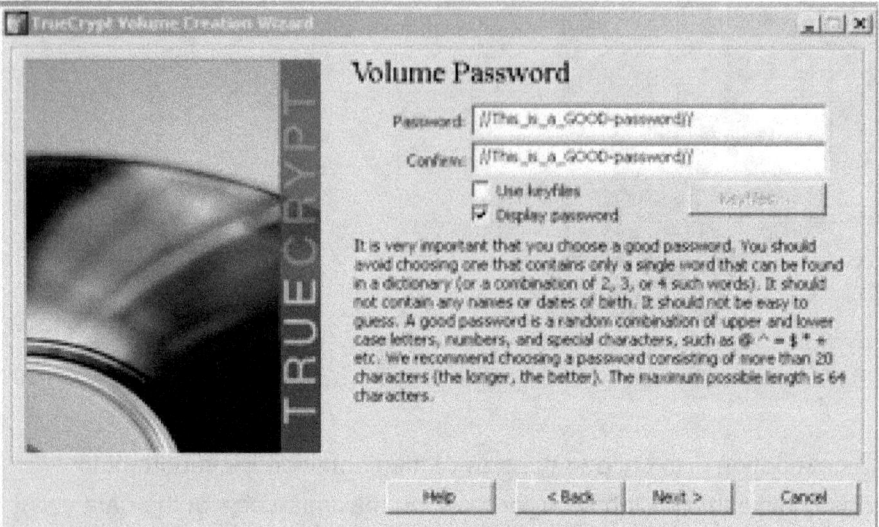

The volume format box lets you select the type of formatting for your file system. Some users prefer to have the formatting match the same formatting on the computer system that is being used. There are some benefits to this, but it isn't required. When the formatting type is selected, you should move the mouse within the box, as indicated, for at least 30 seconds; this helps generate increased security. After you've done this, select the format button.

By default the program will attempt to format the area with a File Allocation Table. This is essentially the recording keeping system for a hard drive. If the

STOP THE INTRUDER™ | KNOWLEDGE IS THE BEST PROTECTION™

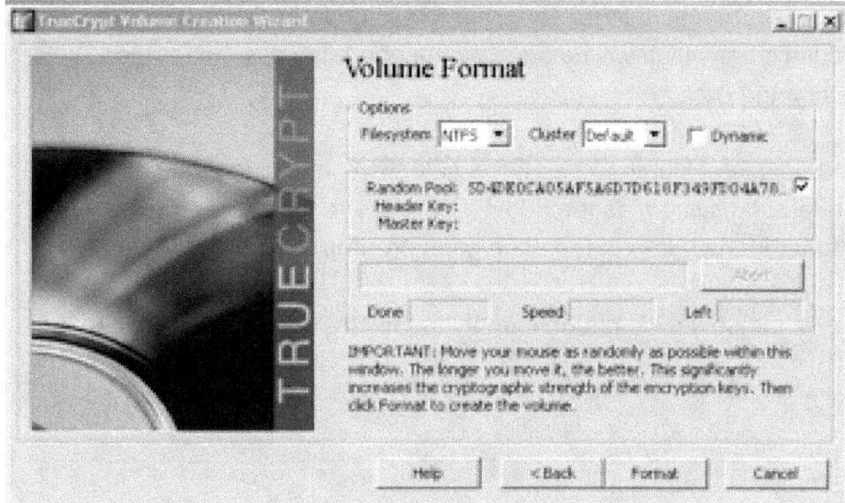

When complete, the following information will be displayed:

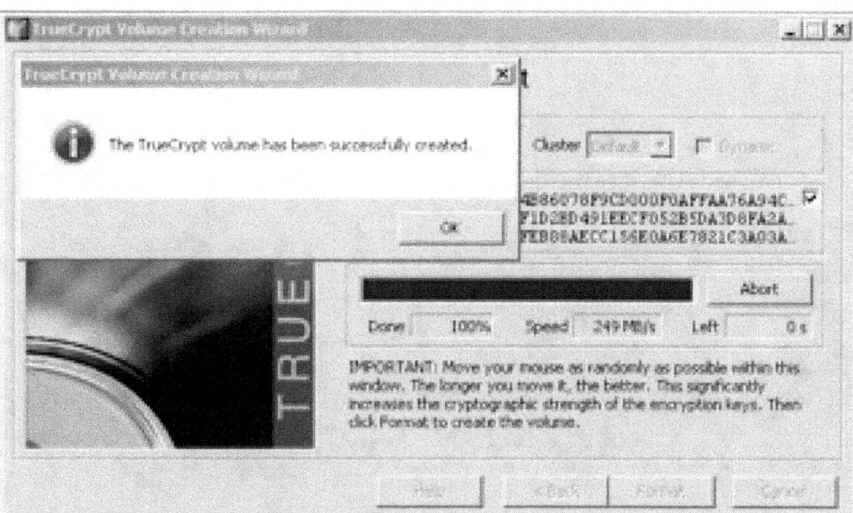

Now that your Truecrypt file is created, it must be opened for the operating system to read it.

Truecrypt calls the file opening process "mounting." Close the current screen to return to the main Truecrypt screen.

71 www.StopTheIntruder.com

Next, select the drive letter you want to assign to the encrypted file. This is the drive letter which will be seen by the operating system for the unencrypted data.

Some people select the letter t; this selection causes the data to be seen by the operating system as the t drive. T is easy to remember because it's the first letter in the name of the encryption program ("Truecrypt").

Click on the select file button identify the file that Truecrypt will open.

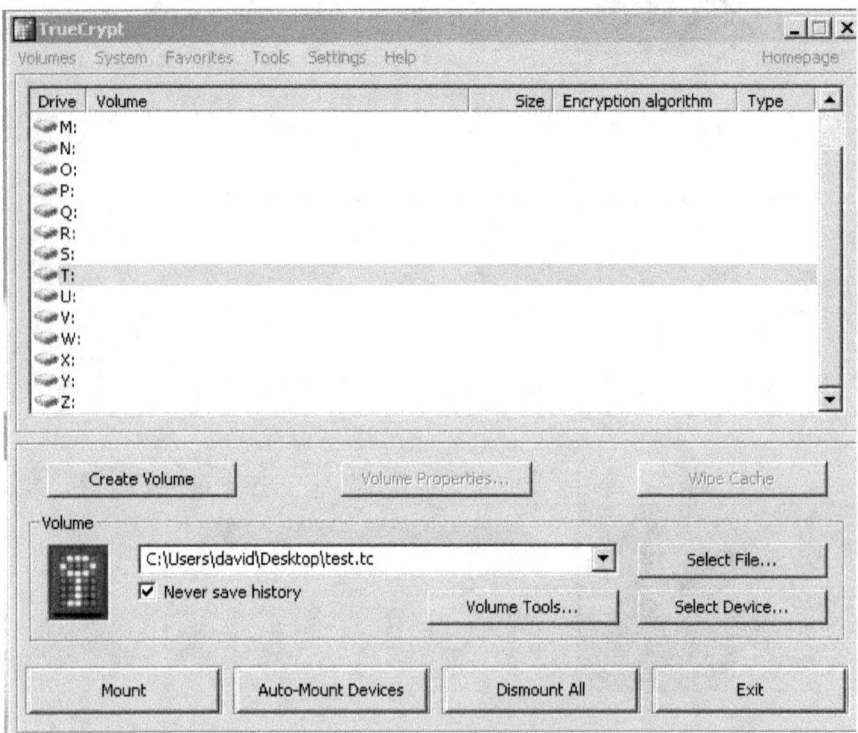

You'll need to type in your password. If the password is long, it's helpful to select the "display password" box. When you've inserted the password, click the "OK" button. It is absolutely imperative that a good password is chosen.

A good password should have the following:

- 13 characters long
- Upper case

STOP THE INTRUDER™ | KNOWLEDGE IS THE BEST PROTECTION™

- ☑ Lower case
- ☑ Numbers
- ☑ Punctuation

The operating system will open the Truecrypt file as whatever drive letter you gave it in the previous screen.

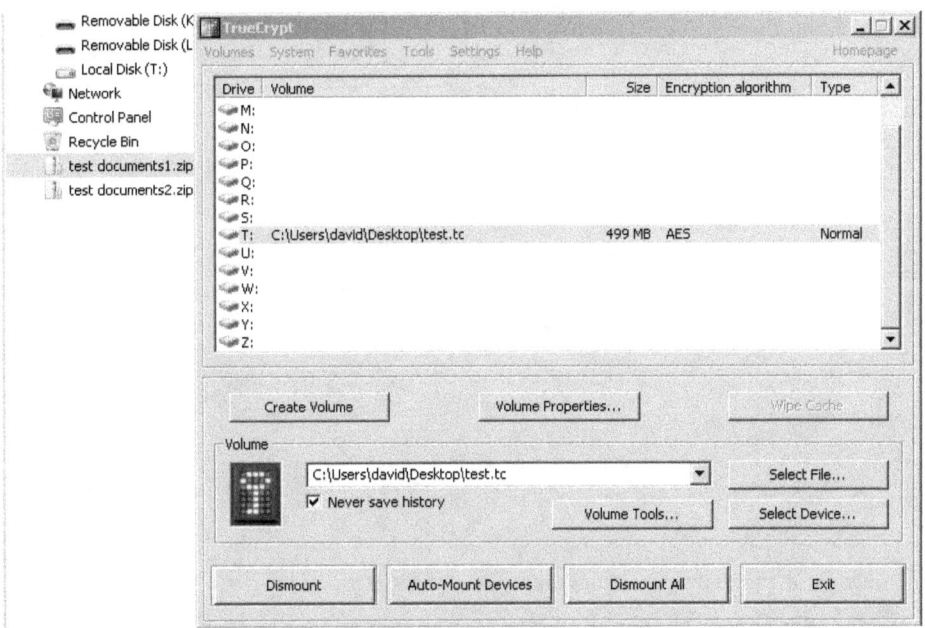

The information can be copied into the Truecrypt container just as if the Truecrypt container were a thumb drive or other device. When finished with the data, it's very important to dismount the container?doing this lets you move the file.

These instructions are not comprehensive and are only intended to provide you an overview of the program. For more information regarding the

STOP THE INTRUDER™ | KNOWLEDGE IS THE BEST PROTECTION™

Truecrypt program, please refer to the online help section at www.truecrypt.org/docs.

Chapter 5
Emergency Disc

Chapter 5 - Emergency Disc

Whenever it becomes necessary to exit a residence or a location quickly with little advance warning, it's completely impractical to carry out a complete full size printed copy of each of your family's important documents: passports, driver's licenses, insurance information, vehicle titles, financial documents and credit cards (to name just a few).

But it is practical to create an electronic copy of these documents in advance to be stored on a compact disc. Copies can be created using a scanner or digital camera.

If there is a concern of identity theft a high end encryption program can provide a high level of protection. A good example is True Crypt. This program will be examined in great detail in a later chapter of this book. Also bear in mind, once documents are encrypted then they will require that they be unencrypted prior to opening them. If the password is forgotten or lost, these documents will be completely useless. Therefore all options should be carefully considered. It is very important to keep a copy of the actual program. The encryption program should also be stored on the disc; this ensures that all necessary information will be available for decryption.

It does you no good if all your data is encrypted and there's no way to download a copy of the decryption program. Once encrypted, your data can be stored in multiple locations or in your vehicles with no fear of compromise.

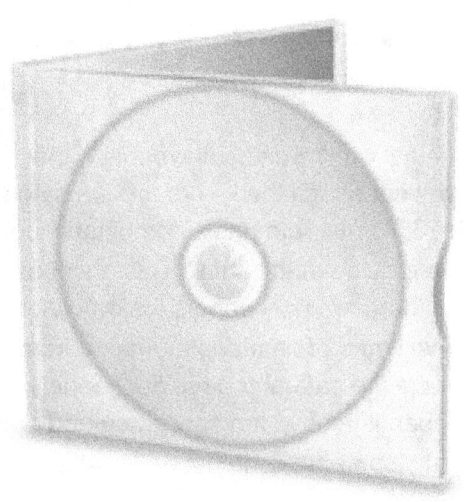

Another possibility is to store a couple copies of this disc in unencrypted containers in a secure location. This could include a safety deposit box, a safe or other location, which is protected from theft.

Security Containers

There are a large number of names for this items. Some people call them a safe or a vault. A full discussion is beyond the scope of this publication. However there are some general principles that should be kept in mind.

There are two types of secured containers.

- ❖ One provides protection from damage caused by the elements.
- ❖ The other provides protection from theft.

Safes designed to protect documents in the event of an environmental event (a residential fire or smoke damage) provide little to no protection during a burglary. Fire safes can be purchased at various home retailers. These safes should be stored next to an exterior wall. In the event of a residential fire, first responders can be directed to the area containing the safe; this will increase its chances of surviving the event.

These types of safes are rated by the number of hours they can sustain a particular heat level during a fire. A fire safe may be taken during a burglary so store only encrypted sensitive information inside a fire safe.
You can take several steps to decrease your chances of a fire safe being confiscated during a burglary. One is to write on the outside "Does not contain items of monetary value."

A criminal likely won't believe this without being able to see for him or herself so why not attach the key to the fire safe so the criminal can see what's inside? (If your safe has a combination lock, you can write the combination on the outside of the safe.) This encourages a burglar to open the safe to prove there are only papers inside. Allowing this decreases the chances he'll remove items of no monetary value from your residence. If a criminal can't open the fire safe at the residence, he'll likely remove it from the premises and open it later with a saw, torch and other tools. This would result in the destruction of the contents and/or their consignment to a landfill.

A high security safe is designed to protect the contents against burglary. High security safes must be installed and used in accordance with the user's manual. It's very important that this safe be secured to a concrete floor. If the safe is not physically anchored, it will be removed from the residence during a burglary and opened somewhere else. This would result in all contents being destroyed. All original physical documents should be stored in a waterproof bag inside a safe deposit box at your financial institution, never here.

Many criminals have developed a keen sense for where their victims store their valuables (usually in the bedroom or a bedroom closet). Never store your valuables in any of the following places:

- Bedroom
- Bedroom closet
- Kitchen
- Kitchen appliances
- Large indoor plant pots
- Behind pictures

Given the opportunity, a criminal will open every box in every bedroom and the master bedroom closet.

The best storage location is a high security safe that is anchored to the floor, carefully following the manufactures instructions. If you try to hide your valuables, do so in less obvious places. (Consider air vents and other obscure places, perhaps in the attic with the holiday decorations.)

Inventory/Marking

It's crucial to have a comprehensive list of your valuables. Taking a home inventory satisfies this requirement. An inventory can include every item you own or just high value items. Use paper or an electronic list, a digital camera, a video camera, or a combination of these. An example inventory sheet is included in the Appendix 1. Your inventory list should include the manufacturer, make/model and serial number (at a minimum). Added other items as you accrue them.

If you keep an electronic inventory, include it with other items on the household compact disc with other important documents. A digital picture is a simple way to prove that you owned certain items prior to a fire or a weather-related event. And a video walkthrough can be a valuable aid when remembering items after the fact.

In addition to making an inventory, permanently mark (etch) your items. There are many ways to mark valuables. Some people put their initials, address, telephone numbers or other identifying information on items. The downfall to doing this: when you move you can't always take your telephone number with you and you definitely leave your address behind.

A good marking system provides a long?term solution to this problem. One option is to use a two letter state abbreviation with your driver license number. Since your driver license number changes if you move out of state, this ensures that the information will remain valid for a longer period of time. Even if you move out of state, your current driver's license number should remain on file for years, even decades. (Some states never reuse a driver's license number.)

Chapter 6
Lethal Force

Chapter 6 - Lethal Force

Some homeowners choose to protect their homes by lethal force. The legality of lethal force varies widely across the United States. Closely examine local laws regarding the lethal use of force. Some states allow it when an intruder enters your home; others are at the other end of the spectrum.

Whenever an individual uses a weapon to inflict (or attempt to inflict) fatal consequences against another person, he or she is employing lethal force. Some states allow the application of lethal force. Some states employ a legal doctrine called "the defense of home (or castle) doctrine". This doctrine allows an individual to use lethal force to defend themselves or their home. Lethal projectile weapons include handguns, shotguns or rifles. Blunt force weapon include baseball bats. Edged weapons include knives.

STOP THE INTRUDER™ | KNOWLEDGE IS THE BEST PROTECTION™

The following states have some form of Castle Doctrine and/or Stand Your Ground law:

- Alabama
- Alaska
- Arizona
- Florida
- Georgia
- Illinois
- Indiana
- Kansas
- Kentucky
- Louisiana
- Maine
- Massachusetts
- Michigan
- Mississippi
- Missouri
- Montana
- North Carolina
- North Dakota
- Ohio
- Oklahoma
- Pennsylvania
- Rhode Island
- South Carolina
- South Dakota
- Tennessee
- Texas
- Utah
- West Virginia
- Wyoming

But it's crucial to check with your local law enforcement officers regarding the meaning and application of lethal force in your location. (This list changes from time to time.) Again, please contact your local law enforcement professionals to get the current information.

Firearms

So you have contemplated purchasing a firearm for personal and home defense. For whatever reason, be it increasing news reports of violence perpetrated against truly innocent victims or some personal knowledge of crime in your own community, you have decided to look into purchasing a gun of some kind; but you don't know where to start.

What type of gun to buy, where to buy it, and how to prepare to use it if the time comes when you might have to do so. These are but a few of the considerations before, during, and after the purchase of a weapon. For most law-abiding citizens the thought of owning a firearm is quite foreign, but some make the mental transition from consideration to actual purchase due to some desire to make themselves less of a potential victim. But this decision ought not be made lightly. Following are suggestions for the first-time gun purchaser.

Research

Besides going online to check out the newest and coolest handguns being released on the market, the potential first-time gun owner needs to go to a reputable gun dealer and actually look around the store at the various gun models available. There are myriad of makes and models out there. Whether you decide to purchase a revolver (wheel gun), semi-automatic pistol, or even a shotgun, you should actually look around at the weapons and even try to get the feel of the weapon in your hand. Gun dealers are great sources of information regarding the various products; and though not all are knowledgeable regarding training with the weapons, they are quite knowledgeable about the guns and how they operate. Take the time to pick their brains and listen to them. Ask follow up questions about each gun you handle.

Take the time to visit the gun store and talk to a dealer. Don't be afraid to admit your inexperience with guns. If you have a friend or family member who has some experience with guns, by all means, take them along. Just be sure they don't begin to push you toward buying something they like. What's right for them may not be right for you. Explain your desire to purchase, but admit your complete lack of knowledge. Then hold several different guns in your hands to get the feel of them. Take note of the grip in your hand, the length of the barrel, the overall weight of the gun as you hold it up and out at eye level (pointing in a safe direction of course—the gun dealer will make sure it is empty, handing it to you with cylinder open, slide to the rear, etc.). After all that, don't buy. Thank the dealer for his or her assistance and ask if he knows of a gun range where you can practice shooting before you purchase. The dealer should know of a place, or maybe there is one right there on sight.

Locate a Firearms Range

There are many indoor gun ranges you can go to practice. The best thing about the ranges is that most have guns you can rent. If you are serious about purchasing a gun, go to a range and practice. If you are the first-time shooter going to a range, it would be safest to hire a trained firearms instructor to give you lessons. Many ranges actually offer safety courses. If you are unsure, do your own research, find a qualified instructor, and talk to him/her beforehand, then meet at the range for a lesson. Be prepared to pay for quality instruction.

Firearms instruction is not cheap (not quality instruction from a certified instructor). But research your instructor as well. There are lots of instructors out there. Check credentials. Civilian National Rifle Association (NRA) certified instructors usually teach to NRA standards (which hold safety as the number one priority to any training environment), but not all instructors are of the same caliber (pun intended). Many law enforcement and military trained firearms instructors also hold seminars or offer one-on-one instruction. If you can find one of them offering courses or available for hire for individual instruction, make contact and hire away. These instructors usually hold themselves to a higher standard simply by the nature of the instruction they give to their respective departments (law enforcement training with firearms is constant and consistent for the officers and deputies and continually under scrutiny by the media, the public, and the courts).

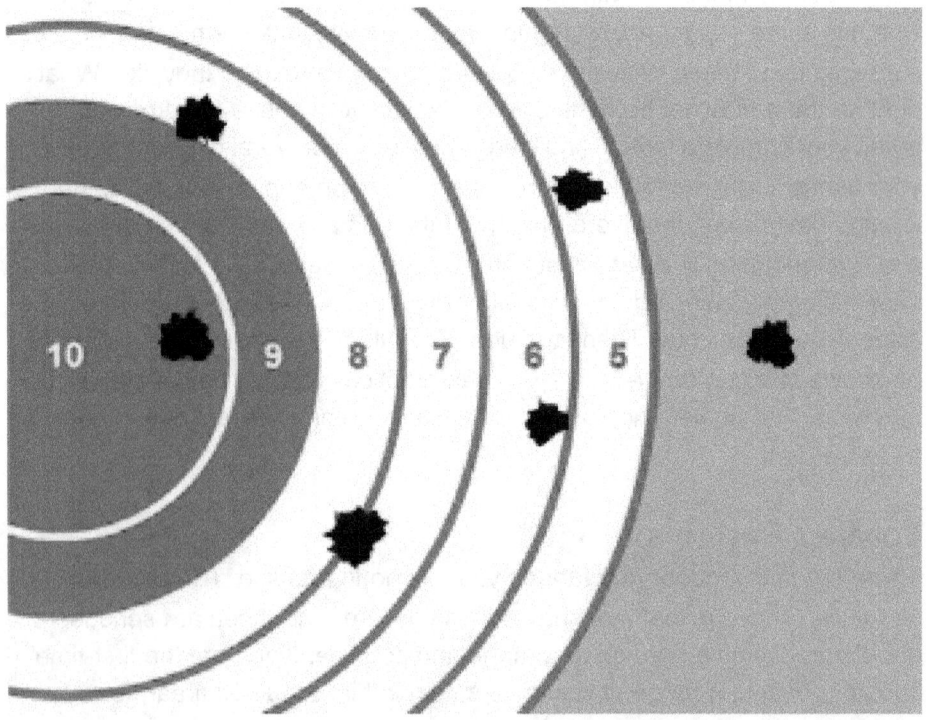

Purchasing Decisions

You've put some time in. You've practiced with different weapons. You've received some limited instruction with a few different types of weapons. Now you want to buy a firearm. How do you decide? It comes down to a few fairly simple yet important factors. The first is to understand what you want as opposed to what you need. You've seen a type of gun in a movie or your friend owns one and you like its look. You may have even rented one at the range a few times. It just looks cool and sounds like a cannon when you fire it. It's just a great, powerful weapon. Whether it be a .45 caliber semi-auto or a .357 Magnum, you just love the power it possesses and you'd love to have one. But when you fired it the first few times you couldn't hit the target. For whatever reason, it was too much for you. You anticipated the recoil, you jerked the trigger, you flinched just before it went "bang," or you simply were afraid of the thing.

So how do you know which weapon is right for you? Again certain questions need to be answered. Why are you buying a weapon? Is it for home protection only? Do you plan on keeping it in the car when you travel? Do you plan on keeping it on your person as you go about your daily routines? How will it be applied if necessary?

If it is for home protection you have a number of options. All handguns are suited for close shooting, but of course some handguns are more powerful than others. The stopping power of a .22 caliber handgun is vastly different than that of a .50 caliber Desert Eagle. If you have been practicing with different types of handguns you will have some knowledge that that a .22 caliber is also a great deal easier to handle than the larger caliber handguns. In the end it comes down to your comfort level, but most recommendations for first first-time gun buyers in this category are to practice with a handgun somewhere in the mid-range of bullet size (caliber). A .32 or .38 caliber revolver is a decent choice in the wheel gun category. Depending on the type of ammunition you purchase (we'll cover the differences in a bit) these weapons can provide enough stopping power for home protection without too much recoil when you fire them.

What exactly is recoil anyway and why do some weapons have more than others? Recoil is the motion of the weapon when the round is fired and leaves the barrel of the gun. A slight understanding of ballistics (the science of projectiles being fired from the weapon) is necessary to give you an idea why different caliber weapons have different levels of recoil. When a weapon (handgun/shotgun/rifle) is fired there are mechanical actions and chemical reactions taking place. The gun is a mechanical tool which, when put to use, causes a chemical reaction in the cartridge (bullet). Before we take on the mechanics of the gun, let's cover the makeup of the cartridge.

Every cartridge (bullet, shotgun shell, etc.) is composed in a similar manner. There are some internal variations that affect the speed of the projectile, but the actual construction is the same. At the base of each cartridge is an area in the center called the primer. The primer is actually an ignition source. Its physical composition is not important to know but its purpose is. When the hammer or firing pin in your weapon strikes the primer it ignites. It is not much more than a spark, and it does not have enough power to push the round out of the weapon. It does, however, start a chain reaction inside the cartridge. If you have an understanding of how explosives work, think of the primer as a blasting cap. Blasting caps are used as ignition sources for dynamite or other explosives. The primer is the "blasting cap" of the cartridge. Within the shell casing (the "brass" which holds all components of the cartridge together) there is additional ignitable material that begins to burn. The solid material within the casing burns at a very rapid pace. As it does it goes through the chemical change from a tightly compacted solid to a rapidly expanding gas.

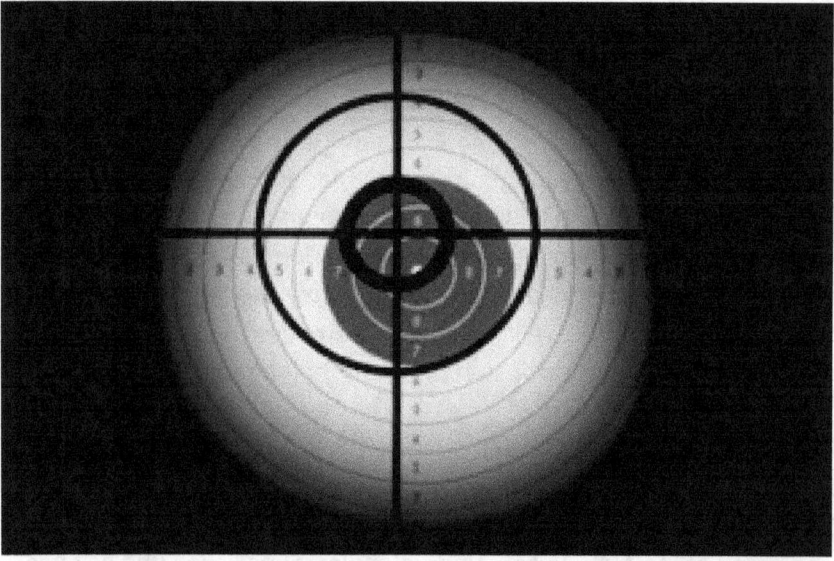

The next thing that happens involves a bit of physics (but not so much as to make your head spin). This rapidly expanding gas has to go somewhere. The way the cartridge fits into the chamber only allows the gas to go one way: forward. It pushes the brass wall of the cartridge outward so that it is airtight in the chamber and then the part of the round that will become the projectile is forced away from the shell casing and into the barrel. The gases continue to expand, pushing the projectile out of the end of the barrel and toward whatever the gun was pointed at. And now we arrive at recoil.

Recoil is not felt when the primer is struck. There is no rearward motion pushing backward on the gun at this point. As the material within the bullet begins to burn and the gases start expanding there is still no rearward motion (remember, the gases are pushing outward and then forward). The bullet is being pushed forward by the rapidly expanding gases. It is not pushing backward. It is not causing recoil. So what causes the weapon to violently recoil in your hand when it is fired? It is the gases…eventually. Once the projectile is out of the weapon and headed toward the target, the gases leave the barrel. Outside the barrel is the air we breathe. The atmosphere. It is itself composed of gases. When the gases leaving the barrel intrude upon the space occupied by the gases in the atmosphere there is a rearward motion. The rather big analogy would be to think about the space shuttle or any rocket for that matter. The solid fuel boosters operate in a similar fashion (though the burn lasts a lot longer than the burn of the round in a gun). The fuel begins to burn and pushes ignited gases out of the rear of the rocket. Those gases push against the atmosphere and cause the rocket to move upward. Jet engines operate on the same principle. When a gun is fired it too has a brief flash of propulsion as the gases push against the atmosphere and force the weapon backward in your hand. So there is recoil.

Why is this important to a shooter? Understanding recoil will help you understand how to become a better shooter. If the greater recoil of a large caliber weapon is not comfortable to you, you may begin to anticipate it and involuntarily begin to work against it. The inexperienced shooter will unconsciously push the weapon forward at the anticipated moment of recoil. That will cause the weapon to come off target before the round leaves the barrel. Lower caliber rounds have smaller projectiles which require less combustible material to propel out of the weapon. That equates to less recoil. Hence the suggestion that less-experienced shooters begin with a lower caliber weapon. A smaller amount of gas is pushed out of the barrel. The larger caliber rounds require more combustible material and therefore produce more gases and more propulsion as the larger amount of gas leaves the barrel. A higher level of comfort with weapons is necessary to shoot these weapons proficiently.

The mechanics of the gun play a part in how you shoot as well. Different types of guns operate slightly differently. They all have a mechanism for igniting the firing pin to cause the round to go off in the chamber, and that mechanism involves pulling a trigger. But all triggers don't feel the same when you pull them. The triggers in revolvers, for example, are usually harder to pull than semi-automatics. Most revolvers don't have a safety mechanism and therefore the trigger has a greater pull. Trigger pull is measured in pounds of pull (the amount of weight required to pull the trigger). Semi-automatic pistols operate a little differently than revolvers. They usually have some sort of externally operated safety mechanism (a lever which usually has to be manipulated in order for the gun to fire) and afterward require much less trigger pull. Some semi-automatics don't have a safety and the trigger pull on these weapons is usually similar to that of a revolver.

Shooting Basics

There are several keys to shooting well. If you do take on a trainer to help you learn to shoot you will learn them in some detail. The greatest of these is trigger control. Some others are grip, stance, breathing, and follow through. These are great to learn and will definitely help you to shoot well on the range. But sight alignment and sight picture play a large role, also. But trigger control is the greatest. The most proficient shooter masters the art of moving nothing but the trigger finger throughout the process of firing the gun while maintaining steady and unwavering sight alignment within a well established sight picture. With practice even the most inexperienced shooter can become extraordinarily proficient at shooting a pistol (or long gun).

As far as purchasing ammunition for the gun you decide upon, there are different types. For practice you should use full metal jacket rounds. These are usually a lot less expensive than hollow point or soft point rounds. The projectile is usually fully encased in metal, which leaves less residue in the barrel of the gun. When practicing with full metal-jacketed rounds be sure to buy the same grain ammunition of specialty rounds (hollow point or soft point). The weight of the round is described as grain. The main reason you want to use the same grain ammunition for your practice round as the defense round is to make sure the round travels the same when practicing as it will when you need to use it for defense. The gun dealer of your choice should be able to give you some guidance with regard to grain. The dealer should also be able to help when choosing a defense round for home protection.

Hollow point and soft point rounds are designed to expand (or mushroom) after contact. Most people think that these rounds are used to cause more damage to the person who is shot, but that is not the case. If you are using your weapon responsibly and appropriately to protect yourself and family from a valid threat, you want to be sure that the round fired from your gun stops the threat to you and yours, and you also want to be sure your rounds don't over-penetrate and have any potential to harm anyone else in your home. An expanding round will have less chance of passing through the threat and doing any harm to your loved ones. As stated before, talk to the gun dealer. He should be able to make some good recommendations. That's a quick overview of ammunition considerations.

Types of Home Protection Firearms

Revolvers, semi-automatic pistols, and shotguns are all weapons one might choose to purchase.

Revolver

The benefits of the revolver are easy to describe. As previously stated most do not have a safety mechanism. In order to fire you simply pull the trigger. Yet not all revolvers are the same. Some are single action, while others are double action. Single action revolvers require two pulls of the trigger to fire a shot (unless you manually cock the hammer with your hand) and double action revolvers set the hammer back and then release it with a single trigger pull. The trigger pull on the revolver is considerable, but with some models you can manually set the hammer back and effectively give the weapon a much slighter trigger pull (as the hammer is set back in the cocked position it effectively eliminates the majority of the heavy trigger pull).

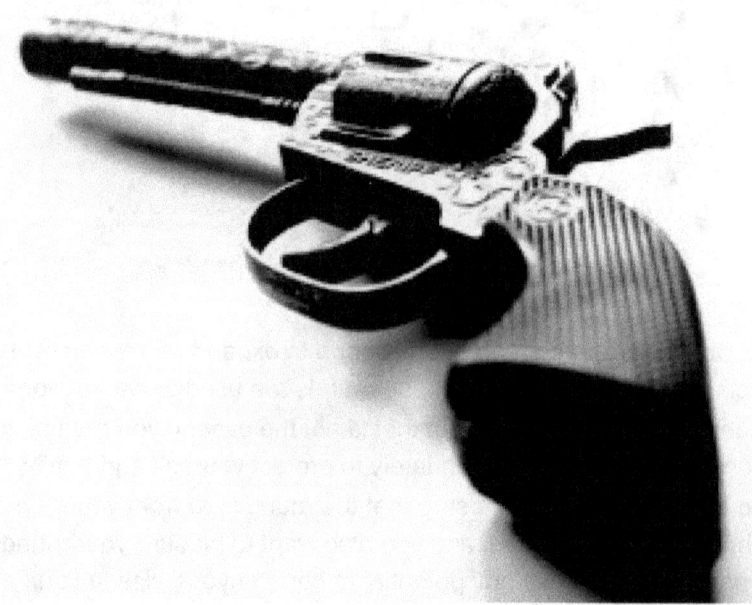

Malfunctions are extremely easy to overcome in a revolver. That portion of the weapon that holds the cartridges is the cylinder. Depending on the model it is easily accessed and loaded. With each pull of the trigger the cylinder rotates and the hammer drops on the next round. Every trigger pull turns the cylinder to the next available round. If a round does not fire for any reason, the shooter simply pulls the trigger and the next available round is fired. But semi-automatic handguns don't operate this way.

Semi-Automatic

A semi-automatic pistol fires every time the trigger is pulled as long as there is a round in the chamber and a magazine (commonly called a clip) loaded with ammunition in the weapon. Handling a malfunction with a semi-automatic pistol is a lot more complicated than that of a revolver. It will take some repeated practice. The shooter will need to practice manipulating the slide as well as understanding the workings of the weapon and magazine. If the trigger is pulled on a semi-automatic pistol and it does not fire the shooter cannot simply pull the trigger again to move to the next round. There is a more in-depth process for clearing the malfunction and getting the next round into the chamber. This is one of the instances a firearms instructor will come in handy. Clearing a malfunction in a semi-automatic pistol is not difficult once the mechanics are practiced with some expert tutelage.

Shotgun

The shotgun is another option available to someone looking to purchase a weapon for home protection. There are different types of shotguns on the market as well. The pump action shotgun is the most common (you've seen them in way too many movies). In order to load a round into the chamber you need to pump the action back then forward. There are also breach-loading shotguns (single shot and double-barreled) in which the shotgun is opened and the chamber is exposed and loaded by hand, semi-automatic shotguns which fire each time the trigger is pulled, and fully automatic shotguns which continue to fire as long as the trigger is held to the rear. The pump action shotgun is a good choice for similar reasons as the revolver. If a shotgun shell fails to fire the shooter only needs to pump the shotgun to eject the bad round and cycle a new shell into the chamber. Breach loading shotguns are good as well but they only can chamber one or two rounds before needing to be reloaded. Most pump action shotguns can hold at least four rounds in the magazine tube. And if you need to use a shotgun for home protection, there is nothing quite like the sound of a shotgun being racked. It is not ideal for outside the home though.

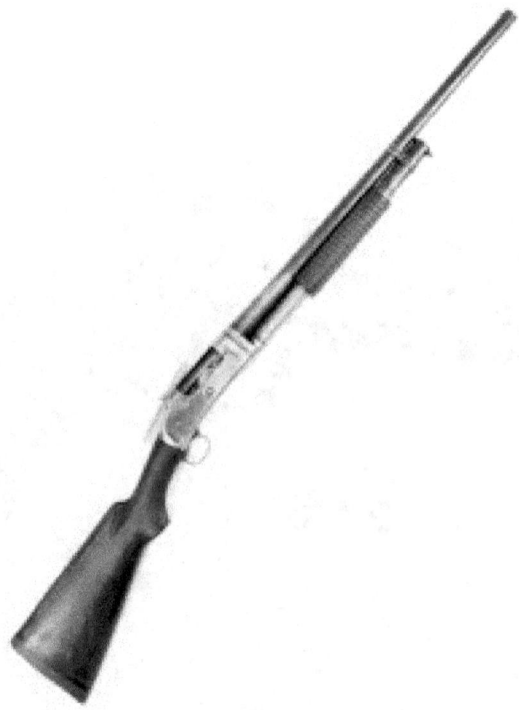

If you have taken the time to practice with different types of weapons and have found yourself to be proficient with more than one caliber then it becomes a question of what you want. Which gun do you like for the purpose you have in mind? You have more options before you if you take the time to practice. Once you become comfortable shooting you only have to decide on which gun you want to have. Or perhaps you will have to decide which guns you want.

Legal Considerations

Once you have decided to purchase a gun it is also important to have a working knowledge of the gun laws in your particular state. The ultimate authority on gun ownership is the 2nd Amendment of the United States Constitution. Each state has its own licensing requirements. The following information relates specifically to Georgia, and if you are contemplating a gun purchase you should check the laws in your own state to be sure you are in line with them.

As of July 2010 there is no longer a Conceal Carry Permit in Georgia: it is simply a license to carry. Georgia no longer makes a distinction between open carry and concealed carry. This means that in the state of Georgia a licensed person can carry a weapon (exposed or concealed) in all but a few prohibited places. In order to get a license to carry a person need only be 21 or older and have no felony convictions (there are a few other restrictions dealing with mental stability, etc). Make sure you read the laws regarding carrying and fully understand them. In a nutshell the Georgia statute indicates that an individual with a valid carry license may carry on his person a loaded gun, exposed or concealed, almost anywhere. The prohibited places are listed as follow: government buildings, courthouses, jails or prisons, places of worship, state mental health facilities, bars, nuclear power facilities, and within 150 feet of any polling place. There are certain caveats to these locations which are best understood if read multiple times with a note pad handy. Generally, the lawful gun carrier will be safe if he keeps his guns away from such locations.

But some gun owners don't want to carry everywhere. Some simply want to be able to defend their families. The good thing about the recently revamped Georgia law is that it made the brief distinction between the licensed gun carrier, the lawful gun owner, and the lawful gun owner eligible for a license.

STOP THE INTRUDER™ | KNOWLEDGE IS THE BEST PROTECTION™

The lawful gun owner is one legally able to own a gun but not of age to obtain a license (over 18 but under 21). The lawful owner eligible for a license is just that: over 21 with no felony conviction, but without a carry license. For any lawful gun owner it is legal to carry a gun on their person while on their own property, in their own home, their own motor vehicle, or their place of business. Outside of those locations the lawful owner must carry the weapon unloaded in a case.

The lawful and eligible person (over 21) may carry in the same as the lawful gun owner with the following exception: he can also carry in any private motor vehicle (not just his own) so long as the owner does not expressly forbid it. Both of these categories are prohibited from carrying outside of the listed places as outlined in Georgia Code 16-11-126. Those places were just provided but it would be a good idea to thoroughly read the code section. Georgia Code 16-11-127 lists the places even licensed persons cannot carry (again, listed above). If you do get a license, by all means become familiar with these locations so that you can remain legal.

The most important part of this is that the lawful gun owner can carry on his person (concealed or open) a loaded weapon from inside his home, onto his driveway (his property), and into his car. The tricky part is once you arrive at your location. Once you step outside your car, depending on your final destination, you need to have a license to carry in order to be legally carrying! If your end point is property you own, you're fine and legal. If it is the parking lot of the local grocery store, not legal! If you have the license to carry, you are fine and legal. But be aware, even if you are licensed to carry, if you are asked by management or ownership to not enter with the gun, you must leave. The 2nd Amendment right and state laws do not override the rights of private property owners to refuse weapons on their property.

Become familiar with the laws of your particular state. Research the laws as well. If you plan on carrying, either with or without a license, know the places you can and cannot carry. There are many websites of organizations that purport to fight for the 2nd Amendment right to bear arms. They maintain lists of various laws from state to state. Some of them are specific to each state while others are more general and broader in scope. Some are more reputable and with less rhetoric. Those more reputable ones refer the reader to the actual laws on the books. To find the laws as necessary for your state, check the Lexis-Nexis website. Lexis-Nexis usually will have the most up-to-date laws on their site.

Self Defense

The next legal consideration is using your gun for defense. Each state has laws on the books regarding protection of self and others. The following is specific to Georgia, but again most state laws are similar. In Georgia there is one code section that outlines the use of force up to and including deadly force (that force which is likely to or will cause death). Per Georgia law, a person is justified in using deadly force if he reasonably believes the application of such force is necessary to prevent death or great bodily harm to himself. In other words if you are being attacked or reasonably perceive an attack is imminent and such attack will cause death or great bodily harm to you, then you can protect yourself by using deadly force.

The next instance deadly force can be used is to protect a third person. Again per Georgia law, a person is justified in using deadly force if he reasonably believes the application of that force is necessary to prevent death or great bodily harm to someone else. This means that you can use deadly force to protect someone other than yourself. This is an important facet of law. Most people don't realize they have the right to not only defend themselves but also to defend others. If someone is being attacked and you have a reasonable belief that that individual is about to be killed or receive great bodily harm then you would be within the law if you intervened by using deadly force.

The next portion covers several instances. Georgia law specifies that a person may use deadly force to prevent the commission of a forcible felony. In general terms, a forcible felony is any felony in which physical harm or the threat of physical harm is applied to a victim. Armed robbery, aggravated assault, rape, and several other crimes fall into this category. Any lawful gun carrier who might intervene in such an instance should take caution. You really need to be sure the crime you are attempting to stop falls into this category. Police officers receive many hours of training to understand the application of deadly force, while the casual gun carrier exercising his 2nd Amendment right to bear arms may have only the briefest introduction to such laws. In many instances it is simply better to be a good witness. But it is also good to be prepared to act if the need should arise.

Perhaps one of the most misunderstood legal concepts around the use of deadly force is its application in protection of the home (Use of force in defense of habitation). The following is a brief summary of Georgia law. A person is justified in using force against another person if he reasonably believes the use of force is necessary to prevent or stop the other person's unlawful entry into or attack upon a habitation. This statement is not inclusive of the use of deadly force. In order for a person to use deadly force to repel an attack upon a habitation certain specific elements must be present.

First, the entry made or attempted by the perpetrator must be of a "violent and tumultuous manner." A door being kicked in or a window being smashed might easily qualify as violent and tumultuous. In addition the person within the home must reasonably believe the entry is being made to assault any person either living or visiting the home and deadly force is necessary to stop the assault. This becomes an issue for some people who think that the assault has to be taking place. According to law the attempted unlawful entry (violent and tumultuous) gives rise to the reasonable person that the assault is imminent. Deadly force can be used if it is reasonable to believe such an assault is the reason for the entry. The question about the threshold sometimes comes up. Homeowners many times are under the mistaken impression that the perpetrator has to be inside the house. This is not true. Whether he be at the door or at the window, his violent attempt to gain entry is just as good as a violent entry. You need not wait for him to get in the house to use deadly force to protect yourself and your family.

There are two additional times offered for consideration as well. Per Georgia law, such deadly force may be employed against the perpetrator provided he is not a member of the family or household and he has unlawfully and forcibly entered the home. The person using deadly force must know or have reason to believe an unlawful and forcible entry has taken place. And yet another instance indicates the person using deadly force must also reasonably believe the entry is made in order to commit a felony and the use of deadly force is necessary to prevent the felony.

The first stated justification for using deadly force to protect the home is an easy one to understand. The violent and tumultuous wording is easy to understand. The bad guy is kicking in the front or back door. He has smashed a window and is climbing inside. That makes sense to most of us. Any logical person would be able to articulate some level of concern for his own safety and the safety of anyone else in the home. But the question arises regarding the burglar. Many wonder if they have the right to employ deadly force just because an unauthorized person enters their home. There has been no violent or tumultuous entry. What should the homeowner do if he comes home early from work one day to find a pair of teenage burglars stealing electronics from his home? Is he legally justified if he draws his weapon and shoots them?

On its face the Georgia law (16-3-23) seems to be on the side of the homeowner in this situation. Burglary is a felony. The law does state the person using deadly force must reasonably believe the entry by the perpetrator was made for the purpose of committing a felony. However, the crux of the law is found in the wording in the first paragraph, which indicates the use of force in general. Any application of force must be used with the reasonable expectation that such "force is necessary to prevent or terminate" the unlawful entry. If our noble homeowner returns home early and finds the two teenage burglars in his home and they immediately drop their ill-gotten goods and begin to attempt an escape, then the use of force, especially deadly force, is not considered reasonable. The homeowner's mere presence has accomplished the termination of the entry as the two miscreants make their escape.

The general terminology to take into account is imminent danger. If a reasonable person would have perceived the given situation in the same way, then it is reasonable to use deadly force. Articulation of one's perception becomes the key to any deadly force encounter. Whether using deadly force to protect yourself, a third person, or your home, you must be able to articulate your perceptions. Not all people are going to perceive each situation exactly the same way. An accomplished mixed martial artist will not perceive an unarmed burglar in the same way an untrained mother of three would. And the reasonable levels of force would be different in those two situations. But an armed intruder levels the playing field. Even the martial artist would be justified in using a handgun to repel an armed intruder. The mother of three most definitely would.

Firearms Safety

There are basic safety rules that every responsible gun owner must abide by. There are only four of them. They are universal and every gun safety course you might take should go over them in some form or fashion. Their importance is paramount, and if they are followed it will be all but impossible for an accident to do harm to you or anyone else.

RULE 1
Treat every gun as if it were loaded.

This rule sets the stage for the other rules. If you mentally perceive that the weapon is loaded and treat it as such you will be careful with it. If it is loaded in your mind you will be less likely to be careless with it. Know that every gun has the potential to cause great bodily harm or death. Remind yourself of this fact again and again. Even if you are 100% sure that the weapon is unloaded, treat it as if it is loaded. People make mistakes all the time. Many accidental discharges occur because of negligence on the part of the gun owner. You might be sure the weapon is unloaded, but what if you are wrong?

Accidental shootings are so very tragic and, sadly, avoidable.

STOP THE INTRUDER™ | KNOWLEDGE IS THE BEST PROTECTION™

Rule 2
Never point your weapon at anything you do not intend to shoot.

This rule follows the first. If you treat the weapon as if it is loaded, hopefully you would not ever point it at anything or anyone you don't intend to shoot. Again, tragedy can be avoided by following this rule. The weapon is not a toy. Even unloaded it should be treated as a serious weapon, as it is.

Rule 3
Keep your finger off the trigger until you are ready to fire

Again the first rule precludes this one. If the weapon is treated as if it is loaded, the responsible gun owner will not place his finger on the trigger unless he is about to fire it. The second rule comes into play as well; the weapon will of course be pointed at an intended target. Whether it is loaded or unloaded these rules remain just as important.

And now the last rule: Be sure of your target and everything behind it.

Make sure the weapon is pointed at what you intend to shoot. And pay special attention to what is near and behind your target. The responsible shooter needs to be aware of what else is nearby. If it is not safe to fire the weapon without possibly hitting an unintended bystander then the decision to fire should be reconsidered. This decision is easy to make when practicing on a gun range, but it might be harder to determine in a home or personal protection situation. This is where practice at a gun range becomes important. The more skillful shooter can be more confident in taking more difficult shots.

Gun safety is more than safely operating the weapon. The responsible gun owner needs a plan for safe storage in the home. Remember, when at home the lawful gun owner can carry a loaded gun on his person. The issue of safety arises when the same gun owner removes the gun from his person. The weapon should be kept out of children's reach and vision. There are reputable and established safety programs for children. That is for the parents to decide.

The NRA has a list of rules for young children (those not considered old enough to be allowed to handle a gun). They are simple and common sense. Even parents opposed to guns in the home can appreciate the safety of these rules. These rules are:

- **STOP;**
- **DON'T TOUCH;**
- **LEAVE THE AREA; and**
- **TELL AN ADULT.**

It is important that children know that guns are not toys. They are never to be played with. If a child finds what is possibly an actual gun, they should immediately leave it alone and find an adult. For the gun owner with children at home, these rules should be explained in grave detail. The rules need to be quizzed into the children to make sure they become second nature.

Once you store the weapon in your home you need to make sure it is not accessible to children. There are many safety mechanisms one can purchase to make the gun safe. Different manufacturers make variations of trigger locking mechanisms, gun locks, gun safes, etc. It is up to you to determine which type of safety mechanism you want to use. The shoebox on a high shelf in your bedroom closet probably is not the safest route to take. Kids are kids and you can't bet on their lives that they won't go snooping through your things and find the loaded weapon. No matter what type of safety mechanism you decide to put to use, be sure you practice unlocking and accessing your weapon on a regular basis. If you find yourself having to defend your family in the middle of the night you won't have time to practice then.

Another safety consideration is whether or not to keep the weapon loaded when you store it at home. A little bit of common sense should come into play. If the gun is locked in a safe that has to be unlocked before the weapon is accessed, it is probably alright to have the weapon loaded. If you do not store it in a safe but instead keep it in a drawer in your nightstand, maybe you should keep it unloaded with a full magazine nearby. That way if you wake up in the middle of the night to check that loud thump downstairs, you'll have to wake up and actually load the weapon first (a conscious act requiring you to wake up a little). Some gun owners keep their weapons unloaded and locked (either in a safe, or tucked away with a trigger lock). Whichever way you store your weapon at home, be sure to practice getting to it and getting it loaded and ready.

In summary, be responsible throughout the gun ownership process. Before you buy, check out all that is available to you. Know what it is you are buying the gun for. Seek assistance in all phases: researching, practicing, buying, personal safety, and home safety. Become gun savvy. Gun ownership is a right afforded to all law abiding U.S. citizens. Get to know and understand your home state's laws. But above all else be safe. Be safe while you practice, while you carry, and once you get your new defense tool home.

Conclusion

This course has offered an array of information to stop the intruder. We've analyzed the four security zones in detail. The outermost zone is the deterrence zone. The goal here is to deter criminals from choosing your residence as a target.

The next zone is the funnel zone. Its goal is to channel visitors and potential criminals to approved access points. The channels should deter others from approaching less-secure areas as much as possible.

The access control points are the third zone. These points let people enter or exit unless you deny them access. Access control points must be reinforced. The final zone is the refuge. This area is designed to provide safety inside your residence in the event of home invasion or other life-threatening incident. You and your family must remain vigilant at all times.

It's very important that your residence does not become a target. Analyze all your daily activities. Apply common sense to all situations. Ensure that your trash doesn't throw a spotlight on your high dollar purchases. Report anyone loitering near your residence to law enforcement professionals and photograph them (to the extent that doing so is practical and safe). Look at your home and its surroundings from the standpoint of a criminal: observe your home during the day and night to locate weak points and vulnerabilities. A great defense is developing friendships with your neighbors. Establish a level of trust with them whenever possible. Invite them over and get to know them. Agree to watch each other's home and property; train your discerning eye on neighboring residences. Finally, apply the other principles ideas you find here as they apply to your specific situation. Work together, stay involved and stay safe!

STOP THE INTRUDER™ | KNOWLEDGE IS THE BEST PROTECTION™

Appendix 1 - Emergency Contact List

In the US - dial 911

Hospital	Address / Telephone
Hospital	Address / Telephone
Sheriff's Office	Address / Telephone (non emergency)
Police Department	Address / Telephone (non emergency)
Fire Department	Address / Telephone (non emergency)
State Patrol	Address / Telephone (non emergency)
Ambulance Service	Address / Telephone (non emergency)

Your Address

_____

Subdivision / Area Name

_____

Nearest Cross Streets

_____ & _____

Global Positioning System Coordinates

_____

STOP THE INTRUDER™ | KNOWLEDGE IS THE BEST PROTECTION™

Appendix 2 - First Aid Equipment

- Abdominal Pads 5"x9"
- After Bite Wipes
- Airways
- Alcohol Wipes
- Ammonia Inhalants
- Antiseptic Wipes
- Assorted Size bandaids
- "Bandage Strips 2x3""
- Blood Clotting Spray
- Blood Pressure Cuff
- Bloodspot Bandages
- Burn Aid
- Burn Spray
- butterfly strips
- Calamine Lotion, 6oz
- Cervical Collar
- CPR mask
- Elastic Bandages 2"
- Elastic Bandages 6"
- Elastic Bandages Gauze 4.5"x 4 yards"
- Emergency Blanket
- EMT Shears
- Eye Pads
- Gauze Sponges 2x2
- Hand Sanitizer
- Instant Glucose
- Instant Ice Packs
- Iodine Wipe
- Irrigation Syringes
- Latex Gloves
- Lip Balm
- Needle Probe
- Pain Reliever
- Pen Light
- Quick Clots
- Safety Pins
- SAM/Universal Splint
- Scalpel Blades
- Scalpel Handle # 3
- Skin & Eye Wash
- Stainless Steel Hemostat
- Sterile Sponges 4x4
- Stethoscope
- Suture Sets
- Tape, Rolls, Adhesives
- Tongue Depressors
- Triangular Bandages
- Triple Antibiotic
- Tweezers

Appendix 3 - State Crime Analysis

STOP THE INTRUDER™ | KNOWLEDGE IS THE BEST PROTECTION™

ALABAMA

Alabama is located in the southeastern part of the United States. It was admitted to the Union on December 14, 1819 and borders Tennessee in the north, Georgia in the east, Florida and Gulf of Mexico in the south and Mississippi on the west. Alabama happens to be the 23rd most populous state in the United States and stretches over an area of 52,419 square miles. It is composed of 67 counties.

Largest cities:
- Birmingham
- Montgomery
- Mobile

Population:
- 4.8 million
- Ranked 23rd

Size:
- 52,419 square miles
- Ranked 30th

Population
According to the 2011 United States Census, Alabama had a population of 4.8 million. The 2000 census reported 4.4 million people. This population is composed of the following:

White	68.5%
African American	26.2%
American Indian	0.6%
Asian	1.1%
Hispanics	3.9%
Other	1.5%

Crime Statistics
The Federal Bureau of Investigation collects a series of crime information from across the country. This information was analyzed to provide the following:

Type	Totals	By 100,000 people	Risk
Murder & Manslaughter	273	5.7	High
Forcible Rape	1,349	28.2	Moderate
Robbery	4,761	99.6	Moderate
Aggravated Assault	11,763	244.2	Moderate
Burglary	42,034	879.4	Moderate
Larceny-Theft	115,458	2,415.6	High

Violent Crime Trends
Violent crimes are composed of murder, non-negligent manslaughter, forcible rape, robbery and aggravated assault. Home invasions are considered a robbery. When combined together there were a total of 18,146 in 2010.

Property Crime Trends
Property crimes are composed of burglary, larceny / theft and motor vehicle theft. When combined together there were a total of 168,092 in 2010.

STOP THE INTRUDER™ | KNOWLEDGE IS THE BEST PROTECTION™

ALASKA

Alaska happens to the largest state in the United States. It is surrounded by Canada on the east, the Arctic Ocean on the north, the Pacific Ocean on the west and the south. Alaska is the least populated state in the U.S. and stretches over an area of 663,268 square miles. It was admitted to the union on January 3, 1959. Alaska does not have any counties but consists of 25 boroughs.

The largest cities:
- Anchorage
- Fairbanks
- Juneau

Population:
- 722,718
- Ranked 47th

Size:
- 663,268 square miles
- Ranked 1st

Population
According to the 2011 United States Census, Alaska had a population of 722,718. The 2000 census reported 626,932 people. This population is composed of the following:

White	66.7%
African American	3.3%
American Indian	14.8%
Asian	5.4%
Hispanics	5.5%
Other	7.3%

Crime Statistics
The Federal Bureau of Investigation collects a series of crime information from across the country. This information was analyzed to provide the following:

Type	Totals	By 100,000 people	Risk
Murder & Manslaughter	31	4.4	Moderate
Forcible Rape	533	75	High
Robbery	594	83.6	Moderate
Aggravated Assault	3,379	475.8	High
Burglary	3,105	437.2	Moderate
Larceny-Theft	15,535	2,187.3	Moderate

Violent Crime Trends
Violent crimes are composed of murder, non-negligent manslaughter, forcible rape, robbery and aggravated assault. Home invasions are considered a robbery. When combined together there were a total of 4,537 in 2010.

Property Crime Trends
Property crimes are composed of burglary, larceny / theft and motor vehicle theft. When combined together there were a total of 20,259 in 2010.

STOP THE INTRUDER™ | KNOWLEDGE IS THE BEST PROTECTION™

ARIZONA

Description
Alaska happens to the largest state in the United States. It is surrounded New Mexico on the east, California on the west, and Nevada, Utah and Colorado on the north. Alaska is the 16th most populous state in the U.S. and stretches over an area of 113,990 square miles. It was admitted to the union on February 14, 1912. Alaska consists of 16 counties.

The largest cities:
- Phoenix
- Tucson
- Mesa

Population:
- 6.4 million
- Ranked 16th

Size:
- 113,990 square miles
- Ranked 6th

Population
According to the 2011 United States Census, Arizona had a population of 6.4 million. The 2000 census reported 5.1 million people. This population is composed of the following:

White	73%
African American	4.1%
American Indian	4.6%
Asian	2.8%
Hispanics	29.6%
Other	3.4%

Crime Statistics
The Federal Bureau of Investigation collects a series of crime information from across the country. This information was analyzed to provide the following:

Type	Totals	By 100,000 people	Risk
Murder & Manslaughter	409	6.4	High
Forcible Rape	2,165	33.9	Moderate
Robbery	6,937	108.5	Moderate
Aggravated Assault	16,574	259.3	Moderate
Burglary	50,771	794.3	Moderate
Larceny-Theft	153,614	2,403.2	High

Violent Crime Trends
Violent crimes are composed of murder, non-negligent manslaughter, forcible rape, robbery and aggravated assault. Home invasions are considered a robbery. When combined together there were a total of 25,545 in 2010.

Property Crime Trends
Property crimes are composed of burglary, larceny / theft and motor vehicle theft. When combined together there were a total of 225,893 in 2010.

STOP THE INTRUDER™ | KNOWLEDGE IS THE BEST PROTECTION™

ARKANSAS

Description
Arkansas is located in the southern part of the United States. It is surrounded by Missouri on the north, Tennessee and Mississippi on the east, Louisiana in the south, Texas in the southwest and Oklahoma to its west. It is the 32nd most populous state in the U.S. and stretched over an area of 53,179 square miles. It was admitted to the union on June 15, 1836. Arkansas consists of 75 counties.

The largest cities:
- Little Rock
- Fort Smith
- Fayetteville

Population:
- 2.9 million
- Ranked 32nd

Size:
- 53,179 square miles
- Ranked 29th

Population
According to the 2011 United States Census, Arkansas had a population of 2.9 million. The 2000 census reported 2.6 million people. This population is composed of the following:

White	77%
African American	15.4%
American Indian	0.8%
Asian	1.2%
Hispanics	6.4%
Other	2.0%

Crime Statistics
The Federal Bureau of Investigation collects a series of crime information from across the country. This information was analyzed to provide the following:

Type	Totals	By 100,000 people	Risk
Murder & Manslaughter	138	4.7	Moderate
Forcible Rape	1,312	45	High
Robbery	2,372	81.3	Moderate
Aggravated Assault	10,193	374.3	High
Burglary	32,511	1,114.9	High
Larceny-Theft	65,720	2,253.8	Moderate

Violent Crime Trends
Violent crimes are composed of murder, non-negligent manslaughter, forcible rape, robbery and aggravated assault. Home invasions are considered a robbery. When combined together there were a total of 14,015 in 2010.

Property Crime Trends
Property crimes are composed of burglary, larceny / theft and motor vehicle theft. When combined together there were a total of 103,775 in 2010.

STOP THE INTRUDER™ | KNOWLEDGE IS THE BEST PROTECTION™

CALIFORNIA

California is located on the western coastal part of the United States. It is surrounded by Oregon on the north, Nevada on the east and Arizona on the southeast. It is the most populous states in the U.S. and stretches over an area of 163,696 square miles. It was admitted to the union on September 9, 1850. California consists of 58 counties.

The largest cities:
- Los Angeles
- San Diego
- San Jose

Population:
- 37.6 million
- Ranked 1st

Size:
- 163,696 square miles
- Ranked 3rd

Population
According to the 2011 United States Census, California had a population of 37.6 million. The 2000 census reported 33.8 million people. This population is composed of the following:

White	57.6%
African American	6.2%
American Indian	1.0%
Asian	13.0%
Hispanics	37.6%
Other	4.9%

Crime Statistics
The Federal Bureau of Investigation collects a series of crime information from across the country. This information was analyzed to provide the following:

Type	Totals	By 100,000 people	Risk
Murder & Manslaughter	1,809	4.9	Moderate
Forcible Rape	8,331	22.4	Moderate
Robbery	58,116	156.0	High
Aggravated Assault	95,877	257.4	Moderate
Burglary	228,857	614.3	Moderate
Larceny-Theft	600,558	1,612.1	Moderate

Violent Crime Trends
Violent crimes are composed of murder, non-negligent manslaughter, forcible rape, robbery and aggravated assault. Home invasions are considered a robbery. When combined together there were a total of 164,133 in 2010.

Property Crime Trends
Property crimes are composed of burglary, larceny / theft and motor vehicle theft. When combined together there were a total of 9,814,939 in 2010.

STOP THE INTRUDER™ | KNOWLEDGE IS THE BEST PROTECTION™

COLORADO

Often known as the centennial state, Colorado is surrounded by Utah on the west, Wyoming and Nebraska in the north, Kansas to its east and New Mexico to its south. Colorado is the 22nd most populous state of the United States and stretches over an area of 104,094 square miles. It was admitted to the union on August 1, 1876. Colorado consists of 64 counties.

The largest cities:
- Denver
- Colorado Springs
- Aurora

Population:
- 5.1 million
- Ranked 22nd

Size:
- 104,094 square miles
- Ranked 8th

Population
According to the 2011 United States Census, Colorado had a population of 5.1 million. The 2000 census reported 4.3 million people. This population is composed of the following:

White	81.3%
African American	4.0%
American Indian	1.1%
Asian	2.8%
Hispanics	20.7%
Other	3.4%

Crime Statistics
The Federal Bureau of Investigation collects a series of crime information from across the country. This information was analyzed to provide the following:

Type	Totals	By 100,000 people	Risk
Murder & Manslaughter	120	2.4	Moderate
Forcible Rape	2,198	43.7	High
Robbery	3,132	62.3	Moderate
Aggravated Assault	10,683	212.4	Moderate
Burglary	26,153	520.0	Moderate
Larceny-Theft	97,592	1,940.5	Moderate

Violent Crime Trends
Violent crimes are composed of murder, non-negligent manslaughter, forcible rape, robbery and aggravated assault. Home invasions are considered a robbery. When combined together there were a total of 16,133 in 2010.

Property Crime Trends
Property crimes are composed of burglary, larceny / theft and motor vehicle theft. When combined together there were a total of 134,992 in 2010.

STOP THE INTRUDER™ | KNOWLEDGE IS THE BEST PROTECTION™

CONNECTICUT

Connecticut is located in the northeastern part of the United States. It was admitted to the Union on Jan. 9, 1788. It is a state in the New England region and is surrounded by Rhode Island on the east, Massachusetts on the north and New York on the west and the south. Connecticut happens to be the 29th most populous state in the United States and stretches over an area of 5,543 square miles. It is composed of 8 counties.

The largest cities:
- Bridgeport
- New Haven
- Hartford

Population:
- 3.5 million
- Ranked 29th

Size:
- 5,543 square miles
- Ranked 48th

Population
According to the 2011 United States Census, Connecticut had a population of 3.5 million. The 2000 census reported 3.4 million people. This population is composed of the following:

White	77.6%
African American	10.1%
American Indian	0.3%
Asian	3.8%
Pacific Islander	5.6%
Other	2.6%

Crime Statistics
The Federal Bureau of Investigation collects a series of crime information from across the country. This information was analyzed to provide the following:

Type	Totals	By 100,000 people	Risk
Murder & Manslaughter	130	3.6	Moderate
Forcible Rape	583	16.3	Low
Robbery	3,553	99.4	Moderate
Aggravated Assault	5,791	162	Moderate
Burglary	15,172	424.5	Low
Larceny-Theft	56,507	1581	Low

Violent Crime Trends
Violent crimes are composed of murder, non-negligent manslaughter, forcible rape, robbery and aggravated assault. Home invasions are considered a robbery. When combined together there were a a total of 10,057 in 2010.

Property Crime Trends
Property crimes are composed of burglary, larceny / theft and motor vehicle theft. When combined together there were a total of 78,386 in 2010.

STOP THE INTRUDER™ | KNOWLEDGE IS THE BEST PROTECTION™

DELAWARE

The largest cities:
- Bridgeport
- New Haven
- Hartford

Delaware is located in the mid-Atlantic region of the United States. It is surrounded by Maryland on the south and west, by New Jersey on the northeast, and by Pennsylvania to its north. It is the 45th most populous state in the U.S. and stretches over an area of 2,490 square miles. It was admitted to the union on December 7, 1787 and consists of 3 counties.

Population:
- 3.5 million
- Ranked 29th

Size:
- 5,543 square miles
- Ranked 48th

Population
According to the 2011 United States Census, Delaware had a population of 3.5 million. The 2000 census reported 3.4 million people. This population is composed of the following:

White	68.9%
African American	21.4%
American Indian	0.5%
Asian	3.2%
Hispanic	8.2%
Other	2.7%

Crime Statistics
The Federal Bureau of Investigation collects a series of crime information from across the country. This information was analyzed to provide the following:

Type	Totals	By 100,000 people	Risk
Murder & Manslaughter	48	5.3	Moderate
Forcible Rape	312	34.7	Moderate
Robbery	1,829	203.7	High
Aggravated Assault	3,386	377.1	High
Burglary	7,515	836.9	Moderate
Larceny-Theft	21,519	2,396.5	High

Violent Crime Trends
Violent crimes are composed of murder, non-negligent manslaughter, forcible rape, robbery and aggravated assault. Home invasions are considered a robbery. When combined together there were a a total of 5,575 in 2010.

Property Crime Trends
Property crimes are composed of burglary, larceny / theft and motor vehicle theft. When combined together there were a total of 30,963 in 2010.

STOP THE INTRUDER™ | KNOWLEDGE IS THE BEST PROTECTION™

FLORIDA

Florida is located in the southeastern part of the United States. To its west lies the Gulf of Mexico, Alabama and Georgia are to its north, and it is bordered by the Atlantic Ocean to its east. It is the 4th most populous state in the U.S. and stretches over an area of 65,755 square miles. Florida was admitted to the union on March 3, 1845. It consists of 67 counties.

The largest cities:
- Jacksonville
- Miami
- Tampa

Population:
- 19 million
- Ranked 4th

Size:
- 65,755 square miles
- Ranked 22nd

Population
According to the 2011 United States Census, Florida had a population of 4.8 million. The 2000 census reported 15.9 million people. This population is composed of the following:

White	75.0%
African American	16.0%
American Indian	0.4%
Asian	2.4%
Hispanics	22.5%
Other	2.5%

Crime Statistics
The Federal Bureau of Investigation collects a series of crime information from across the country. This information was analyzed to provide the following:

Type	Totals	By 100,000 people	Risk
Murder & Manslaughter	987	5.2	Moderate
Forcible Rape	5,373	28.6	Moderate
Robbery	26,086	138.7	High
Aggravated Assault	69,523	369.8	High
Burglary	169,119	899.5	Moderate
Larceny-Theft	458,454	2,438.4	High

Violent Crime Trends
Violent crimes are composed of murder, non-negligent manslaughter, forcible rape, robbery and aggravated assault. Home invasions are considered a robbery. When combined together there were a total of 94,969 in 2010.

Property Crime Trends
Property crimes are composed of burglary, larceny / theft and motor vehicle theft. When combined together there were a total of 669,035 in 2010.

STOP THE INTRUDER™ | KNOWLEDGE IS THE BEST PROTECTION™

GEORGIA

The state of Georgia is located in the southeastern part of the United States. It was admitted to the union on January 2, 1788 and borders Florida in the south, the Atlantic Ocean and South Carolina on the east, Alabama in the west and by Tennessee and North Carolina on the north. Georgia is the 9th most populous state in the United States and stretches over an area of 59,425 square miles. It has 159 counties.

The largest cities:
- Atlanta
- Augusta
- Columbus

Population:
- 9.8 million
- Ranked 9th

Size:
- 59,425 square miles
- Ranked 24th

Population
According to the 2011 United States Census, Georgia had a population of 9.8 million. The 2000 census reported 8.1 million people. This is an increase of 1,628,757. This population is composed of the following:

White	59.7%
African American	30.5%
American Indian	0.3%
Asian	3.2%
Hispanics	8.8%
Other	2.1%

Crime Statistics
The Federal Bureau of Investigation collects a series of crime information from across the country. This information was analyzed to provide the following:

Type	Totals	By 100,000 people	Risk
Murder & non-negligent manslaughter	558	5.8	High
Forcible Rape	2,093	21.6	Low
Robbery	12,373	127.7	Moderate
Aggravated Assault	24,048	248.2	Moderate
Burglary	96,723	998.4	High
Larceny-Theft	225,651	2,329.3	Moderate

Violent Crime Trends
Violent crimes are composed of murder, non-negligent manslaughter, forcible rape, robbery and aggravated assault. Home invasions are considered a robbery. When combined together there were a total of 24,048 in 2010.

Property Crime Trends
Property crimes are composed of burglary, larceny / theft and motor vehicle theft. When combined together there were a total of 352,679 in 2010.

STOP THE INTRUDER™ | KNOWLEDGE IS THE BEST PROTECTION™

HAWAII

Hawaii happens to be the sole U.S. state that is entirely made up of islands. It is surrounded by the Pacific Ocean about 2,400 miles southwest of the Continental United States. It is the 40th most populous states in the U.S. and stretches over an area of 10,931 square miles. It was admitted to the union on August 21, 1959. Hawaii consists of 5 counties.

The largest cities:
- Honolulu
- Hilo
- Kailua

Population:
- 1.3 million
- Ranked 40th

Size:
- 10,931 square miles
- Ranked 43rd

Population
According to the 2011 United States Census, Hawaii had a population of 1.3 million. The 2000 census reported 1.2 million people. This population is composed of the following:

White	24.7%
African American	1.6%
American Indian	0.3%
Asian	38.6%
Hispanics	8.9%
Other	23.6%

Crime Statistics
The Federal Bureau of Investigation collects a series of crime information from across the country. This information was analyzed to provide the following:

Type	Totals	By 100,000 people	Risk
Murder & Manslaughter	24	1.8	Low
Forcible Rape	365	26.8	Moderate
Robbery	1,054	77.5	Moderate
Aggravated Assault	2,131	156.7	Moderate
Burglary	8,663	636.8	Moderate
Larceny-Theft	31,320	2,302.4	Moderate

Violent Crime Trends
Violent crimes are composed of murder, non-negligent manslaughter, forcible rape, robbery and aggravated assault. Home invasions are considered a robbery. When combined together there were a total of 3,574 in 2010.

Property Crime Trends
Property crimes are composed of burglary, larceny / theft and motor vehicle theft. When combined together there were a total of 45,083 in 2010.

STOP THE INTRUDER™ | KNOWLEDGE IS THE BEST PROTECTION™

IDAHO

Since Idaho is located in the Rocky Mountain region, it is often known as the mountain state. It is surrounded by Utah and Nevada on the south, Oregon on the west, Washington on the northwest, Wyoming on the east and Montana to its east. It is the 39th most populous state in the U.S. and stretches over an area of 83,570 square miles. It was admitted to the union on July 3, 1980. It consists of 44 counties.

The largest cities:
- Boise
- Nampa
- Meridian

Population:
- 1.5 million
- Ranked 39th

Size:
- 83,570 square miles
- Ranked 14th

Population
According to the 2011 United States Census, Idaho had a population of 1.5 million. The 2000 census reported 1.3 million people. This population is composed of the following:

White	89.1%
African American	0.6%
American Indian	1.4%
Asian	1.2%
Hispanics	11.2%
Other	2.5%

Crime Statistics
The Federal Bureau of Investigation collects a series of crime information from across the country. This information was analyzed to provide the following:

Type	Totals	By 100,000 people	Risk
Murder & Manslaughter	21	1.3	Low
Forcible Rape	525	33.5	Moderate
Robbery	214	13.7	Low
Aggravated Assault	2,705	172.6	Moderate
Burglary	6,502	414.8	Low
Larceny-Theft	23,642	1,4969.7	Low

Violent Crime Trends
Violent crimes are composed of murder, non-negligent manslaughter, forcible rape, robbery and aggravated assault. Home invasions are considered a robbery. When combined together there were a total of 3,465 in 2010.

Property Crime Trends
Property crimes are composed of burglary, larceny / theft and motor vehicle theft. When combined together there were a total of 31,469 in 2010.

STOP THE INTRUDER™ | KNOWLEDGE IS THE BEST PROTECTION™

ILLINOIS

The state of Illinois is surrounded by Iowa on the west, Missouri on the southwest, Wisconsin on the north, Indiana on the east, Michigan on the northeast and Kentucky to its south. It is 5th most populous state in the United States and stretches over an area of 57,914 square miles. It was admitted to the union on December 3, 1818 and consists of 102 counties.

The largest cities:
- Chicago
- Aurora
- Rockford

Population:
- 12.8 million
- Ranked 5th

Size:
- 57,914 square miles
- Ranked 25th

Population
According to the 2011 United States Census, Illinois had a population of 12.8 million. The 2000 census reported 12.4 million people. This population is composed of the following:

African American	14.5%
American Indian	0.3%
Asian	4.6%
Caucasian	71.5%
Hispanics	15.8%
Other	2.3%

Crime Statistics
The Federal Bureau of Investigation collects a series of crime information from across the country. This information was analyzed to provide the following:

Type	Totals	By 100,000 people	Risk
Murder & non-negligent manslaughter	706	5.5	Moderate
Forcible Rape	3,033	23.6	Moderate
Robbery	20,054	156.3	High
Aggravated Assault	32,042	249.7	Moderate
Burglary	75,399	587.6	Moderate
Larceny-Theft	239,794	1,868.9	Moderate

Violent Crime Trends
Violent crimes are composed of murder, non-negligent manslaughter, forcible rape, robbery and aggravated assault. Home invasions are considered a robbery. When combined together there were a total of 55,835 in 2010.

Property Crime Trends
Property crimes are composed of burglary, larceny / theft and motor vehicle theft. When combined together there were a total of 343,989 in 2010.

www.StopTheIntruder.com

STOP THE INTRUDER™ | KNOWLEDGE IS THE BEST PROTECTION™

INDIANA

Indiana is a U.S. state that is located in the Midwestern region of North America. It is surrounded by Illinois on the west, Michigan on the north, Pennsylvania and Ohio on the east and Kentucky to its south. It is the 15th most populous state in the United States and stretches over an area of 36,418 square miles. It was admitted to the union on December 11, 1816 and consists of 92 counties.

The largest cities:
- Indianapolis
- Fort Wayne
- Evansville

Population:
- 6.5 million
- Ranked 15th

Size:
- 36,418 square miles
- Ranked 38th

Population
According to the 2011 United States Census, Indiana had a population of 6.5 million. The 2000 census reported 6 million people. This population is composed of the following:

African American	9.1%
American Indian	0.3%
Asian	1.6%
Caucasian	84.3%
Hispanics	6.0%
Other	2.0%

Crime Statistics
The Federal Bureau of Investigation collects a series of crime information from across the country. This information was analyzed to provide the following:

Type	Totals	By 100,000 people	Risk
Murder & non-negligent manslaughter	292	4.5	Moderate
Forcible Rape	1,761	27.2	Moderate
Robbery	6,219	95.9	Moderate
Aggravated Assault	12,117	186.9	Moderate
Burglary	47,115	726.7	Moderate
Larceny-Theft	137,027	2,113.4	Moderate

Violent Crime Trends
Violent crimes are composed of murder, non-negligent manslaughter, forcible rape, robbery and aggravated assault. Home invasions are considered a robbery. When combined together there were a total of 20,389 in 2010.

Property Crime Trends
Property crimes are composed of burglary, larceny / theft and motor vehicle theft. When combined together there were a total of 197,260 in 2010.

STOP THE INTRUDER™ | KNOWLEDGE IS THE BEST PROTECTION™

IOWA

Iowa is a U.S. state that is located in the Midwestern region of North America. It is surrounded on the west by Nebraska, Minnesota on the north, North Dakota on the northwest, Illinois and Wisconsin on the east and Missouri on the south. It is the 30th most populous state in the U.S. and stretches over an area of 56,272 square miles. It was admitted to the union on December 28, 1846 and consists of 99 counties.

The largest cities:
- Des Moines
- Cedar Rapids
- Davenport

Population:
- 3.06 million
- Ranked 30th

Size:
- 56,272 square miles
- Ranked 26th

Population
According to the 2011 United States Census, Iowa had a population of 3.06 million. The 2000 census reported 2.9 million people. This population is composed of the following:

African American	2.9%
American Indian	0.4%
Asian	1.7%
Caucasian	91.3%
Hispanics	5.0%
Other	1.8%

Crime Statistics
The Federal Bureau of Investigation collects a series of crime information from across the country. This information was analyzed to provide the following:

Type	Totals	By 100,000 people	Risk
Murder & non-negligent manslaughter	39	1.3	Low
Forcible Rape	836	27.4	Moderate
Robbery	1,011	33.2	Low
Aggravated Assault	6,447	211.6	Moderate
Burglary	16,656	546.8	Moderate
Larceny-Theft	47,883	1,571.8	Low

Violent Crime Trends
Violent crimes are composed of murder, non-negligent manslaughter, forcible rape, robbery and aggravated assault. Home invasions are considered a robbery. When combined together there were a total of 8,333 in 2010.

Property Crime Trends
Property crimes are composed of burglary, larceny / theft and motor vehicle theft. When combined together there were a total of 68,315 in 2010.

STOP THE INTRUDER™ | KNOWLEDGE IS THE BEST PROTECTION™

KANSAS

Kansas is located in the Midwestern part of the United States. It is surrounded by Colorado on the west, Nebraska and Iowa on the north, Missouri on the east and Oklahoma and Arkansas to its south. It is the 33rd most populous state in the U.S. and stretches over an area of 82,277 square miles. It was admitted to the union on January 29, 1861 and consists of 105 counties.

The largest cities:
- Wichita
- Overland Park
- Kansas City

Population:
- 2.8 million
- Ranked 33rd

Size:
- 82,277 square miles
- Ranked 15th

Population
According to the 2011 United States Census, Kansas had a population of 2.8 million. The 2000 census reported 2.6 million people. This population is composed of the following:

African American	5.9%
American Indian	1.0%
Asian	2.4%
Caucasian	83.8%
Hispanics	10.5%
Other	3.0%

Crime Statistics
The Federal Bureau of Investigation collects a series of crime information from across the country. This information was analyzed to provide the following:

Type	Totals	By 100,000 people	Risk
Murder & non-negligent manslaughter	100	3.5	Moderate
Forcible Rape	1,107	38.8	High
Robbery	1,544	54.1	Moderate
Aggravated Assault	7,780	272.7	Moderate
Burglary	19,404	680.1	Moderate
Larceny-Theft	63,602	2,229.2	Moderate

Violent Crime Trends
Violent crimes are composed of murder, non-negligent manslaughter, forcible rape, robbery and aggravated assault. Home invasions are considered a robbery. When combined together there were a total of 10,531 in 2010.

Property Crime Trends
Property crimes are composed of burglary, larceny / theft and motor vehicle theft. When combined together there were a total of 89,015 in 2010.

STOP THE INTRUDER™ | KNOWLEDGE IS THE BEST PROTECTION™

KENTUCKY

Kentucky is located in the upper southern part of North America. It is surrounded by Ohio and Pennsylvania in the north, Virginia and West Virginia on the east, Tennessee on the south and Missouri and Illinois to its east. It is the 26th most populous state in the United States and stretches over an area of 40,409 square miles. It was admitted to the union on June 1, 1792 and consists of 120 counties.

The largest cities:
- Louisville
- Lexington
- Bowling Green

Population:
- 4.3 million
- Ranked 26th

Size:
- 40,409 square miles
- Ranked 37th

Population
According to the 2011 United States Census, Kentucky had a population of 4.3 million. The 2000 census reported 4.04 million people. This population is composed of the following:

African American	7.8%
American Indian	0.2%
Asian	1.1%
Caucasian	87.8%
Hispanics	3.1%
Other	1.7%

Crime Statistics
The Federal Bureau of Investigation collects a series of crime information from across the country. This information was analyzed to provide the following:

Type	Totals	By 100,000 people	Risk
Murder & non-negligent manslaughter	187	4.3	Moderate
Forcible Rape	1,381	31.8	Moderate
Robbery	3,748	86.4	Moderate
Aggravated Assault	5,212	120.1	Low
Burglary	30,311	698.5	Moderate
Larceny-Theft	74,189	1,709.7	Moderate

Violent Crime Trends
Violent crimes are composed of murder, non-negligent manslaughter, forcible rape, robbery and aggravated assault. Home invasions are considered a robbery. When combined together there were a total of 10,528 in 2010.

Property Crime Trends
Property crimes are composed of burglary, larceny / theft and motor vehicle theft. When combined together there were a total of 110,709 in 2010.

STOP THE INTRUDER™ | KNOWLEDGE IS THE BEST PROTECTION™

LOUISIANA

The largest cities:
- New Orleans
- Baton Rouge
- Shreveport

Description
Louisiana is located in the southern part of North America. It is surrounded on the west by Texas, Oklahoma and Arkansas in the north and Mississippi on the east. It is the 25th most populous state in the U.S. and stretches over an area of 51,843 square miles. It was admitted to the union on April 30, 1812 and is the only state in the U.S. that does not have any counties. It has political subdivisions, instead and they are termed as parishes.

Population:
- 4.5 million
- Ranked 25th

Size:
- 51,843 square miles
- Ranked 31st

Population
According to the 2011 United States Census, Louisiana had a population of 4.5 million. The 2000 census reported 4.4 million people. This population is composed of the following:

White	62.6%
African American	32.0%
American Indian	0.7%
Asian	1.5%
Hispanics	4.2%
Other	1.6%

Crime Statistics
The Federal Bureau of Investigation collects a series of crime information from across the country. This information was analyzed to provide the following:

Type	Totals	By 100,000 people	Risk
Murder & Manslaughter	510	11.2	High
Forcible Rape	1,233	27.2	Moderate
Robbery	5,211	114.9	Moderate
Aggravated Assault	17,932	395.6	High
Burglary	45,435	1,002.2	High
Larceny-Theft	110,029	2,427.1	High

Violent Crime Trends
Violent crimes are composed of murder, non-negligent manslaughter, forcible rape, robbery and aggravated assault. Home invasions are considered a robbery. When combined together there were a total of 24,866 in 2010.

Property Crime Trends
Property crimes are composed of burglary, larceny / theft and motor vehicle theft. When combined together there were a total of 165,357 in 2010.

STOP THE INTRUDER™ | KNOWLEDGE IS THE BEST PROTECTION™

MAINE

A state in the New England region, Maine is located in the northeaster part of the United States. It is surrounded by the Atlantic Ocean on the east and the south, New Hamphire on the west, Quebec on the northwest and New Brunswick on the northeast. It was admitted to the union on March 15, 1820. Maine is the 41st most populous state in the United States and stretches over an area of 35,385 square miles. Maine consists of 16 counties.

The largest cities:
- Portland
- Lewiston
- Bangor

Population:
- 1.3 million
- Ranked 41st

Size:
- 35,385 square miles
- Ranked 39th

Population

According to the 2011 United States Census, Maine had a population of 1.3 million. The 2000 census reported 1.2 million people. This population is composed of the following:

Non-Hispanic White	94.4%
African American	1.1%
American Indian	0.6%
Asian	1%
Hispanics	1.3%
Other	0.1%

Crime Statistics

The Federal Bureau of Investigation collects a series of crime information from across the country. This information was analyzed to provide the following:

Type	Totals	By 100,000 people	Risk
Murder & non-negligent manslaughter	24	1.8	Low
Forcible Rape	389	29.3	Moderate
Robbery	414	31.2	Low
Aggravated Assault	794	59.8	Low
Burglary	7,359	554	Moderate
Larceny-Theft	24,585	1,850	Moderate

Violent Crime Trends

Violent crimes are composed of murder, non-negligent manslaughter, forcible rape, robbery and aggravated assault. Home invasions are considered a robbery. When combined together there were a total of 1,621 in 2010.

Property Crime Trends

Property crimes are composed of burglary, larceny / theft and motor vehicle theft. When combined together there were a total of 78,386 in 2010.

STOP THE INTRUDER™ | KNOWLEDGE IS THE BEST PROTECTION™

MARYLAND

Maryland is located in the mid-Atlantic region of the United States. It is surrounded by Pennsylvania in the north, Delaware on the east, Virginia and West Virginia to its south and District of Columbia on the west. It is the 19th most populous state in the U.S. and stretches over an area of 12,407 square miles. It was admitted to the union on April 28, 1788 and consists of 24 counties.

The largest cities:
- Baltimore
- Frederick
- Rockville

Population:
- 5.8 million
- Ranked 19th

Size:
- 12,407 square miles
- Ranked 42nd

Population
According to the 2011 United States Census, Maryland had a population of 5.8 million. The 2000 census reported 5.3 million people. This population is composed of the following:

African American	29.4%
American Indian	0.4%
Asian	5.5%
Caucasian	58.2%
Hispanics	8.2%
Other	2.9%

Crime Statistics
The Federal Bureau of Investigation collects a series of crime information from across the country. This information was analyzed to provide the following:

Type	Totals	By 100,000 people	Risk
Murder & non-negligent manslaughter	430	7.4	High
Forcible Rape	1,227	21.3	Low
Robbery	11,054	191.5	High
Aggravated Assault	18,909	327.5	Moderate
Burglary	36,542	632.9	Moderate
Larceny-Theft	118,458	2,051.7	Moderate

Violent Crime Trends
Violent crimes are composed of murder, non-negligent manslaughter, forcible rape, robbery and aggravated assault. Home invasions are considered a robbery. When combined together there were a total of 31,620 in 2010.

Property Crime Trends
Property crimes are composed of burglary, larceny / theft and motor vehicle theft. When combined together there were a total of 173,051 in 2010.

STOP THE INTRUDER™ | KNOWLEDGE IS THE BEST PROTECTION™

MASSACHUSETTS

A state in the New England region, Massachusetts is located in the northeaster part of the United States. It is surrounded by Rhode Island and Connecticut on the south, New York on the west, Vermont and New Hampshire on the north, and the Atlantic Ocean on the east. It was admitted to the union on Feb. 6, 1788. Maine is the 14th most populous state in the United States and stretches over an area of 10,555 square miles. Massachusetts consists of 14 counties.

The largest cities:
- Boston
- Worcester
- Springfield

Population:
- 6.5 million
- Ranked 14th

Size:
- 10,555 square miles
- Ranked 44th

Population
According to the 2011 United States Census, Massachusetts had a population of 6.5 million. The 2000 census reported 6.3 million people. This population is composed of the following:

White	80.4%
African American	6.6%
American Indian	0.3%
Asian	5.3%
Hispanics	9.6%
Other	4.7%

Crime Statistics
The Federal Bureau of Investigation collects a series of crime information from across the country. This information was analyzed to provide the following:

Type	Totals	By 100,000 people	Risk
Murder & non-negligent manslaughter	210	3.2	Moderate
Forcible Rape	1,745	26.7	Moderate
Robbery	6,874	105	Moderate
Aggravated Assault	21,724	331.8	Moderate
Burglary	37,767	576.8	Moderate
Larceny-Theft	104,685	1,598.8	Low

Violent Crime Trends
Violent crimes are composed of murder, non-negligent manslaughter, forcible rape, robbery and aggravated assault. Home invasions are considered a robbery. When combined together there were a total of 30,553 in 2010.

Property Crime Trends
Property crimes are composed of burglary, larceny / theft and motor vehicle theft. When combined together there were a total of 153,90 in 2010.

MICHIGAN

Michigan is located in the Great Lakes region of the United States. It is surrounded on the west by Wisconsin, Ohio and Indiana on the south, and consists of two peninsulas: the Upper Peninsula and the Lower Peninsula. It is the 8th most populous state in the U.S. and stretches over an area of 96,716 square miles. It was admitted to the union on January 26, 1837 and consists of 83 counties.

The largest cities:
- Baltimore
- Frederick
- Rockville

Population:
- 9.8 million
- Ranked 8th

Size:
- 96,716 square miles
- Ranked 11th

Population
According to the 2011 United States Census, Michigan had a population of 9.8 million. The 2000 census reported 9.9 million people. This population is composed of the following:

African American	14.2%
American Indian	0.6%
Asian	2.4%
Caucasian	78.9%
Hispanics	4.4%
Other	2.3%

Crime Statistics
The Federal Bureau of Investigation collects a series of crime information from across the country. This information was analyzed to provide the following:

Type	Totals	By 100,000 people	Risk
Murder & non-negligent manslaughter	567	5.7	Moderate
Forcible Rape	4,673	47.3	High
Robbery	11,493	116.3	Moderate
Aggravated Assault	31,727	321.0	Moderate
Burglary	73,868	747.4	Moderate
Larceny-Theft	166,980	1,689.5	Moderate

Violent Crime Trends
Violent crimes are composed of murder, non-negligent manslaughter, forcible rape, robbery and aggravated assault. Home invasions are considered a robbery. When combined together there were a total of 48,460 in 2010.

Property Crime Trends
Property crimes are composed of burglary, larceny / theft and motor vehicle theft. When combined together there were a total of 268,201 in 2010.

STOP THE INTRUDER™ | KNOWLEDGE IS THE BEST PROTECTION™

MINNESOTA

Minnesota is located in the Midwestern part of the United States. It is surrounded by South Dakota and North Dakota in the west, Iowa on the south and Wisconsin to its east. It is the 21st most populous state in the U.S. and stretches over an area of 86,939 square miles. It was admitted to the union on May 11, 1858 and consists of 874 counties.

The largest cities:
- Detroit
- Grand Rapids
- Warren

Population:
- 5.3 million
- Ranked 21st

Size:
- 86,939 square miles
- Ranked 12th

Population
According to the 2011 United States Census, Minnesota had a population of 5.3 million. The 2000 census reported 4.9 million people. This population is composed of the following:

African American	5.2%
American Indian	1.1%
Asian	4.0%
Caucasian	85.3%
Hispanics	4.7%
Other	2.4%

Crime Statistics
The Federal Bureau of Investigation collects a series of crime information from across the country. This information was analyzed to provide the following:

Type	Totals	By 100,000 people	Risk
Murder & non-negligent manslaughter	96	1.8	Low
Forcible Rape	1,798	33.9	Moderate
Robbery	3,388	63.9	Moderate
Aggravated Assault	7,233	136.4	Low
Burglary	24,415	460.3	Moderate
Larceny-Theft	103,429	1,950.0	Moderate

Violent Crime Trends
Violent crimes are composed of murder, non-negligent manslaughter, forcible rape, robbery and aggravated assault. Home invasions are considered a robbery. When combined together there were a total of 12,515 in 2010.

Property Crime Trends
Property crimes are composed of burglary, larceny / theft and motor vehicle theft. When combined together there were a total of 136,431 in 2010.

STOP THE INTRUDER™ | KNOWLEDGE IS THE BEST PROTECTION™

MISSISSIPPI

Mississippi is located on the southern part of the United States. It is surrounded by Alabama on the east, Tennessee on the north, Louisiana on the southwest and Arkansas on the west. It is the 25th most populated state in the U.S. and stretches over an area of 48,430 square miles. It was admitted to the union on December 10, 1817 and consists of 82 counties.

The largest cities:
- Jackson
- Gulfport
- Hattiesburg

Population:
- 2.9 million
- Ranked 25th

Size:
- 48,430 square miles
- Ranked 32nd

Population
According to the 2011 United States Census, Mississippi had a population of 2.9 million. The 2000 census reported 2.8 million people. This population is composed of the following:

White	59.1%
African American	37.0%
American Indian	0.5%
Asian	0.9%
Hispanics	2.7%
Other	1.1%

Crime Statistics
The Federal Bureau of Investigation collects a series of crime information from across the country. This information was analyzed to provide the following:

Type	Totals	By 100,000 people	Risk
Murder & Manslaughter	208	7.0	High
Forcible Rape	927	31.2	Moderate
Robbery	2,779	93.7	Moderate
Aggravated Assault	4,089	137.8	Low
Burglary	30,444	1,026.0	High
Larceny-Theft	52,770	1,778.4	Moderate

Violent Crime Trends
Violent crimes are composed of murder, non-negligent manslaughter, forcible rape, robbery and aggravated assault. Home invasions are considered a robbery. When combined together there were a total of 8,003 in 2010.

Property Crime Trends
Property crimes are composed of burglary, larceny / theft and motor vehicle theft. When combined together there were a total of 88,574 in 2010.

STOP THE INTRUDER™ | KNOWLEDGE IS THE BEST PROTECTION™

MISSOURI

Description
Missouri is located in the Midwestern part of the United States. It is surrounded by Arkansas on the south, Kansas on the west, Iowa to the north, Illinois on the east and Kentucky on the southeast. It is the 18th most populous state in the U.S. and stretches over an area of 69,704 square miles. It was admitted to the union on August 10, 1821 and consists of 114 counties.

The largest cities:
- Kansas City
- Saint Louis
- Springfield

Population:
- 6.01 million
- Ranked 18th

Size:
- 69,704 square miles
- Ranked 21st

Population
According to the 2011 United States Census, Missouri had a population of 6.01 million. The 2000 census reported 5.6 million people. This population is composed of the following:

White	82.8%
African American	11.6%
American Indian	0.5%
Asian	1.6%
Hispanics	3.5%
Other	2.1%

Crime Statistics
The Federal Bureau of Investigation collects a series of crime information from across the country. This information was analyzed to provide the following:

Type	Totals	By 100,000 people	Risk
Murder & Manslaughter	420	7.0	High
Forcible Rape	1,432	23.9	Moderate
Robbery	6,312	102.4	Moderate
Aggravated Assault	19,628	321.7	Moderate
Burglary	44,043	735.4	Moderate
Larceny-Theft	140,320	2,343.0	Moderate

Violent Crime Trends
Violent crimes are composed of murder, non-negligent manslaughter, forcible rape, robbery and aggravated assault. Home invasions are considered a robbery. When combined together there were a total of 27,792 in 2010.

Property Crime Trends
Property crimes are composed of burglary, larceny / theft and motor vehicle theft. When combined together there were a total of 200,414 in 2010.

STOP THE INTRUDER™ | KNOWLEDGE IS THE BEST PROTECTION™

MONTANA

Description
Montana is located in the western part of the United States. It is surrounded by Wyoming in the south, Idaho on the west and southwest, and by North Dakota and South Dakota to its east. It is the 44th most populous state in the U.S. and stretches over an area of 147,042 square miles. It was admitted to the union on November 8, 1889 and consists of 56 counties.

The largest cities:
- Billings
- Missoula
- Great Falls

Population:
- 998,199
- Ranked 44th

Size:
- 147,042 square miles
- Ranked 4th

Population
According to the 2011 United States Census, Montana had a population of 998,199. The 2000 census reported 902,195 people. This population is composed of the following:

White	89.4%
African American	0.4%
American Indian	6.3%
Asian	0.6%
Hispanics	2.9%
Other	2.5%

Crime Statistics
The Federal Bureau of Investigation collects a series of crime information from across the country. This information was analyzed to provide the following:

Type	Totals	By 100,000 people	Risk
Murder & Manslaughter	26	2.6	Moderate
Forcible Rape	321	32.4	Moderate
Robbery	157	15.9	Low
Aggravated Assault	2,189	221.2	Moderate
Burglary	3,654	369.3	Low
Larceny-Theft	19,989	2,020.3	Moderate

Violent Crime Trends
Violent crimes are composed of murder, non-negligent manslaughter, forcible rape, robbery and aggravated assault. Home invasions are considered a robbery. When combined together there were a total of 2,690 in 2010.

Property Crime Trends
Property crimes are composed of burglary, larceny / theft and motor vehicle theft. When combined together there were a total of 25,169 in 2010.

STOP THE INTRUDER™ | KNOWLEDGE IS THE BEST PROTECTION™

NEBRASKA

Description
Nebraska is located in the Midwestern part of the United States. It is surrounded by South Dakota on the north, Kansas and Colorado on the south, Wyoming to its west and Iowa to its east. It is the 38th most populous state in the U.S. and stretches over an area of 77,354 square miles. It was admitted to the union on March 1, 1867 and consists of 93 counties.

The largest cities:
- Omaha
- Lincoln
- Bellevue

Population:
- 1.8 million
- Ranked 38th

Size:
- 77,354 square miles
- Ranked 16th

Population
According to the 2011 United States Census, Nebraska had a population of 1.8 million. The 2000 census reported 1.7 million people. This population is composed of the following:

White	86.1%
African American	4.5%
American Indian	1.0%
Asian	1.8%
Hispanics	9.2%
Other	2.2%

Crime Statistics
The Federal Bureau of Investigation collects a series of crime information from across the country. This information was analyzed to provide the following:

Type	Totals	By 100,000 people	Risk
Murder & Manslaughter	54	3.0	Moderate
Forcible Rape	672	36.8	High
Robbery	1,025	56.1	Moderate
Aggravated Assault	3,353	183.6	Moderate
Burglary	8,326	455.9	Moderate
Larceny-Theft	36,881	2,019.4	Moderate

Violent Crime Trends
Violent crimes are composed of murder, non-negligent manslaughter, forcible rape, robbery and aggravated assault. Home invasions are considered a robbery. When combined together there were a total of 5,104 in 2010.

Property Crime Trends
Property crimes are composed of burglary, larceny / theft and motor vehicle theft. When combined together there were a total of 48,821 in 2010.

STOP THE INTRUDER™ | KNOWLEDGE IS THE BEST PROTECTION™

NEVADA

Description
Nevada is located in the western and southwestern part of the United States. It is surrounded by California on the west and southwest, Oregon and Idaho on the north, Utah on the east and Arizona on the southeast. It is the 35th most populous state in the U.S. and stretches over an area of 110,622 square miles. It was admitted to the union on October 21, 1864 and consists of 17 counties.

The largest cities:
- Las Vegas
- Henderson
- North Las Vegas

Population:
- 2.7 million
- Ranked 35th

Size:
- 110,622 square miles
- Ranked 7th

Population
According to the 2011 United States Census, Nevada had a population of 2.7 million. The 2000 census reported 2.0 million people. This population is composed of the following:

White	66.2%
African American	8.1%
American Indian	1.2%
Asian	7.2%
Hispanics	26.5%
Other	4.7%

Crime Statistics
The Federal Bureau of Investigation collects a series of crime information from across the country. This information was analyzed to provide the following:

Type	Totals	By 100,000 people	Risk
Murder & Non-negligent Manslaughter	158	5.9	High
Forcible Rape	965	35.7	Moderate
Robbery	5,298	196.2	High
Aggravated Assault	11,420	422.9	High
Burglary	22,226	823.0	Moderate
Larceny-Theft	42,521	1,574.5	Low

Violent Crime Trends
Violent crimes are composed of murder, non-negligent manslaughter, forcible rape, robbery and aggravated assault. Home invasions are considered a robbery. When combined together there were a total of 17,841 in 2010.

Property Crime Trends
Property crimes are composed of burglary, larceny / theft and motor vehicle theft. When combined together there were a total of 74,932 in 2010.

STOP THE INTRUDER™ | KNOWLEDGE IS THE BEST PROTECTION™

NEW HAMPSHIRE

A state in the New England region, New Hampshire is located in the northeastern part of the United States. It is surrounded by Massachusetts on the south, on the west by Vermont, the Atlantic Ocean and Maine on the east and in the north by Quebec. It was admitted to the union on June 21, 1788. It is the 42nd most populous state in the United States and stretches over an area of 9,304 square miles. New Hampshire consists of 10 counties.

The largest cities:
- Manchester
- Nashua
- Concord

Population:
- 1.3 million
- Ranked 21st

Size:
- 9,304 square miles
- Ranked 46th

Population
According to the 2011 United States Census, New Hampshire had a population of 1.3 million. The 2000 census reported 1.2 million people. This population is composed of the following:

White	93.9%
African American	1.1%
American Indian	0.2%
Asian	2.2%
Hispanics	1.3%

Crime Statistics
The Federal Bureau of Investigation collects a series of crime information from across the country. This information was analyzed to provide the following:

Type	Totals	By 100,000 people	Risk
Murder & non-negligent manslaughter	13	1.0	Low
Forcible Rape	412	31.3	Moderate
Robbery	451	34.3	Low
Aggravated Assault	1,322	100.4	Low
Burglary	5,441	413.3	Low
Larceny-Theft	22,373	1,699.5	Moderate

Violent Crime Trends
Violent crimes are composed of murder, non-negligent manslaughter, forcible rape, robbery and aggravated assault. Home invasions are considered a robbery. When combined together there were a total of 2198 in 2010.

Property Crime Trends
Property crimes are composed of burglary, larceny / theft and motor vehicle theft. When combined together there were a total of 28,752 in 2010.

STOP THE INTRUDER™ | KNOWLEDGE IS THE BEST PROTECTION™

NEW JERSEY

New Jersey is a state in the northeastern part of the United States. It is surrounded by New York on the north and east, by Atlantic Ocean on the south and southeast. Pennsylvania lies on its west and to its southwest is the state of Delaware. New Jersey is the 11th most populous state in the United States and stretches over an area of 8,721 square miles. It was admitted to the union on December 17, 1787. New Jersey consists of 21 counties.

The largest cities:
- Newark
- Jersey City
- Paterson

Population:
- 8.8 million
- Ranked 11th

Size:
- 8,721 square miles
- Ranked 47th

Population
According to the 2011 United States Census, New Jersey had a population of 8.8 million. The 2000 census reported 8.4 million people. This population is composed of the following:

White	68.6%
African American	13.7%
American Indian	0.3%
Asian	8.3%
Hispanics	17.7%
Other	2.7%

Crime Statistics
The Federal Bureau of Investigation collects a series of crime information from across the country. This information was analyzed to provide the following:

Type	Totals	By 100,000 people	Risk
Murder & non-negligent manslaughter	371	4.2	Moderate
Forcible Rape	981	11.2	Low
Robbery	11,818	134.4	High
Aggravated Assault	13,885	157.9	Moderate
Burglary	38,732	440.5	Moderate
Larceny-Theft	128,754	1,464.5	Low

Violent Crime Trends
Violent crimes are composed of murder, non-negligent manslaughter, forcible rape, robbery and aggravated assault. Home invasions are considered a robbery. When combined together there were a total of 27,055 in 2010.

Property Crime Trends
Property crimes are composed of burglary, larceny / theft and motor vehicle theft. When combined together there were a total of 183,042 in 2010.

NEW MEXICO

New Mexico is located in the southwestern and western part of the United States. It is surrounded by Arizona on the west, Colorado on the north and Texas on the east and southeast. It is the 36th most populous state in the U.S. and stretches over an area of 121,589 square miles. It was admitted to the union on January 6, 1912 and consists of 33 counties.

The largest cities:
- Albuquerque
- Las Cruces
- Rio Rancho

Population:
- 2.08 million
- Ranked 36th

Size:
- 121,589 square miles
- Ranked 5th

Population
According to the 2011 United States Census, New Mexico had a population of 2.08 million. The 2000 census reported 1.8 million people. This population is composed of the following:

White	68.4%
African American	2.1%
American Indian	9.4%
Asian	1.4%
Hispanics	46.3%
Other	3.7%

Crime Statistics
The Federal Bureau of Investigation collects a series of crime information from across the country. This information was analyzed to provide the following:

Type	Totals	By 100,000 people	Risk
Murder & non-negligent manslaughter	142	6.9	High
Forcible Rape	958	46.5	High
Robbery	1,614	78.4	Moderate
Aggravated Assault	9,412	457.1	High
Burglary	21,014	1,020.5	High
Larceny-Theft	44,481	2,160.1	Moderate

Violent Crime Trends
Violent crimes are composed of murder, non-negligent manslaughter, forcible rape, robbery and aggravated assault. Home invasions are considered a robbery. When combined together there were a total of 12,126 in 2010.

Property Crime Trends
Property crimes are composed of burglary, larceny / theft and motor vehicle theft. When combined together there were a total of 70,742 in 2010.

STOP THE INTRUDER™ | KNOWLEDGE IS THE BEST PROTECTION™

NEW YORK

The largest cities:
- New York City
- Brooklyn
- Manhattan

New York is a state in the northeastern part of the United States. It is surrounded by New Jersey and Pennsylvania on the south, by Connecticut, Massachusetts and Vermont on the east, Ontario on the west and north and Quebec to its north. It is the 3rd most populous states in the U.S. and stretches over an area of 54,566 square miles. New York was admitted to the union on July 26, 1788. New York consists of 62 counties.

Population:
- 19.4 million
- Ranked 3rd

Size:
- 54,556 square miles
- Ranked 27th

Population
According to the 2011 United States Census, New York had a population of 19.4 million. The 2000 census reported 18.9 million people. This population is composed of the following:

White	65.7%
African American	5.9%
American Indian	0.6%
Asian	7.3%
Hispanics	17.6%
Other	3.0%

Crime Statistics
The Federal Bureau of Investigation collects a series of crime information from across the country. This information was analyzed to provide the following:

Type	Totals	By 100,000 people	Risk
Murder & non-negligent manslaughter	866	4.5	Moderate
Forcible Rape	2,771	14.3	Low
Robbery	28,473	146.9	High
Aggravated Assault	43,867	226.4	Moderate
Burglary	64,973	335.3	Low
Larceny-Theft	290,755	1,500.4	Low

Violent Crime Trends
Violent crimes are composed of murder, non-negligent manslaughter, forcible rape, robbery and aggravated assault. Home invasions are considered a robbery. When combined together there were a total of 75,977 in 2010.

Property Crime Trends
Property crimes are composed of burglary, larceny / theft and motor vehicle theft. When combined together there were a total of 376,131 in 2010.

STOP THE INTRUDER™ | KNOWLEDGE IS THE BEST PROTECTION™

NORTH CAROLINA

North Carolina is located in the southeastern region of the United States. It is surrounded by South Carolina and Georgia on the south, Tennessee on the west, and Virginia to its north. It is the 10th most populous state in the U.S. and stretches over an area of 53,819 square miles. It was admitted to the union on November 21, 1789 and consists of 100 counties.

The largest cities:
- Charlotte
- Raleigh
- Greensboro

Population:
- 9.6 million
- Ranked 10th

Size:
- 53,819 square miles
- Ranked 28th

Population
According to the 2011 United States Census, North Carolina had a population of 9.6 million. The 2000 census reported 8.04 million people. This population is composed of the following:

White	68.5%
African American	21.5%
American Indian	1.3%
Asian	2.2%
Hispanics	8.4%
Other	2.2%

Crime Statistics
The Federal Bureau of Investigation collects a series of crime information from across the country. This information was analyzed to provide the following:

Type	Totals	By 100,000 people	Risk
Murder & non-negligent manslaughter	476	5.0	Moderate
Forcible Rape	2,013	21.1	Low
Robbery	9,610	100.8	Moderate
Aggravated Assault	22,554	236.5	Moderate
Burglary	102,690	1,076.9	High
Larceny-Theft	207,719	2,178.4	Moderate

Violent Crime Trends
Violent crimes are composed of murder, non-negligent manslaughter, forcible rape, robbery and aggravated assault. Home invasions are considered a robbery. When combined together there were a total of 34,653 in 2010.

Property Crime Trends
Property crimes are composed of burglary, larceny / theft and motor vehicle theft. When combined together there were a total of 328,719 in 2010.

STOP THE INTRUDER™ | KNOWLEDGE IS THE BEST PROTECTION™

NORTH DAKOTA

North Dakota is located in the Midwestern region of the United States. It is surrounded by Manitoba and Saskatchewan on the north, by Minnesota to its east, South Dakota on the south and to its west by Montana. It is the 48th most populous state in the U.S. and stretches over an area of 70,700 square miles. It was admitted to the union on November 2, 1889 and consists of 53 counties.

The largest cities:
- Fargo
- Bismarck
- Grand Forks

Population:
- 683,932
- Ranked 48th

Size:
- 70,700 square miles
- Ranked 19th

Population
According to the 2011 United States Census, North Dakota had a population of 9.6 million. The 2000 census reported 8.04 million people. This population is composed of the following:

White	90.0%
African American	1.2%
American Indian	5.4%
Asian	1.0%
Hispanics	2.0%
Other	1.8%

Crime Statistics
The Federal Bureau of Investigation collects a series of crime information from across the country. This information was analyzed to provide the following:

Type	Totals	By 100,000 people	Risk
Murder & non-negligent manslaughter	10	1.5	Low
Forcible Rape	237	35.2	Moderate
Robbery	90	13.4	Low
Aggravated Assault	1,176	174.8	Moderate
Burglary	1,966	292.3	Low
Larceny-Theft	9,070	1,348.5	Low

Violent Crime Trends
Violent crimes are composed of murder, non-negligent manslaughter, forcible rape, robbery and aggravated assault. Home invasions are considered a robbery. When combined together there were a total of 1,513 in 2010.

Property Crime Trends
Property crimes are composed of burglary, larceny / theft and motor vehicle theft. When combined together there were a total of 11,895 in 2010.

STOP THE INTRUDER™ | KNOWLEDGE IS THE BEST PROTECTION™

OHIO

Ohio is located in the Midwestern region of the United States. It is surrounded on the west by Indiana, on the south by Kentucky, Pennsylvania and West Virginia on the east and Michigan to its north. It is the 7th most populous state in the U.S. and stretches over an area of 44,825 square miles. It was admitted to the union on March 1, 1803 and consists of 88 counties.

Population
According to the 2011 United States Census, Ohio had a population of 11.5 million. The 2000 census reported 11.3 million people. This population is composed of the following:

The largest cities:
- Columbus
- Cleveland
- Cincinnati

Population:
- 11.5 million
- Ranked 7th

Size:
- 44,825 square miles
- Ranked 34th

White	82.7%
African American	12.2%
American Indian	0.2%
Asian	1.7%
Hispanics	3.1%
Other	2.1%

Crime Statistics
The Federal Bureau of Investigation collects a series of crime information from across the country. This information was analyzed to provide the following:

Type	Totals	By 100,000 people	Risk
Murder & non-negligent manslaughter	476	4.1	Moderate
Forcible Rape	3,699	32.1	Moderate
Robbery	16,479	142.8	High
Aggravated Assault	15,712	136.2	Low
Burglary	106,521	923.3	High
Larceny-Theft	246,742	2,138.8	Moderate

Violent Crime Trends
Violent crimes are composed of murder, non-negligent manslaughter, forcible rape, robbery and aggravated assault. Home invasions are considered a robbery. When combined together there were a total of 36,366 in 2010.

Property Crime Trends
Property crimes are composed of burglary, larceny / theft and motor vehicle theft. When combined together there were a total of 374,381 in 2010.

STOP THE INTRUDER™ | KNOWLEDGE IS THE BEST PROTECTION™

OKLAHOMA

Oklahoma is located in the south central part of the United States. It is bordered on the south and west by Texas, on the northwest by New Mexico, Kansas to its north and Arkansas on the east. It is the 28th most populous state in the U.S. and stretches over an area of 69,898 square miles. It was admitted to the union on November 16, 1907 and consists of 77 counties.

The largest cities:
- Oklahoma City
- Tulsa
- Norman

Population:
- 3.8million
- Ranked 28th

Size:
- 69,898 square miles
- Ranked 20th

Population
According to the 2011 United States Census, Oklahoma had a population of 3.8 million. The 2000 census reported 3.4 million people. This population is composed of the following:

White	72.2%
African American	7.4%
American Indian	8.6%
Asian	1.7%
Hispanics	8.9%
Other	5.9%

Crime Statistics
The Federal Bureau of Investigation collects a series of crime information from across the country. This information was analyzed to provide the following:

Type	Totals	By 100,000 people	Risk
Murder & non-negligent manslaughter	195	5.2	Moderate
Forcible Rape	1,450	38.7	High
Robbery	3,337	89.0	Moderate
Aggravated Assault	13,005	346.7	High
Burglary	37,476	999.0	High
Larceny-Theft	80,460	2,144.8	Moderate

Violent Crime Trends
Violent crimes are composed of murder, non-negligent manslaughter, forcible rape, robbery and aggravated assault. Home invasions are considered a robbery. When combined together there were a total of 17,987 in 2010.

Property Crime Trends
Property crimes are composed of burglary, larceny / theft and motor vehicle theft. When combined together there were a total of 128,126 in 2010.

STOP THE INTRUDER™ | KNOWLEDGE IS THE BEST PROTECTION™

OREGON

Oregon is located in the Pacific northwestern region of the United States. It is surrounded by Washington on the north, California on the south, Nevada to its southeast and Idaho on its east. It is the 27th most populous state in the U.S. and stretches over an area of 98,381 square miles. It was admitted to the union on February 14, 1859 and consists of 36 counties.

The largest cities:
- Portland
- Eugene
- Salem

Population:
- 3.8 million
- Ranked 27th

Size:
- 98,381 square miles
- Ranked 9th

Population
According to the 2011 United States Census, Oregon had a population of 3.4 million. The 2000 census reported 3.4 million people. This population is composed of the following:

White	83.6%
African American	1.8%
American Indian	1.4%
Asian	3.7%
Hispanics	11.7%
Other	3.8%

Crime Statistics
The Federal Bureau of Investigation collects a series of crime information from across the country. This information was analyzed to provide the following:

Type	Totals	By 100,000 people	Risk
Murder & non-negligent manslaughter	91	2.4	Moderate
Forcible Rape	1,214	31.7	Moderate
Robbery	2,390	62.4	Moderate
Aggravated Assault	5,960	155.6	Moderate
Burglary	19,637	512.6	Moderate
Larceny-Theft	86,879	2,267.7	Moderate

Violent Crime Trends
Violent crimes are composed of murder, non-negligent manslaughter, forcible rape, robbery and aggravated assault. Home invasions are considered a robbery. When combined together there were a total of 9,655 in 2010.

Property Crime Trends
Property crimes are composed of burglary, larceny / theft and motor vehicle theft. When combined together there were a total of 115,428 in 2010.

STOP THE INTRUDER™ | KNOWLEDGE IS THE BEST PROTECTION™

PENNSYLVANIA

Pennsylvania is officially known as the Commonwealth of Pennsylvania. It is located in the northeastern and mid-Atlantic regions of the United States. It is surrounded by Delaware on the southeast, Maryland on the south, West Viriginia on the southwest, Ohio on the west, New York on the north and New Jersey to its east. It is the 6th most populous state in the U.S. and stretches over an area of 46,055 square miles. It was admitted to the union on December 12, 1787. Pennsylvania consists of 67 counties.

The largest cities:
- Philadelphia
- Pittsburgh
- Allentown

Population:
- 12.7 million
- Ranked 6th

Size:
- 46,055 square miles
- Ranked 33rd

Population
According to the 2011 United States Census, Pennsylvania had a population of 12.7 million. The 2000 census reported 12.2 million people. This population is composed of the following:

White	81.9%
African American	10.8%
American Indian	0.2%
Asian	2.7%
Hispanics	5.7%
Other	1.9%

Crime Statistics
The Federal Bureau of Investigation collects a series of crime information from across the country. This information was analyzed to provide the following:

Type	Totals	By 100,000 people	Risk
Murder & non-negligent manslaughter	657	5.2	Moderate
Forcible Rape	3,415	26.9	Moderate
Robbery	16,362	128.8	Moderate
Aggravated Assault	26,080	205.3	Moderate
Burglary	55,171	434.3	Low
Larceny-Theft	204,183	1,607.4	Moderate

Violent Crime Trends
Violent crimes are composed of murder, non-negligent manslaughter, forcible rape, robbery and aggravated assault. Home invasions are considered a robbery. When combined together there were a total of 46,514 in 2010.

Property Crime Trends
Property crimes are composed of burglary, larceny / theft and motor vehicle theft. When combined together there were a total of 276,023 in 2010.

STOP THE INTRUDER™ | KNOWLEDGE IS THE BEST PROTECTION™

RHODE ISLAND

A state in the New England region, Rhode Island is officially known as the State of Rhode Island and Providence Plantations. It is surrounded by Connecticut, Massachusetts in the north and the east. Long Island happens to share a water boundary with Rhode Island on the southwest. It was admitted to the union on May 29, 1790. It is the 43rd most populous state in the United States and stretches over an area of 1,214 square miles. Rhode Island consists of 5 counties.

The largest cities:
- Providence
- Warwick
- Cranston

Population:
- 1.5 million
- Ranked 41st

Size:
- 35,385 square miles
- Ranked 43rd

Population
According to the 2011 United States Census, Rhode Island had a population of 1.5 million. The 2000 census reported 1.04 million people. This population is composed of the following:

White	81.4%
African American	5.7%
American Indian	0.6%
Asian	2.9%
Hispanics	12.4%
Other	6%

Crime Statistics
The Federal Bureau of Investigation collects a series of crime information from across the country. This information was analyzed to provide the following:

Type	Totals	By 100,000 people	Risk
Murder & non-negligent manslaughter	29	2.8	Moderate
Forcible Rape	296	28.1	Moderate
Robbery	780	74.1	Moderate
Aggravated Assault	1,596	151.6	Moderate
Burglary	6,121	581.5	Moderate
Larceny-Theft	18,390	1,747.2	Moderate

Violent Crime Trends
Violent crimes are composed of murder, non-negligent manslaughter, forcible rape, robbery and aggravated assault. Home invasions are considered a robbery. When combined together there were a total of 2,701 in 2010.

Property Crime Trends
Property crimes are composed of burglary, larceny / theft and motor vehicle theft. When combined together there were a total of 26,910 in 2010.

STOP THE INTRUDER™ | KNOWLEDGE IS THE BEST PROTECTION™

SOUTH CAROLINA

South Carolina is located in the southeastern part of the United States. It is surrounded on the north by North Carolina, by Georgia on the south and west, and on the east by the Atlantic Ocean. It is the 24th most populous state in the U.S. and stretches over a period of 32,020 square miles. It was admitted to the union on May 23, 1788 and consists of 46 counties.

The largest cities:
- Columbia
- Charleston
- North Charleston

Population:
- 4.6 million
- Ranked 24th

Size:
- 32,020 square miles
- Ranked 40th

Population
According to the 2011 United States Census, South Carolina had a population of 4.6 million. The 2000 census reported 4.01 million people. This population is composed of the following:

White	66.2%
African American	27.9%
American Indian	0.4%
Asian	1.3%
Hispanics	5.1%
Other	1.7%

Crime Statistics
The Federal Bureau of Investigation collects a series of crime information from across the country. This information was analyzed to provide the following:

Type	Totals	By 100,000 people	Risk
Murder & non-negligent manslaughter	280	6.1	High
Forcible Rape	1,466	31.7	Moderate
Robbery	4,982	107.7	Moderate
Aggravated Assault	20,920	452.3	High
Burglary	46,156	997.9	High
Larceny-Theft	121,054	2,617.2	High

Violent Crime Trends
Violent crimes are composed of murder, non-negligent manslaughter, forcible rape, robbery and aggravated assault. Home invasions are considered a robbery. When combined together there were a total of 27,648 in 2010.

Property Crime Trends
Property crimes are composed of burglary, larceny / theft and motor vehicle theft. When combined together there were a total of 180,407 in 2010.

STOP THE INTRUDER™ | KNOWLEDGE IS THE BEST PROTECTION™

SOUTH DAKOTA

South Dakota is located in the Midwestern part of the United States. It is surrounded by North Dakota in the north, Minnesota in the east, Nebraska on the south, Wyoming on the southwest and Montana on the northwest. It is the 46th most populous state in the U.S. and stretches over an area of 77,116 square miles. It was admitted to the union on November 2, 1889 and consists of 66 counties.

The largest cities:
- Sioux Falls
- Rapid City
- Aberdeen

Population:
- 824,082
- Ranked 46th

Size:
- 77,116 square miles
- Ranked 17th

Population
According to the 2011 United States Census, South Dakota had a population of 824,082. The 2000 census reported 754,844 people. This population is composed of the following:

White	85.9%
African American	1.3%
American Indian	8.8%
Asian	0.9%
Hispanics	2.7%
Other	2.1%

Crime Statistics
The Federal Bureau of Investigation collects a series of crime information from across the country. This information was analyzed to provide the following:

Type	Totals	By 100,000 people	Risk
Murder & non-negligent manslaughter	23	2.8	Moderate
Forcible Rape	390	47.9	High
Robbery	154	18.9	Low
Aggravated Assault	1,619	198.9	Moderate
Burglary	3,181	390.7	Low
Larceny-Theft	11,106	1,364.1	Low

Violent Crime Trends
Violent crimes are composed of murder, non-negligent manslaughter, forcible rape, robbery and aggravated assault. Home invasions are considered a robbery. When combined together there were a total of 2,186 in 2010.

Property Crime Trends
Property crimes are composed of burglary, larceny / theft and motor vehicle theft. When combined together there were a total of 15,082 in 2010.

STOP THE INTRUDER™ | KNOWLEDGE IS THE BEST PROTECTION™

TENNESSEE

Tennessee is located in the southeaster part of the United States. It is surrounded on the north by Kentucky and Virginia, North Carolina on the east, to the south by Georgia, Alabama and Mississippi and to its west by Arkansas and Missouri. It is the 17th most populous state in the U.S. and stretches over an area of 42,143 square miles. It was admitted to the union on June 1, 1796 and consists of 95 counties.

The largest cities:
- Memphis
- Nashville
- Knoxville

Population:
- 6.4 million
- Ranked 17th

Size:
- 42,143 square miles
- Ranked 36th

Population
According to the 2011 United States Census, Tennessee had a population of 6.4 million. The 2000 census reported 5.7 million people. This population is composed of the following:

White	77.6%
African American	16.7%
American Indian	0.3%
Asian	1.4%
Hispanics	4.6%
Other	1.7%

Crime Statistics
The Federal Bureau of Investigation collects a series of crime information from across the country. This information was analyzed to provide the following:

Type	Totals	By 100,000 people	Risk
Murder & non-negligent manslaughter	357	5.6	Moderate
Forcible Rape	2,138	33.7	Moderate
Robbery	8,366	131.8	High
Aggravated Assault	28,060	442.2	High
Burglary	64,235	1,012.2	High
Larceny-Theft	153,062	2,411.9	High

Violent Crime Trends
Violent crimes are composed of murder, non-negligent manslaughter, forcible rape, robbery and aggravated assault. Home invasions are considered a robbery. When combined together there were a total of 38,921 in 2010.

Property Crime Trends
Property crimes are composed of burglary, larceny / theft and motor vehicle theft. When combined together there were a total of 232,132 in 2010.

TEXAS

Texas is located in the south-central region of the United States. It is surrounded on the east by Louisiana, Oklahoma on the north, Arkansas on the northeast and New Mexico on the west. It is the 2nd most populated state in the U.S. and stretches over an area of 268,581 square miles. It was admitted to the union on December 29, 1845 and consists of 254 counties.

The largest cities:
- Houston
- San Antonio
- Dallas

Population:
- 25.6 million
- Ranked 2nd

Size:
- 268,581 square miles
- Ranked 2nd

Population
According to the 2011 United States Census, Tennessee had a population of 25.6 million. The 2000 census reported 20.8 million people. This population is composed of the following:

White	70.4%
African American	11.8%
American Indian	0.7%
Asian	3.8%
Hispanics	37.6%
Other	2.7%

Crime Statistics
The Federal Bureau of Investigation collects a series of crime information from across the country. This information was analyzed to provide the following:

Type	Totals	By 100,000 people	Risk
Murder & non-negligent manslaughter	1,249	5.0	Moderate
Forcible Rape	7,622	30.3	Moderate
Robbery	32,843	130.6	Moderate
Aggravated Assault	71,517	284.4	Moderate
Burglary	228,597	909.1	Moderate
Larceny-Theft	654,626	2,603.3	High

Violent Crime Trends
Violent crimes are composed of murder, non-negligent manslaughter, forcible rape, robbery and aggravated assault. Home invasions are considered a robbery. When combined together there were a total of 113,231 in 2010.

Property Crime Trends
Property crimes are composed of burglary, larceny / theft and motor vehicle theft. When combined together there were a total of 951,246 in 2010.

STOP THE INTRUDER™ | KNOWLEDGE IS THE BEST PROTECTION™

UTAH

Utah is located in the western part of the United States. It is surrounded on the south by Arizona, on the east by Colorado, on the northeast by Wyoming, Idaho on the north and Nevada to its west. It is the 34th most populous state in the U.S. and stretches over an area of 84,899 square miles. It was admitted to the union on January 4, 1896 and consists of 29 counties.

The largest cities:
- Salt Lake City
- West Valley City
- Provo

Population:
- 2.8 million
- Ranked 34th

Size:
- 84,899 square miles
- Ranked 13th

Population
According to the 2011 United States Census, Utah had a population of 2.8 million. The 2000 census reported 2.2 million people. This population is composed of the following:

White	86.1%
African American	1.1%
American Indian	1.2%
Asian	2.0%
Hispanics	13.0%
Other	2.7%

Crime Statistics
The Federal Bureau of Investigation collects a series of crime information from across the country. This information was analyzed to provide the following:

Type	Totals	By 100,000 people	Risk
Murder & non-negligent manslaughter	53	1.9	Low
Forcible Rape	948	34.3	Moderate
Robbery	1,268	45.9	Moderate
Aggravated Assault	3,610	130.6	Low
Burglary	15,017	543.3	Moderate
Larceny-Theft	66,914	2,421.0	High

Violent Crime Trends
Violent crimes are composed of murder, non-negligent manslaughter, forcible rape, robbery and aggravated assault. Home invasions are considered a robbery. When combined together there were a total of 5,879 in 2010.

Property Crime Trends
Property crimes are composed of burglary, larceny / theft and motor vehicle theft. When combined together there were a total of 87,880 in 2010.

STOP THE INTRUDER™ | KNOWLEDGE IS THE BEST PROTECTION™

VERMONT

A state in the New England region, Vermont is located in the northeaster part of the United States. It is surrounded by Massachusetts in the south, New Hampshire on the east, New York on the west and Quebec on the north. It was admitted to the union on May 29, 1790. It is the 49th most populous state in the United States and stretches over an area of 9,620 square miles. Vermont consists of 14 counties.

The largest cities:
- Burlington
- South Burlington
- Rutland

Population:
- 626,431
- Ranked 49th

Size:
- 9,620 square miles
- Ranked 45th

Population
According to the 2011 United States Census, Vermont had a population of 626,431. The 2000 census reported 608,827 people. This population is composed of the following:

White	95.3%
African American	1.0%
American Indian	0.4%
Asian	1.3%
Hispanics	1.5%
Other	1.7%

Crime Statistics
The Federal Bureau of Investigation collects a series of crime information from across the country. This information was analyzed to provide the following:

Type	Totals	By 100,000 people	Risk
Murder & non-negligent manslaughter	7	1.1	Low
Forcible Rape	132	21.1	Low
Robbery	74	11.8	Low
Aggravated Assault	602	96.2	Low
Burglary	3,366	537.9	Moderate
Larceny-Theft	10,474	1,673.9	Moderate

Violent Crime Trends
Violent crimes are composed of murder, non-negligent manslaughter, forcible rape, robbery and aggravated assault. Home invasions are considered a robbery. When combined together there were a total of 815 in 2010.

Property Crime Trends
Property crimes are composed of burglary, larceny / theft and motor vehicle theft. When combined together there were a total of 14,281 in 2010.

STOP THE INTRUDER™ | KNOWLEDGE IS THE BEST PROTECTION™

VIRGINIA

Virginia is located in the South Atlantic region of the United States. It is known as the Commonwealth of Virginia. It is surrounded on the south by North Carolina and Tennessee, on the west by West Virginia and Kentucky and on the north by Maryland. It is the 12th most populous state in the U.S. and stretches over an area of 42,774.2 square miles. It was admitted to the union on June 25, 1788 and consists of 95 counties.

The largest cities:
- Virginia Beach
- Norfolk
- Chesapeake

Population:
- 8.09 million
- Ranked 12th

Size:
- 42,774.2 square miles
- Ranked 35th

Population
According to the 2011 United States Census, Virginia had a population of 8.09 million. The 2000 census reported 7.07 million people. This population is composed of the following:

White	68.6%
African American	19.4%
American Indian	0.4%
Asian	5.5%
Hispanics	7.9%
Other	2.9%

Crime Statistics
The Federal Bureau of Investigation collects a series of crime information from across the country. This information was analyzed to provide the following:

Type	Totals	By 100,000 people	Risk
Murder & non-negligent manslaughter	369	4.6	Moderate
Forcible Rape	1,532	19.1	Low
Robbery	5,657	70.7	Moderate
Aggravated Assault	9,529	119.1	Moderate
Burglary	30,629	382.8	Low
Larceny-Theft	145,019	1,812.5	Low

Violent Crime Trends
Violent crimes are composed of murder, non-negligent manslaughter, forcible rape, robbery and aggravated assault. Home invasions are considered a robbery. When combined together there were a total of 17,087 in 2010.

Property Crime Trends
Property crimes are composed of burglary, larceny / theft and motor vehicle theft. When combined together there were a total of 186,196 in 2010.

STOP THE INTRUDER™ | KNOWLEDGE IS THE BEST PROTECTION™

WASHINGTON

Washington is located in the Pacific Northwestern region of the United States. It is surrounded by Oregon on the south, and on the east and southeast by Idaho. It is the 13th most populous state in the U.S. and stretches over an area of 71,300 square miles. It was admitted to the union on November 11, 1889 and consists of 39 counties.

The largest cities:
- Seattle
- Spokane
- Tacoma

Population:
- 6.8 million
- Ranked 13th

Size:
- 71,300 square miles
- Ranked 18th

Population
According to the 2011 United States Census, Washington had a population of 6.8 million. The 2000 census reported 5.9 million people. This population is composed of the following:

White	77.3%
African American	3.6%
American Indian	1.5%
Asian	7.2%
Hispanics	11.2%
Other	4.7%

Crime Statistics
The Federal Bureau of Investigation collects a series of crime information from across the country. This information was analyzed to provide the following:

Type	Totals	By 100,000 people	Risk
Murder & non-negligent manslaughter	152	2.3	Moderate
Forcible Rape	2,562	38.1	High
Robbery	5,929	88.2	Moderate
Aggravated Assault	12,458	185.3	Moderate
Burglary	55,164	820.3	Moderate
Larceny-Theft	168,360	2,503.7	High

Violent Crime Trends
Violent crimes are composed of murder, non-negligent manslaughter, forcible rape, robbery and aggravated assault. Home invasions are considered a robbery. When combined together there were a total of 21,101 in 2010.

Property Crime Trends
Property crimes are composed of burglary, larceny / theft and motor vehicle theft. When combined together there were a total of 249,253 in 2010.

STOP THE INTRUDER™ | KNOWLEDGE IS THE BEST PROTECTION™

WEST VIRGINIA

West Virginia is located the Appalachian region of the eastern part of United States. It is surrounded on the southeast by Virginia, on the southwest by Kentucky, to the northwest by Ohio, on the northeast by Pennsylvania and on the east by Maryland. It is the 37th most populous state in the U.S. and stretches over an area of 24,230 square miles. It was admitted to the union on June 20, 1863 and consists of 55 counties.

The largest cities:
- Charleston
- Huntington
- Parkersburg

Population:
- 1.8 million
- Ranked 37th

Size:
- 24,230 square miles
- Ranked 41st

Population
According to the 2011 United States Census, West Virginia had a population of 1.85 million. The 2000 census reported 1.8 million people. This population is composed of the following:

White	93.9%
African American	3.4%
American Indian	0.2%
Asian	0.7%
Hispanics	1.2%
Other	1.5%

Crime Statistics
The Federal Bureau of Investigation collects a series of crime information from across the country. This information was analyzed to provide the following:

Type	Totals	By 100,000 people	Risk
Murder & non-negligent manslaughter	62	3.3	Moderate
Forcible Rape	354	19.1	Low
Robbery	828	44.7	Low
Aggravated Assault	4,586	247.5	Moderate
Burglary	10,756	580.5	Moderate
Larceny-Theft	28,383	1,531.7	Low

Violent Crime Trends
Violent crimes are composed of murder, non-negligent manslaughter, forcible rape, robbery and aggravated assault. Home invasions are considered a robbery. When combined together there were a total of 5,830 in 2010.

Property Crime Trends
Property crimes are composed of burglary, larceny / theft and motor vehicle theft. When combined together there were a total of 41,500 in 2010.

STOP THE INTRUDER™ | KNOWLEDGE IS THE BEST PROTECTION™

WISCONSIN

Wisconsin is located in the north-central region of the United States. It is also a part of the Great Lakes and the Midwest regions. It is surrounded on the west by Minnesota, on the southwest by Iowa, to the south by Illinois, on the east by Lake Michigan, on the northeast by Michigan and on the north by Lake Superior. It is the 20th most populous state in the U.S. and stretches over an area of 65,497.82 square miles. It was admitted to the union on May 26, 1848 and consists of 72 counties.

The largest cities:
- Milwaukee
- Madison
- Green Bay

Population:
- 5.7 million
- Ranked 20th

Size:
- 65,497.82 square miles
- Ranked 23rd

Population

According to the 2011 United States Census, Wisconsin had a population of 5.7 million. The 2000 census reported 5.3 million people. This population is composed of the following:

White	86.2%
African American	6.3%
American Indian	1.0%
Asian	2.3%
Hispanics	5.9%
Other	1.8%

Crime Statistics

The Federal Bureau of Investigation collects a series of crime information from across the country. This information was analyzed to provide the following:

Type	Totals	By 100,000 people	Risk
Murder & non-negligent manslaughter	155	2.7	Moderate
Forcible Rape	1,187	20.9	Low
Robbery	4,504	79.2	Moderate
Aggravated Assault	8,296	145.9	Low
Burglary	26,566	467.1	Moderate
Larceny-Theft	107,908	1,897.5	Moderate

Violent Crime Trends

Violent crimes are composed of murder, non-negligent manslaughter, forcible rape, robbery and aggravated assault. Home invasions are considered a robbery. When combined together there were a total of 14,142 in 2010.

Property Crime Trends

Property crimes are composed of burglary, larceny / theft and motor vehicle theft. When combined together there were a total of 142,612 in 2010.

STOP THE INTRUDER™ | KNOWLEDGE IS THE BEST PROTECTION™

WYOMING

Wyoming is located in the mountainous region of the western part of United States. It is surrounded on the north by Montana, on the northeast by South Dakota, on the southeast by Nebraska, on the south by Utah and Colorado and Idaho on the west. It is the least populated state in the U.S. and stretches over an area of 97,814 square miles. It was admitted to the union on July 10, 1890 and consists of 23 counties.

The largest cities:
- Cheyenne
- Casper
- Laramie

Population:
- 568,158
- Ranked 50th

Size:
- 97,814 square miles
- Ranked 10th

Population
According to the 2011 United States Census, Wyoming had a population of 568,158. The 2000 census reported 493,782 people. This population is composed of the following:

White	90.7%
African American	0.8%
American Indian	2.4%
Asian	0.8%
Hispanics	8.9%
Other	2.2%

Crime Statistics
The Federal Bureau of Investigation collects a series of crime information from across the country. This information was analyzed to provide the following:

Type	Totals	By 100,000 people	Risk
Murder & non-negligent manslaughter	8	1.4	Low
Forcible Rape	164	29.1	Moderate
Robbery	76	13.5	Low
Aggravated Assault	856	151.9	Moderate
Burglary	2,149	381.3	Low
Larceny-Theft	11,134	1,975.4	Moderate

Violent Crime Trends
Violent crimes are composed of murder, non-negligent manslaughter, forcible rape, robbery and aggravated assault. Home invasions are considered a robbery. When combined together there were a total of 1,104 in 2010.

Property Crime Trends
Property crimes are composed of burglary, larceny / theft and motor vehicle theft. When combined together there were a total of 13,874 in 2010.

STOP THE INTRUDER™ | KNOWLEDGE IS THE BEST PROTECTION™

Historical Information
Murder and Manslaughter

This following chart provides a year over year analysis of the reported crimes.

Year	Population	Violent Crime	Violent Crime Rate	Murder/ Manslaughter	Murder/ Manslaughter Rate
1991	252,153,092	1,911,767	758.2	24,703	9.8
1992	255,029,699	1,932,274	757.7	23,760	9.3
1993	257,782,608	1,926,017	747.1	24,526	9.5
1994	260,327,021	1,857,670	713.6	23,326	9.0
1995	262,803,276	1,798,792	684.5	21,606	8.2
1996	265,228,572	1,688,540	636.6	19,645	7.4
1997	267,783,607	1,636,096	611.0	18,208	6.8
1998	270,248,003	1,533,887	567.6	16,974	6.3
1999	272,690,813	1,426,044	523.0	15,522	5.7
2000	281,421,906	1,425,486	506.5	15,586	5.5
2001	285,317,559	1,439,480	504.5	16,037	5.6
2002	287,973,924	1,423,677	494.4	16,229	5.6
2003	290,788,976	1,383,676	475.8	16,528	5.7
2004	293,656,842	1,360,088	463.2	16,148	5.5
2005	296,507,061	1,390,745	469.0	16,740	5.6
2006	299,398,484	1,435,123	479.3	17,309	5.8
2007	301,621,157	1,422,970	471.8	17,128	5.7
2008	304,059,724	1,394,461	458.6	16,465	5.4
2009	307,006,550	1,325,896	431.9	15,399	5.0
2010	308,745,538	1,246,248	403.6	14,748	4.8

Historical Information
Forcible Rape

This following chart provides a year over year analysis of the reported crimes.

Year	Population	Violent Crime	Violent Crime Rate	Forcible Rape	Forcible Rape Rate
1991	252,153,092	1,911,767	758.2	106,593	42.3
1992	255,029,699	1,932,274	757.7	109,062	42.8
1993	257,782,608	1,926,017	747.1	106,014	41.1
1994	260,327,021	1,857,670	713.6	102,216	39.3
1995	262,803,276	1,798,792	684.5	97,470	37.1
1996	265,228,572	1,688,540	636.6	96,252	36.3
1997	267,783,607	1,636,096	611.0	96,153	35.9
1998	270,248,003	1,533,887	567.6	93,144	34.5
1999	272,690,813	1,426,044	523.0	89,411	32.8
2000	281,421,906	1,425,486	506.5	90,178	32.0
2001	285,317,559	1,439,480	504.5	90,863	31.8
2002	287,973,924	1,423,677	494.4	95,235	33.1
2003	290,788,976	1,383,676	475.8	93,883	32.3
2004	293,656,842	1,360,088	463.2	95,089	32.4
2005	296,507,061	1,390,745	469.0	94,347	31.8
2006	299,398,484	1,435,123	479.3	94,472	31.6
2007	301,621,157	1,422,970	471.8	92,160	30.6
2008	304,059,724	1,394,461	458.6	90,750	29.8
2009	307,006,550	1,325,896	431.9	89,241	29.1
2010	308,745,538	1,246,248	403.6	84,767	27.5

STOP THE INTRUDER™ | KNOWLEDGE IS THE BEST PROTECTION™

Historical Information
Robbery

This following chart provides a year over year analysis of the reported crimes.

Year	Population	Violent Crime	Violent Crime Rate	Robbery	Robbery Rate
1991	252,153,092	1,911,767	758.2	687,732	272.7
1992	255,029,699	1,932,274	757.7	672,478	263.7
1993	257,782,608	1,926,017	747.1	659,870	256.0
1994	260,327,021	1,857,670	713.6	618,949	237.8
1995	262,803,276	1,798,792	684.5	580,509	220.9
1996	265,228,572	1,688,540	636.6	535,594	201.9
1997	267,783,607	1,636,096	611.0	498,534	186.2
1998	270,248,003	1,533,887	567.6	447,186	165.5
1999	272,690,813	1,426,044	523.0	409,371	150.1
2000	281,421,906	1,425,486	506.5	408,016	145.0
2001	285,317,559	1,439,480	504.5	423,557	148.5
2002	287,973,924	1,423,677	494.4	420,806	146.1
2003	290,788,976	1,383,676	475.8	414,235	142.5
2004	293,656,842	1,360,088	463.2	401,470	136.7
2005	296,507,061	**1,390,745**	469.0	417,438	140.8
2006	299,398,484	1,435,123	479.3	449,246	150.0
2007	301,621,157	1,422,970	471.8	447,324	148.3
2008	304,059,724	1,394,461	458.6	443,563	145.9
2009	307,006,550	1,325,896	431.9	408,742	133.1
2010	308,745,538	1,246,248	403.6	367,832	119.1

STOP THE INTRUDER™ | KNOWLEDGE IS THE BEST PROTECTION™

Historical Information
Aggravated Assault

This following chart provides a year over year analysis of the reported crimes.

Year	Population	Violent Crime	Violent Crime Rate	Aggravated Assault	Aggravated Assault Rate
1991	2.5215E+08	1,911,767	758.2	1,092,739	433.4
1992	2.5503E+08	1,932,274	757.7	1,126,974	441.9
1993	2.5778E+08	1,926,017	747.1	1,135,607	440.5
1994	2.6033E+08	1,857,670	713.6	1,113,179	427.6
1995	2.6280E+08	1,798,792	684.5	1,099,207	418.3
1996	2.6523E+08	1,688,540	636.6	1,037,049	391.0
1997	2.6778E+08	1,636,096	611.0	1,023,201	382.1
1998	2.7025E+08	1,533,887	567.6	976,583	361.4
1999	2.7269E+08	1,426,044	523.0	911,740	334.3
2000	2.8142E+08	1,425,486	506.5	911,706	324.0
2001	2.8532E+08	1,439,480	504.5	909,023	318.6
2002	2.8797E+08	1,423,677	494.4	891,407	309.5
2003	2.9079E+08	1,383,676	475.8	859,030	295.4
2004	2.9366E+08	1,360,088	463.2	847,381	288.6
2005	2.9651E+08	1,390,745	469.0	862,220	290.8
2006	2.9940E+08	1,435,123	479.3	874,096	292.0
2007	3.0162E+08	1,422,970	471.8	866,358	287.2
2008	3.0406E+08	1,394,461	458.6	843,683	277.5
2009	3.0701E+08	1,325,896	431.9	812,514	264.7
2010	3.0875E+08	1,246,248	403.6	778,901	252.3

STOP THE INTRUDER™ | KNOWLEDGE IS THE BEST PROTECTION™

Historical Information
Burglary

This following chart provides a year over year analysis of the reported crimes.

Year	Population	Property Crime	Property Crime Rate	Burglary	Bruglary Rate
1991	2.5215E+08	12,961,116	5,140.2	3,157,150	1,252.1
1992	2.5503E+08	12,505,917	4,903.7	2,979,884	1,168.4
1993	2.5778E+08	12,218,777	4,740.0	2,834,808	1,099.7
1994	2.6033E+08	12,131,873	4,660.2	2,712,774	1,042.1
1995	2.6280E+08	12,063,935	4,590.5	2,593,784	987.0
1996	2.6523E+08	11,805,323	4,451.0	2,506,400	945.0
1997	2.6778E+08	11,558,475	4,316.3	2,460,526	918.8
1998	2.7025E+08	10,951,827	4,052.5	2,332,735	863.2
1999	2.7269E+08	10,208,334	3,743.6	2,100,739	770.4
2000	2.8142E+08	10,182,584	3,618.3	2,050,992	728.8
2001	2.8532E+08	10,437,189	3,658.1	2,116,531	741.8
2002	2.8797E+08	10,455,277	3,630.6	2,151,252	747.0
2003	2.9079E+08	10,442,862	3,591.2	2,154,834	741.0
2004	2.9366E+08	10,319,386	3,514.1	2,144,446	730.3
2005	2.9651E+08	10,174,754	3,431.5	2,155,448	726.9
2006	2.9940E+08	10,019,601	3,346.6	2,194,993	733.1
2007	3.0162E+08	9,882,212	3,276.4	2,190,198	726.1
2008	3.0406E+08	9,774,152	3,214.6	2,228,887	733.0
2009	3.0701E+08	9,337,060	3,041.3	2,203,313	717.7
2010	3.0875E+08	9,082,887	2,941.9	2,159,878	699.6

STOP THE INTRUDER™ | KNOWLEDGE IS THE BEST PROTECTION™

Historical Information
Larceny-Theft

This following chart provides a year over year analysis of the reported crimes.

Year	Population	Property Crime	Property Crime Rate	Larceny-Theft	Larceny-Theft Rate
1991	252,153,092	12,961,116	5,140.2	8,142,228	3,229.1
1992	255,029,699	12,505,917	4,903.7	7,915,199	3,103.6
1993	257,782,608	12,218,777	4,740.0	7,820,909	3,033.9
1994	260,327,021	12,131,873	4,660.2	7,879,812	3,026.9
1995	262,803,276	12,063,935	4,590.5	7,997,710	3,043.2
1996	265,228,572	11,805,323	4,451.0	7,904,685	2,980.3
1997	267,783,607	11,558,475	4,316.3	7,743,760	2,891.8
1998	270,248,003	10,951,827	4,052.5	7,376,311	2,729.5
1999	272,690,813	10,208,334	3,743.6	6,955,520	2,550.7
2000	281,421,906	10,182,584	3,618.3	6,971,590	2,477.3
2001	285,317,559	10,437,189	3,658.1	7,092,267	2,485.7
2002	287,973,924	10,455,277	3,630.6	7,057,379	2,450.7
2003	290,788,976	10,442,862	3,591.2	7,026,802	2,416.5
2004	293,656,842	10,319,386	3,514.1	6,937,089	2,362.3
2005	296,507,061	10,174,754	3,431.5	6,783,447	2,287.8
2006	299,398,484	10,019,601	3,346.6	6,626,363	2,213.2
2007	301,621,157	9,882,212	3,276.4	6,591,542	2,185.4
2008	304,059,724	9,774,152	3,214.6	6,586,206	2,166.1
2009	307,006,550	9,337,060	3,041.3	6,338,095	2,064.5
2010	308,745,538	9,082,887	2,941.9	6,185,867	2,003.5

STOP THE INTRUDER™ | KNOWLEDGE IS THE BEST PROTECTION™

Historical Information
Burglary

This following chart provides a year over year analysis of the reported crimes.

Year	Population	Property Crime	Property Crime Rate	Motor Vehicle Theft	Motor Vehicle Theft Rate
1991	252,153,092	12,961,116	5,140.2	1,661,738	659.0
1992	255,029,699	12,505,917	4,903.7	1,610,834	631.6
1993	257,782,608	12,218,777	4,740.0	1,563,060	606.3
1994	260,327,021	12,131,873	4,660.2	1,539,287	591.3
1995	262,803,276	12,063,935	4,590.5	1,472,441	560.3
1996	265,228,572	11,805,323	4,451.0	1,394,238	525.7
1997	267,783,607	11,558,475	4,316.3	1,354,189	505.7
1998	270,248,003	10,951,827	4,052.5	1,242,781	459.9
1999	272,690,813	10,208,334	3,743.6	1,152,075	422.5
2000	281,421,906	10,182,584	3,618.3	1,160,002	412.2
2001	285,317,559	10,437,189	3,658.1	1,228,391	430.5
2002	287,973,924	10,455,277	3,630.6	1,246,646	432.9
2003	290,788,976	10,442,862	3,591.2	1,261,226	433.7
2004	293,656,842	10,319,386	3,514.1	1,237,851	421.5
2005	296,507,061	10,174,754	3,431.5	1,235,859	416.8
2006	299,398,484	10,019,601	3,346.6	1,198,245	400.2
2007	301,621,157	9,882,212	3,276.4	1,100,472	364.9
2008	304,059,724	9,774,152	3,214.6	959,059	315.4
2009	307,006,550	9,337,060	3,041.3	795,652	259.2
2010	308,745,538	9,082,887	2,941.9	737,142	238.8

STOP THE INTRUDER™ | KNOWLEDGE IS THE BEST PROTECTION™

Locksmiths by State

ALABAMA
A & E Lock and Key
dba GLS Locksmith
www.glslocksmith.net

A Absolute Security Tech
aasecuritytech.com

Aaron's Lock Service
3757 Gulf Shores Pkwy Ste E
Gulf Shores AL 36542
www.aaronslockservice.com

Alabama Lock & Key
1800 Green Springs Highway S
Birmingham AL 35205
www.alabamalock.com

American Lock & Key Inc.
1974 Mall Boulevard
Auburn AL 36830
www.american-lockandkey.com

Armor Lock & Key
alexlocks.com

Brooks Lock & Key
411 6th St SE
Decatur AL 35601
www.brookslock.com

Clifton Lock & Key
8935 Holt Springer Road
Athens AL 35611
shoalslocksmith.com

Coast Safe & Lock Company
P.O. Box 66257
457 Dauphin Island Parkway
Mobile AL 36606
www.coastsafelock.com

Cullman Locksmith & Safe Co
301 3rd Ave. SW.
Cullman AL 35055
www.cullmanlocksmith.com

David's Lock & Key
106 Kent Street
Montgomery AL 36109
www.davidslocknkey.com

Harbison Lock & Key, Inc.
1704 28th Ave S
Homewood AL 35209
www.harbisonlock.com

Hoover Lock & Key
3229 Lorna Road
Hoover AL 35216
www.hooverlockandkeyinc.com

Lamar's Lock & Key
Dothan AL
www.lamarslockandkey.com

Leak's Lock & Key
1140 North Brindlee Parkway
Arab AL 35016
www.leakslockandkey.com

Montgomery Lock & Key
131 Eastdale Rd. South
Montgomery AL 36117
www.montgomerylockandkey.com

ALASKA
Able Locksmiths
511 E. Northern Lights
Anchorage AK 99503
www.ablelocksmith.net

STOP THE INTRUDER™ | KNOWLEDGE IS THE BEST PROTECTION™

Action Security Inc.
243 East 5th Ave.
Anchorage AK 99501
www.actionsecurity.com

Doaks Lock & Key
8800 Glacier Why #119
Juneau AK 99801
doaks.com

Larson's Locksmith & Security, Inc
1249 Noble Street
Fairbanks AK 99701
www.larsonslocksmith.com

ARIZONA
A -1 Locksmith & Security Ctr
1707 E. Weber Drive, Suite 1
Tempe AZ 85281
www.a1locksmith.com

A American Key & Safe / A Top Notch Locksmith
6055 E Southern Ave #103
Mesa AZ 85206
www.americankeyandsafe.com

A Professional Locks
940 N Alma School Rd
Chandler AZ 85224
aprofessionallocks.com

ACME Locksmith
2735 E Main St, STE 10
Mesa AZ 85213
www.acmelocksmith.com

Advanced Lock & Safe
PO Box 10532
Fort Mohave AZ 86427
advancedlocknsafe.com

Alcatraz Locksmith
610 E Bell Rd, Ste 2-372
Phoenix AZ 85022
www.alcatrazlock.com

AIS Locksmith Service
1911 West Broadway Rd.
Mesa AZ 85202
locksmith-mesa.com

Always Secure Locksmithing
12621 N 39Th Way
Phoenix AZ 85032
www.alwayssecurelocksmithing.com

Anderson Lock & Safe, LLC
6146 N. 35th Ave. #101
Phoenix AZ 85017
www.andersonlockandsafe.com

Anytime Lock and Safe
306 N Evergreen St
Chandler AZ 85225
www.anytimelock.net

Arizona School Of Locksmithing
3832 West Davidson Lane
Phoenix AZ 85051
www.azschooloflocksmithing.org

Avid Locksmith LLC
P.O. Box 965
Gilbert AZ 85299
www.avidlocksmith.com

AZ REO Locksmith
34315 N 81st St
Scottsdale AZ 85266
www.azreolocksmith.com

Bill's Key & Lock Service Inc
148 W. Orion Street, Suite C2
Tempe AZ 85283
www.billskey.com

STOP THE INTRUDER™ | KNOWLEDGE IS THE BEST PROTECTION™

Blue Knight Lock & Key
7102 N 11th Ave
Phoenix AZ 85021
blueknightlock.com

Commercial Door & Hardware
708 W. 22nd St.
Tempe AZ 85282
www.cdhsecurity.com

Critical Locksmith
3149 S Larkspur St
Gilbert AZ 85295
criticallocksmithaz.com

Dean's Village Locksmith, Inc
4225 N. Scottsdale Road
Scottsdale AZ 85251
www.locksmithaz.com

Eagle Locksmith, LLC
1827 E. Indian School Rd
Phoenix AZ 85016
www.eaglelocksmithaz.com

Local Locksmith
995 W. 4th Street
Suite G
Benson AZ 85602
www.locallocksmithaz.com

Lockaid USA LLC
4350 East Palm Lane
Phoenix AZ 85008
www.locksmith-lockaid.com

Locksmith Charley
4024 N. 84Th Lane
Phoenix AZ 85037
www.locksmithcharley.com

Mercury Lock & Safe
10893 N Scottsdale Rd
Scottsdale AZ 85254
www.mercurylock.com

Metro Lock Service Inc
10209 North 35th Avenue
Phoenix AZ 85051
www.metrolockandsafe.com

Moss Lock and Key
9266 E. Lobo Ave.
Mesa AZ 85209
www.agentlocksmith.com

Paul's Lock Service
4009 East 17th Street
Tucson AZ 85711
paulslockservice.com

Pinnacle Lock and Safe
7755 E Redfield Rd.
Scottsdale AZ 85260
www.pinnaclelock.com

Pop-a-Lock Of Phoenix
5115 N. Dysart Rd Ste 202 #609
Litchfield Park AZ 85340
www.popalock.com/franchise/maricopa_county_az_locksmith

Red Rock Lock
PO Box 2931
Sedone AZ 86339
redrocklock.net

Roadrunner Lock & Safe
4444 E Grant Rd.
Tucson AZ 85712
www.roadrunnerlock.com

Safeco Security Inc
2636 W. Townley Avenue
Phoenix AZ 85021
www.safecosecurity.com

Shamrock Brothers Lock & Safe
PO Box 6045
Goodyear AZ 85338
www.shamrockbros.com

STOP THE INTRUDER™ | KNOWLEDGE IS THE BEST PROTECTION™

The Locke Shoppe LLC
2062 E. Southern Ave.
Tempe AZ 85282
www.thelockeshoppe.com

Tucson Mobile Lock & Key
5425 E. Broadway # 314
Tucson AZ 85747
www.tucsonmobilelocksmith.com

University Lock Co Inc
1031 W University Dr
Tempe AZ 85281
www.ulssecurity.com

ARKANSAS

Bill's Lock & Safe Inc
1001 Pike Avenue North
Little Rock AR 72114
www.billslockandsafe.com

Bob's Lock n Key
1166 Hwy 178 W
Midway AR 72651
www.bobslock-n-key.com

C & E Lock & Safe Inc.
2337 N. College
Fayetteville AR 72703
candelockandsafe.com

Casey Lock & Key Inc
1117 Southeast 33rd Street
Bentonville AR 72712
caseylockandkey.com

Marie's Lock & Safe Inc
9608 Rogers Avenue
Fort Smith AR 72903
www.marieslockandsafe.com

Robert's Lock
424 Main Street
Malvern AR 72104
robertslocks.com

CALIFORNIA

Aames Lock & Safe Co
818 W Chapman Ave
Orange CA 92868
www.aameslock.com

Accurate Security Pro's, Inc.
9919 Hibert St Suite D
San Diego CA 92131
www.accuratesecuritypros.com

Agoura Lock Technologies Inc
29134 Roadside Drive Unit #108
Agoura Hills CA 91301
www.agouralock.com

All City Locksmith
161 Del Vale Avenue
San Francisco CA 94127
www.allcitylocksmith.com

Aviation Lock & Key
1316 Aviation Blvd
Redondo Beach CA 90278
www.aviationlock.com

Bay Cities Lock & Safe Co
1155 Chess Drive Unit 117
Foster City CA 94404
www.baycitieslock.com

Consolidated Security Systems
510 W Macarthur Blvd.
Oakland CA 94609
www.css510.com

Cypress Lock And Safe
5663 Lincoln Ave. Suite A
Cypress CA 90630
www.cypresslockandsafe.com

Door Systems, Inc.
9434 Chesapeake Drive
Suite 1210
San Diego CA 92123
www.doorsystemsinc.net

STOP THE INTRUDER™ | KNOWLEDGE IS THE BEST PROTECTION™

Foothill Locksmiths Inc
595 East Lewelling Blvd.
Hayward CA 94541
foothilllocksmithsinc.com

Foster Brothers Security Systems
555 South Murphy Ave.
Sunnyvale CA 94086
www.fosterbrothers.com

Grah Safe & Lock Inc
939 University Ave
San Diego CA 92103
www.grahsecurity.com

Havens For Total Security
459 N. Blackstone Ave
Fresno CA 93701
www.havenslock.com

Ingersoll-Rand Security Technologies
5417 E. Ebell St.
Long Beach CA 90808
www.integratedsystems.ingersollrand.com

J P Locks Inc.
1843 Saint Lucia Way
Vista CA 92081
www.jplocks.com

KEEDEX, Inc
510 Cameron St
Placentia CA 92870
www.keedex.com

King's Total Security
3585 E Keswick Rd
Redding CA 96003
locksmithredding.com

La Jolla Lock & Safe
1122 Wall Street
La Jolla CA 92037
www.lajollalock.com

Lee's Lock And Safe
386 N El Camino Real
Encinitas CA 92024
www.leeslock.com

Lightning Lock & Key, LLC
P.O. Box 10803
Truckee CA 96162
lightninglockandkey.com

Locksmith-USA
8941 Atlanta Ave # 155
Huntingdon Beach CA 92646
www.locksmith-usa.com

Lockworks Unlimited
2671 El Camino Real
Redwood City CA 94061
www.lockworksunlimited.com

Mainline Security
617 7Th Street
San Francisco CA 94103
www.mainline-security.com

Martin Lock & Safe Co
26072 Merit Circle, Suite 108
Laguna Hills CA 92653
www.martinlock.com

Mid Valley Lock & Key
26873 Sierra Hwy #245
Santa Clarita CA 91321
www.midvalleylocknkey.com

STOP THE INTRUDER™ | KNOWLEDGE IS THE BEST PROTECTION™

Millbrae Lock
311 El Camino Real
Millbrae CA 94030
www.millbraelock.com

Muenzer's Inc
221 5th Street
Hollister CA 95023
www.muenzers.com

Nason's Lock & Safe Inc
2418 Saviers Rd
Oxnard CA 93033
www.nasonslock.com

Valley Lock & Safe
68100 Ramon Rd
Suite C-11
Cathedral City CA 92234
www.valleylock.com

COLORADO
Acoma Locksmith Service
421 Perry St
Castle Rock CO 80104
www.acomalocksmithservice.com

Blackhawk Products
25913 Road T.5
Dolores CO 81323
www.blackhawk7.com

Doorway Solutions
3333 East 52nd Ave.
Denver CO 80216
www.doorwaysolutions.com

Englewood Lock and Safe
4310 S Broadway
Englewood CO 80113
www.englewoodlock.com/compact

Henley's Key Service Inc
117 E Boulder St
Colorado Springs CO 80903
www.henleyskeyservice.com

LockSafe Systems
326 Walnut St
Fort Collins CO 80524
www.locksafesystems.com

Premier Security Svcs
7931 S Broadway 323
Littleton CO 80122
www.premiersecuritysvcs.com

Racine's Locksmithing & Security
408 N. Santa Fe Ave.
Peublo CO 81003
keyalarms.com

Security Concepts Inc
3478 E. Jamison Ave.
Centennial CO 80122
www.keycuff.com

State-Wide Lock & Safe
7500 E Colfax Ave
Denver CO 80220
wemovesafes.com

CONNECTICUT
AA Lock & Key Inc
1055 Colonel Ledyard Hwy.
Ledyard CT 06339
www.aalockkey.com

Aable Locksmith
47 Marlboro Drive
Milford CT 06461
www.aablelocksmiths.com

STOP THE INTRUDER™ | KNOWLEDGE IS THE BEST PROTECTION™

Amity Safe & Lock Co
1336 Whalley Ave
New Haven CT 06515
www.amitysafeandlock.com

Calvert Safe & Lock Ltd
40 Caroline Street
Derby CT 06418
calvertsafeandlock.com

Charles Stuttig Locksmith Inc
158 Greenwich Ave
Greenwich CT 06830
stuttiglocksmith.com/History.htm

Hartford Safe & Lock
36 Silas Deane Highway
Wethersfield CT 06109
www.locksmithhartfordct.com

Hartley Lock & Key
26 Edrow Rd
Bristol CT 06010
hartleylockandkey.com

Karpilow Safe & Lock Co
4490 Main Street
Bridgeport CT 06606
www.karpilowlock.com

Rackliffe Lock & Safe
P. O. Box 331
Trumbull CT 06611
www.rackliffelock.com

Southington Security Services
2211 Meriden-Waterbury
Turnpike, Route 322
P.O. Box 354
Marion CT 06444
www.southingtonsecurity.com

DELAWARE
Allied Lock Safe
709 N Shipley St
Wilmington DE 19801
www.allied-lock.com

Certified Lock & Access
3 Germay Drive, Suite 7
Wilmington DE 19804
www.certifiedlockandaccess.com

Pop-A-Lock
4142 Stanton-Ogletown Rd
Newark DE 19713
www.popalock.com/franchise/
wilmington_de_locksmith.php

FLORIDA
A All-Safe, Safe & Lock, Inc
1141 East Blue Heron
Riviera Beach FL 33404
www.yoursecurityexperts.com

About Town Lock & Safe Co, Inc
2404 N. Dixie Hwy.
Fort Lauderdale FL 33305
www.abouttownlockandsafe.liveonatt.com

Access Safe & Lock Co
5532 US HWY 98
North Lakeland FL 33809
www.accesssafeandlock.com

Acme SecuritySolutions
P.O. Box 17944
Tampa FL 33682
www.affordablelock.com

Acorn Safe & Lock
409 Lake Avenue
Lake Worth FL 33460
acornlock.com

STOP THE INTRUDER™ | KNOWLEDGE IS THE BEST PROTECTION™

AHC Safe &Lock/Ormond Hdwe
54 W. Granada Blvd.
Ormond Beach FL 32174
www.ahcsafe.com

Benny's Security Solutions
3245 W Bay to Bay Blvd
Tampa FL 33629
www.bennykey.com

Plant City Lock & Key
1002 South Collins Street
Plant City FL 33566
www.plantcitylock.com/plantcit

Pop-A-Lock Of Tampa
405 S Dale Mabry Hwy. Ste 383
Tampa FL 33609
www.popalocktampafl.com

TCB Locksmith, Inc.
712 South US Hwy 27
Minneola FL 34715
locks-locksmith.com

GEORGIA
A-1 Lock & Key Inc
1933 Dawson Road
Albany GA 31707
www.keyedup.com

All Pro Alarm LLC
P.O. Box 33
Tiger GA 30576
www.allproalarm.com

All Secure Inc.
107 Independence Drive
Warner Robins GA 31088
www.allsecuresafe.com

Arrowhead Lock & Safe Inc.
2211 Marietta Blvd. NW
Atlanta GA 30318
www.arrowheadlockandsafe.com

East Point Cycle & Key Inc
2834 Church Street
East Point GA 30344
www.cycleandkey.com

Kevin Wilson Master Locksmith
4155 Lawrenceville Highway
#8181
Lilburn GA 30047
www.kevinwilsonlocksmith.com

Lock Doctor Inc
95 Peachtree Industrial Blvd
Sugar Hill GA 30518
www.lockdoctorinc.com

LockPro Locksmith, LLC
2973 River Road
Elberton GA 30635
www.lockprolocksmith.com

Precision Locksmith
25 Syracuse Lane
Covington GA 30016
www.precision-locksmith.com

Tebarco Door & Metal Services Inc
1905 Grassland Parkway
Alpharetta GA 30004
tebarcodoor.com

HAWAII
Affordable Locksmith & Son
1018 Lunalilo St
Honolulu HI 96822
affordablelocksmithandsons.com

Baker T Lock & Key
3-2600 KAUMUALII HWY 1300
Lihue HI 96766
bakertlockandkey.net

STOP THE INTRUDER™ | KNOWLEDGE IS THE BEST PROTECTION™

JBL Hawaii, Ltd
905 Kokea St
Honolulu HI 96817
www.jblhawaii.com

Lockout Specialists of Hawaii
2110 Kamehameha Ave
Honolulu HI 96822
www.lockoutspec.com

Pacific Lock & Safe
2290 Alahao Pl. #201
Honolulu HI 96819
www.pacificlock.net

Pop-A-Lock Of Honolulu
3133 Waialae Avenue #3721
Honolulu HI 96816
www.popalock.com/franchise/
honolulu_hi_locksmith.php

Ray's Lock & Key Service Inc
85-791 Farrington Highway
Waianae HI 96792
www.rayslockandkey.com

Salz Lock & Safe
3012 Waialae Ave, #3
Honolulu HI 96816
www.salzlock.com

The Key Guy
1684 Ala Moana Blvd 253
Honolulu HI 96815
www.keyguyhawaii.com

IDAHO
AAA-1 Lock & Key
1507 N. Midland Blvd
Nampa ID 83651
aaa1lock.com

Advanced Lock and Key LLC
10966 W Highlander Rd
Boise ID 83709
www.unlockidaho.com

Anytime Lock & Key
6216 Fairview Avenue
Boise ID 83704
www.anytimelockandkey.com

ARK Security & Electronics
47 East Main Street
Rexburg ID 83440
www.arksecurity.com

Daves Lock Shop
111 3rd St
South Nampa ID 83651
www.daveslockshop.com

May Hardware
809 N 3rd Street
McCall ID 83638
www.mayhardware.com

Pop-A-Lock Of Utah
2467 Fairview Rd
American Falls ID 83211
www.popalock.com/franchise/
idaho_falls_id_locksmith.php

The Safe House
6224 N. Park Meadow Way #305
Boise ID 83713
thesafehouse.info

ILLINOIS
A-Paul's Lock Service
9S020 Frontage Rd.
Willowbrook IL 60527
www.paulslocksmithservice.com

STOP THE INTRUDER™ | KNOWLEDGE IS THE BEST PROTECTION™

Anderson Lock Company
850 Oakton Street
Des Plaines IL 60018
www.andersonlock.com

Archway Locksmith
1218 North 17th Street
Swansea IL 62226
www.archwaylocksmith.com

I Spinello Locksmiths
225 S 6th St # B
Rockford IL 61104
spinello.com

Keyway Lock & Security Company
3820 W 79th Street
Chicago IL 60652
www.keywaylockandsecurityinc.com

Omega Locksmith
4329 WEST 26TH STREET
Chicago IL 60623
www.omegalocksmith.com

Plainfield Lock Techs
14730 S Naperville Rd
Plainfield IL 60544
plainfieldlocktechs.com

Rite Lock & Safe
3508 Dempster
Skokie IL 60076
www.ritelocksmith.com

Security Shop
1605 E. 55th St.
Chicago IL 60615
www.securityshopinc.com

Silverton Lock & Key LLC
PO Box 1024
Bedford Park IL 60499
www.silvertonlock.com

INDIANA
Hood's Locksmith Service, LLC
176 West Logan St., Box #217
Noblesville IN 46060
www.hoodslock.com

Lents Lock & Safe, Inc.
PO Box 108
11 W Main St
Washington IN 47501
www.lentslock.com

Lock Specialty
1780 E. Poplar Road
Columbia City IN 46725
www.lockspecialty.com

Lockout Express LLC
748 U.S. Highway 41 Unit A
Schererville IN 46375
lockoutexpress.net/index.htm

Michiana Lock & Key Inc
621 East Jefferson Blvd.
South Bend IN 46617
www.michianalock.com

Murphy's Lock & Key
Greenwood IN 46143
murphyslockandkey.com

Troy's Lockshop
5220 W Troy AVE
Indianapolis IN 46241
www.123locksmith.com

IOWA
Fred's Lock and Key
1005 3rd Ave SW,
Suite B
Cedar Rapids IA 52404
fredslockandkey.com

Strauss Security Solutions
4663 121st Street
Urbandale IA 50323
strausslock.com

The Locksmith Express
450 Central Ave
Dubuque IA 52001
www.locksmithexpress.com

KANSAS
Central Key & Safe Co, Inc
305 N. Market
Wichita KS 67202
www.centralkeyandsafe.com

Middle American Lockout
9421 Pflumm Rd. #100
Lenexa KS 66215
www.midamlockkc.com

Steve's Lock Out
1806 MAIN
Parsons KS 67357
www.steveslockout.com

KENTUCKY
AAA Systems
1101 Shive Lane
Bowling Green KY 42103
www.aaasystems.com

ARG Locks
Bowling Green KY 42104
www.arglocks.com

Bates Security Lock & Safe
213 Walton Ave
Lexington KY 40502
www.batessecurity.com

Dan's Lock & Key Co
1639 Greenland Park
Shelbyville KY 40065
www.danslock.com

Grott Locksmith Center Inc
1112 Winchester Road
Lexington KY 40505
www.grottsecurity.com

J Webb Lock & Key Svc
8003 Blue Lick Rd
Louisville KY 40219
www.jwebblockandkey.com

Tri-State Lock
8347 Dixie Highway
Florence KY 41042
www.tri-statelock.com

W C & D Locksmith
71 Nunn Blvd
Cadiz KY 42211
www.wcdlocksmith.com

LOUISIANA
A-1 Key & Lock LLC
2289 Louisville Ave
Monroe LA 71201
www.a1keyandlock.net

Bradford Lock & Key
PO Box 1702
Denham Springs LA 70727
bradfordlockandkey.com

Captains Lock & Key LLC
P.O. Box 796
St.Amant LA 70774
www.captlocknkey.com

Lafayette Locksmith Service Inc
411 Kaliste Saloom Rd
Lafayette LA 70508
www.lafayettelocksmith.com

Pop A Lock of New Orleans
4300 South I-10 Service Rd
Suite P
Metarie LA 70001

STOP THE INTRUDER™ | KNOWLEDGE IS THE BEST PROTECTION™

Pop-a-Lock
425 N Claiborne Ave
New Orleans LA 70112
www.popalocknola.com

Pop-A-Lock / Northshore Inc.
P.O. Box 2887
Sidell LA 70459
www.popalock.com/franchise/
slidell_la_locksmith.php

MAINE
Burts Security Center Inc
49 Water Street
Hallowell ME 04347
www.burtsinc.com

Lock Stock & Barrel Inc
PO Box 939
Portland ME 04104
www.lockstock.net

MARYLAND
Ace & Fathers Lock & Safe
7303 Timmons Street
Pittsville MD 21850
www.locksmithmdde.com

Baldino's Lock & Key
111 Chinquapin Round Rd Ste 105
Annapolis MD 21401
www.baldinos.com

Bear Lock & Safe Service
205 Cleveland Ave
Baltimore MD 21222
www.bearlock.com/
ALOA_Link.html

Bill Lorenz Locksmith
437 Westside Blvd
Catonville MD 21228
www.lorenzlocks.com

Brad's Safe & Lock Service, Inc
PO Box 675
Reisterstown MD 21136
www.bradssafeandlock.com

Dave's Lock & Key
4314 Dover Dr
Frederick MD 21703
www.daveslockandkey.net

Easter Lock & Access Systems
1713 E Joppa Rd
Baltimore MD 21234
www.easterslock.com

Emergency Lock & Key Service
8407 Tachbrook Rd
Baltimore MD 21236
www.elkssafeservice.com

Maryon's Locksmiths Co Inc
14800 Main Street Upper
Marlboro MD 20772
www.maryonslock.com

Sure-Fit Security
8213 Fenton St.
Silver Spring MD 20910
www.surefitsecurity.com

MASSACHUSSETTS
A W Gifford, Inc (Since 1866)
11 Lyman Street
Springfield MA 01103
www.giffordlock.com

Alden Lock & Security Inc
48 Lantern Rd
Belmont MA 02178
www.aldenlockandsecurity.com

Amherst Lockworks
64 Montague Rd
Amherst MA 01002
amherstlockworks.net

Boston Car Keys, Inc.
P.O.Box 489
East Boston MA 02128
www.bostoncarkeys.com

Bradfords Ace Hardware
231 Main St
P.O. Box 760
Hyannis MA 02601
www.bradfordsace.com

Florence Lock & Key
51 East St
Easthampton MA 01027
www.florencelock.com

Integrated Security Inc
369 Central St Unit 9
Foxboro MA 02035
www.isi-security.com

John DeCosta Jr Inc
PO Box 490 447 North Main Street
West Bridgewater MA 02379
www.jdecosta.biz

Pride Locksmith
321 Chestnut Street
North Attleboro MA 02760
https://www.pridelocksmith.com

The Flying Locksmiths Inc
1115 N Main St
Randolph MA 02368
www.flyinglocksmiths.com

MICHIGAN
American Atlas Locksmith
51105 Washington
Oakland Macomb MI 48047
www.atlaslocksmith.com

Apex Lock & Safe Service
4697 Tote Road
Comins MI 48619
www.apexlock.com

Fenton Lock & Safe
17195 Silver Parkway #305
Fenton MI 48430
www.fentonlockandsafe.com

Huizen's Locksmith Ser Inc
5389 School Avenue
Hudsonville MI 49426
www.huizenslock.com

JK Locksmith Co
47705 West Rd #B101
Wixom MI 48393
www.jklocksmith.com

JP's Lock & Key
PO Box 712
Roseville MI 48066
jpslockandkey.com

Livonia Lock & Key
33861 Five Mile Road
Livonia MI 48154
livonialock.com

Lock Doc LLC
P.O. BOX 654
Kalamazoo MI 49004
www.mylockdoc.com

Marx Locksmith Service,Inc.
12821 S. Saginaw St D-17
Grand Blanc MI 48439
marxlocksmith.com

Premier Lock and Security
Grand Blanc MI 48439
www.premierlockandsecurity.com

STOP THE INTRUDER™ | KNOWLEDGE IS THE BEST PROTECTION™

MINNESOTA
A Dave's Lock & Safe
2019 Emerson Ave. No.
Minneapolis MN 55411
www.adaveslock.com

Assured Security, Inc.
6144 Olson Memorial Highway
Golden Valley MN 55422
www.assuredsecurityinc.com

Bankers Service Co Inc
604 Suzanne Avenue
St.Paul MN 55126
site.bankersserviceco.com

Bonded Lock & Key
1321 Bemidji Avenue
Bemidji MN 56601
www.bondedlock.com

Floyd Total Security
9036 Grand Ave S
Bloomington MN 55420
www.floydtotalsecurity.com

Foty Lock & Safe
619 E. Blue Earth Avenue
P.O. Box 464
Fairmont MN 56031
www.fotylock.com

Lockguard
4512 Williston Rd
Minneapolis MN 55345
www.lockguard.com

Locksmith Services
Duluth MN 55810
www.keys4locks.com

Rhode's Lock & Glass, Inc.
39 NE 77th Ave
Fridley MN 55432
www.rhodeslockandglass.com

Sellers Lock & Key
303 5th Place NW
Austin MN 55912
www.sellerslock.com

Tom's Lock Service
215 E 3rd St
Winona MN 55987
www.tomslockservice.com

MISSISSIPPI
Birmingham Lock & Key and/or
Locksmiths Inc
P O Box 1289
Meridian MS 39302
www.oddlocks.com

Guardian Lock And Key
Starkville MS 39759
www.guardianlockandkeyms.com

MISSOURI
American Locksmiths
8619 Manchester Rd
St.Louis MO 63144
fixmylock.com

Beishir Lock & Security Inc.
5423 S Lindbergh Blvd
St.Louis MO 63123
www.stlsecurity.com

Kenton Brothers Inc
1718 Baltimore Avenue
Kansas City MO 64108
www.kentonbrothers.com

McGuire Lock & Safe
4800 NE Vivion Rd,
PO Box 25373
Kansas City MO 64119
mcguirelock.com

STOP THE INTRUDER™ | KNOWLEDGE IS THE BEST PROTECTION™

Peterson Lock & Key
608 Frisco St
Monett MO 65708
petersonlockandkey.com

Precision Lock & Key
15 Golf Tee Lane
Maryville MO 4468
precisionlockandkey.com

Sure Lock And Key
11019 Manchester Rd
St.Louis MO 63122
www.surelockandkey.net

MONTANA
Bozeman Safe & Lock
2304 North 7th Ave
Bozeman MT 59715
www.bozemansafeandlock.com

NEBRASKA
Big Red Locksmiths, Inc
629 N 46th St
Omaha NE 68132
www.bigredlocksmiths.com

NEVADA
Desert Locksmiths
836 W. 5th St.
Reno NV 89503
www.desertlock.com

Lock Specialties
1914 Highland Ave
Las Vegas NV 89102
lasvegascarkeys.com

Lockmaster Security Services, Inc.
1435 N. Jones Blvd.
Las Vegas NV 89108
www.lockmasterlv.com

Pop A Lock of Las Vegas
6280 S Valley View Ste 102
Las Vegas NV 89118
www.popalocklv.com

NEW HAMPSHIRE
Allsafe & Lock Inc
399 So. Main St.
Manchester NH 03102
www.allsafenh.com

New Hampshire Safe & Lock Co
78 Northeastern Blvd. #3
Nashua NH 03062
www.nhsafeandlock.com

Zizza Lock & Safe, LLC
PO Box 45 8 Frontier Way
Colebrook NH 03576
www.zizzalock.com

NEW JERSEY
Acme Locksmith Service
261B East Main Street
Oceanport NH 7757
www.acmelocksmithnj.com

Arnold's Safe & Lock Co., Inc.
3615 Haddonfield Rd.
Pennsauken NJ 08109
www.arnoldslock.com

Bob Fraser Security Center
129 Watchung Ave.
Montclair NJ 07043
bob-fraser.com

Bullet Lock & Safe Co Inc
181 Broadway
Long Branch NJ 07740
www.bulletlock.com

CLC Locksmiths
2103 Branch Pike Unit 5
Cinnaminson NJ 08077
www.clclocksmiths.com

STOP THE INTRUDER™ | KNOWLEDGE IS THE BEST PROTECTION™

Dunlap Locksmith Inc
60 White St
Red Bank NJ 07701
www.dunlaplocksmith.com

Maffey's Security Group
1172 E Grand St
Elizabeth NJ 07201
www.maffeys.com

Sterling Investigative Service
84 Moorage Ave
Bayville NJ 08721
www.sterlingis.com

The Lock Doctor Inc
433 S Main St
Phillipsburg NJ 08865
www.thelockdoctor.com

Top Security Locksmiths, Inc.
2401 Bridge Ave. Point
Pleasant NJ 08742
www.topsecuritylocksmiths.com

NEW MEXICO
A & E Locksmith
Albuquerque NM 87111
www.aelocksmith.com

Angel Fire Lock & Key Inc.
PO Box 411
Angel Fire NM 87710
www.angelfirelockandkey.com

Heights Key Lock & Safe Inc
920 San Mateo NE
Albuquerque NM 87108
www.heightskey.com

Territorial Key Lock & Safe Inc
1005 St. Francis Suite 109
Santa Fe NM 87501
www.territorialsafe.com

NEW YORK
Aaron Neil's Locksmith Service
253 Russell Rd
Fulton NY 13069
www.aaronneilslocksmithservice.com

Abbey Locksmiths Inc
1558 2nd Ave
New York NY 10028
www.abbeylock.com

All Access Lock And Security
4F Adrian Court
Cortlandt Manor NY 10567
www.allaccesslock.com

All Alert Alarm & Locksmiths Ltd.
P.O. Box 5
Putnam Valley NY 10579
www.allalertalarm.com

Barrys City Lock & Safe Co
1657 Hannington Avenue
Wantagh NY 11793
www.barrylockandsafe.com

Billy's Lock & Alarm Co., Inc.
8 Bedford Ave
Brooklyn NY 11222
www.billyslocksmith.com

Finger Lakes Lock & Security LLC
512 East Ave
Newark NY 14513
www.fingerlakeslock.com

Gladd Security Inc
5390 South Bay Rd
Syracuse NY 13212
www.gladdsecurity.com

Jack's Security Depot
6848 East Genesee Street
Fayetteville NY 13066
https://safes-lo.accountsupport.com

STOP THE INTRUDER™ | KNOWLEDGE IS THE BEST PROTECTION™

Woodstock Lock And Safe, Inc.
1440-1 Rt 28
PO Box 243
West Hurley NY 12491
woodstocklock.com

NORTH CAROLINA
Ace Locksmithing
680 Island Ford RD.
Statesville NC 28625
www.ace-locksmithing.com

Apex Lock & Key
PO Box 1041
Apex NC 27502
www.apexlockandkey.com

BC Lock & Key Inc
1537 Brookdale Ave
Charlotte NC 28210
bclockandkey.com

Estridge Lock & Key Co
209 N. Rutherford Street
Wadesboro NC 28170
estridgelockandkey.com

Marshall Locksmith Svc Inc
4205 Poole Road
Poole Road NC 27610
www.marshallslocks.com

North Carolina Locksmith Inc
8107 Keating Ct.
Oak Ridge NC 27310
www.nclocksmithinc.com

Protec U Corp
200 South Main Street
Waynesville NC 28786
www.protec-u.com

NORTH DAKOTA
Curt's Lock & Key Svc Inc
1102 Main Ave
Fargo ND 58103
curtslock.com

OHIO
A B Bonded Locksmiths Co, Inc
4344 Montgomery Road
Cincinnati OH 45212
ablocks.com

AGP Lock & Security LLC
3481 Dixie Highway
Suite 109
Franklin OH 45005
www.agplock.com

Buckeye Lock Service
130 Carter Cir
Boardman OH 44512
www.buckeyelockservice.com

Cleveland Lock Service, Ltd
2410 Brookview Blvd
Cleveland OH 44134
www.clevelandlockservice.com

Duman's Lock & Safe Inc.
6779 Engle Road, Suite L
Middleburg Heights OH 44130
www.dumanslock.com

Golden Bear Lock & Safe Inc
7445 Daron Court
Plain City OH 43064
www.goldenbearlock.com

Lockmaster Key & Safe
1355 Logan Ave
Youngstown OH 44505
lockmasterkeyandsafe.com

STOP THE INTRUDER™ | KNOWLEDGE IS THE BEST PROTECTION™

Prestige Locksmith
1287 N. Fairfield Road
Beavercreek OH 45432
prestigelocksmith.com

Rick's Locksmithing
394 N Main St
Youngstown OH 44514
www.rickslock.com

South Side Lock & Key
5818 Wilmington Pike #188
Dayton OH 45459
www.southsidelockandkey.com

OKLAHOMA
Charleys Southside Lock & Safe
5123 S. Peoria
Tulsa OK 74105
charleyslock.com

Don's Mobil Lock Shop
323 E Daws
Norman OK 73069
donsmobillockshop.com

Holder's Inc
7027 E 40th St.
Tulsa OK 74145
www.holdersecurity.com

OREGON
A Act Fast Locksmith
16621 SE
82nd Drive
Clackamas OR 97015
aactfastlocksmith.com

A-A Bowman Lock Safe & Key
36036 Airport Drive
Lebanon OR 97355
www.aabowmanlock.com

A-Max Security Solutions, Inc
9050 SW Barbur Blvd.
Portland OR 97219
www.amaxsecurity.com

Davis Lock & Safe
PO Box 6507
Beaverton OR 97007
www.davislock.com

Emerald City Locksmith
1229 W 7th Ave
Eugene OR 97402
https://sites.google.com/site/ecleugene/

Emerald City Locksmith
1229 7th Avenue
Eugene OR 97402
emeraldlock.com

Key Concepts Locksmith and
Master SafeCracker
P.O. Box 4774
Salem OR 97302
www.keyconceptslock.com

Mark's Locksmith
13470 SW Allen Blvd
Beaverton OR 97005
www.markslocksmith.com

Pop-A-Lock Of Portland
2848 NE Everett St
Portland OR 97232
www.popalockportlandor.com

Precision Locksmith Service
10345 SW Canyon Rd
Beaverton OR 97005
www.precisionlocksmith.com

PENNSYLVANIA

A1 Security Center
13 Coffman Avenue
Malvern PA 19355
www.a1securitycenter.com

Assa Technical Services, Inc
6174 State Route 88
Finleyville PA 15332
www.assatechnicalservicesinc.com

Dayton Lock Co
324 West Lancaster Avenue
Wayne PA 19087
www.daytonlock.com

Keystone Lock & Key Service
PO Box 270 Clarks
Summit PA 18411
www.keystonelockandkey.com

Neff's Safe Lock & Security Inc
1039 N Christian St
Lancaster PA 17602
www.askyourlocksmith.com

Reed's Lock & Access Control Systems Inc
700 E. Main St.
Annville PA 17003
www.reedslock.com

Schoell's Lock & Safe Service
PO Box 175
Confluence PA 15424
schoellslockandsafe.com

Shearer Locksmith
5450 Derry Street
Harrisburg PA 17111
www.shearerlocksmith.com

South Penn Lock & Safe Co
936 N Providence Rd
Media PA 19063
www.southpennlock.com

Wizard Lock & Safe Co
218 North Prince St.
Lancaster PA 17603
www.wizardlock.com

RHODE ISLAND

Atlantic Locksmiths
549 Killingly St.
Johnston RI 02919
www.locksmithri.com

SOUTH CAROLINA

Areawide Lock & Key
106 Arrow Head
Hilton Head SC 29928
areawidedecorativehardware.com

POP-A-LOCK of Upstate S.C.
367 S. Pine Street
Spartanburg SC 29302
www.popalock.com/franchise/upstate_sc_locksmith.php

The Key Shop Inc
1000 Taylor St
Columbia SC 29201
www.keyshopinc.com

SOUTH DAKOTA

Hansen Locksmithing
300 W 4th St
Yankton SD 57078
www.hansenlocksmithing.com

TENNESSEE

A-1 Locksmith Inc
3005 Nolensville Pike
Nashville TN 37211
www.a1locksmith247.com

STOP THE INTRUDER™ | KNOWLEDGE IS THE BEST PROTECTION™

ABC Lock & Key Inc
2424 Nolensville Pike
Nashville TN 37211
www.456lock.com

CompuKey Lock And Safe
PO Box 330849
Nashville TN 37203
www.compukeylocksmith.com

Douglas Lock & Safe
PO Box 90571
Nashville TN 37209
douglaslockandsafe.com

Johnny's Locksmiths
615 E Andrew Johnson Hwy
1800 Cox Hill Rd
Greensville TN 37745
www.johnnyslocksmith.com

K & L Locksmith
9540 Hwy 196
Collierville TN 38017
www.kandllocksmith.com

Mid-State Lock & Key
104 Teelia Dr.
Old Hickory TN 37138
www.midstatelock.com

Peifer Safe & Lock
5287 Knight Arnold Rd
Memphis TN 38118
www.peiferlock.com

The LockWorks
3619 Rocky Glade Rd
Eagleville TN 37060
www.thelockworks-tn.com

Tullahoma Lock & Key Service
P.O Box 1898
Tullahoma TN 37388
www.tullahomalock.com/

TEXAS
1st Choice Locksmith, LLC
17117 Westheimer Ste 31
Houston TX 77082
www.houston1stchoicelocksmith.com

24 Hr Lock & Key
P.O. Box 38222
Houston TX 77091
www.24hrlocksmith.net

AMERIKEYS
16274 San Pedro Ave
(Hwy 281 N.)
San Antonio TX 78232
www.amerikeys.com

Anytime Lock & Safe Inc
PO Box 911
LaMarque TX 77568
www.anytimelockandsafe.com

Brock Lock & Key
8014 Elkhart Ave
Lubbock TX 79424
www.brocklockkey.com

Liberty Lock Shop
4002 Nasa Parkway
Seabrook TX 77586
www.libertylockshop.com

Lock Doc Inc
3506 W Loop 281,
Ste. 101
Longview TX 75604
locksmithlongview.com

Locksmith Services of Tyler
241 S. Broadway Ave
Tyler TX 75702
www.locksmithservicesoftyler.com

STOP THE INTRUDER™ | KNOWLEDGE IS THE BEST PROTECTION™

Lubbock Lock & Key Inc
2434 34Th St
Lubbock TX 79411
lubbocklockandkey.com

Saylor Safe & Lock Inc
11035 Cypress N Houston
Houston TX 77065
www.saylorsafe.com

UTAH
Action Locksmith
245 East 3900 South
Salt Lake City UT 84107
www.actionlocksmith.com

Bob's Lock Safe & Key
3112 W. 3500 So.
West Valley City UT 84119
www.bobslockshop.com

Glens Keys Inc
1147 South State Street
Salt Lake City UT 84111
www.glenskey.com

VERMONT
George's Locks & Security
884 Old Hollow Rd N
Ferrisburg VT 05473
www.georgeslocks.com

VIRGINIA
AAA Locksmith Solutions
3219 Columbia Pike
Arlington VA 22204
www.servicelocksmith.com

Area Safe & Lock
3301 Mt Vernon Ave
Alexandria VA 22305
www.areasafe.com

Baldino's Lock & Key
1001-B N. Fillmore St
Arlington VA 22201
www.baldinos.com

Buckley's SecuritySmiths
124 W Tabb St
Petersburg VA 23803
securitysmiths.com

Eastern Safe & Lock Co Inc
6826 Hill Park Drive
Lorton VA 22079
www.easternsafe.com

Federal Lock & Safe Inc
5130 Wilson Boulevard
Arlington VA 22205
www.flslock.com

Precision Locksmith Co., LLC.
3211 Peoples Drive Suite 120
Harrisonburg VA 22801
www.precisionlocksmithco.com

Shorty Wallin Lock & Security
1971 E. Pembroke Ave.
Hampton VA 23663
www.shortywallin.com

Total Security Locksmith
300 Yoakum pkwy
Alexandria VA 22304
www.total-security-va.com

WASHINGTON
A-1 Mobile Lock & Key
1956 South Burlington Blvd.
Burlington WA 98233
www.a1mobilelock.com

Affordable Lock Express
15118 E Sprague Avenue
Spokane WA 99037
affordablelockexpress.com

STOP THE INTRUDER™ | KNOWLEDGE IS THE BEST PROTECTION™

Anytime Lock & Safe
5050 State Hwy 303, #109
Bremerton WA 98311
www.anytimelock.com

ClearStar Security Network
4454 Lopez Ave
Port Townsend WA 98368
www.clearstar.com

E-Z Key Locksmith Inc
811 S. Montesano Street
Westport WA 98595
www.ezkeylocksmith.com

Guardian Security Group Inc
5424 South Tacoma Way
Tacoma WA 98409
www.securityrus.com

RAC Locksmith Services, LLC/
Salmon Creek Locksmith
PO Box 3015
Vancouver WA 98668
www.raclocksmithservices.com

Robblee's Total Security Inc.
751 Tacoma Ave S.
Tacoma WA 98402
www.robblees.com

Watson Security
2106 3rd Avenue
Seattle WA 98121
www.watsonsecurity.com

Wise Locksmith
7018 NE Bothwell Way, Ste A
Kenmore WA 98028
www.wiselocks.com

WEST VIRGINIA
Blue Ridge Locksmithing
P.O. Box 272 Charles
Town WV 25414
www.blueridgelocksmithing.com

WISCONSIN
A & A Lock Service
633 S 3rd Ave
Wausau WI 54401
www.a-a-lock.com

American Locksmiths LLC
2120 E. Moreland Blvd
Waukesha WI 53186
www.autolocksmithing.com

American Pride Services Inc
501 Wisconsin St
Eau Claire WI 54702
www.changemylocks.com

Bill's Locksmith Service Inc.
W1598 Lee Road
Lee Road WI 54843
www.billslocksmithinc.com

J & K Security Solutions
1605 S Park St
Madison WI 53715
jksecurity.com

LKMAN Inc DBA Chucks Lock & Safe
3851 8th Ave.
Wisconsin Dells WI 53965
www.chuckslockandsafe.com

Locks and Unlocks, Inc
PO Box 59
Stoughton WI 53589
www.locksandunlocks.com

Pop-A-Lock Of Milwaukee
544 E. Ogden Ave,
Suite 700-382
Milwaukee WI 53202
www.popalock.com/franchise/
milwaukee_wi_locksmith.php

Tru-Lock & Security Inc
2080 Traux Blvd
Eau Claire WI 54703
www.tru-lock.com

Urich Lock
360 Security 16540 W. Rogers Dr
New Berlin WI 53151
www.urichlock.com/

WYOMING
McCumber Locksmith Shop
1026 Alger Ave
Cody WY 82414
www.mccumberlocksmith.com

STOP THE INTRUDER™ | KNOWLEDGE IS THE BEST PROTECTION™

Alarm Companies by State

ALABAMA
ESC Central, Inc.
3050 Guess Park Dr.
Birmingham, AL 35215
www.esccentral.com

Hunter Security Inc.
28228 N. Main St.
Daphne, AL 36526
www.huntersecurity.net

Ion247 Interactive Video Security
2101 Highland Ave., South,
Suite 100
Birmingham, AL 35205
www.ion247.com

ARIZONA
Axis Communications
9910 N. 47 Pl.
Phoenix, AZ 85028
www.axis.com

Safeguard Security and
Communications, Inc.
8454 N. 90th Street
Scottsdale, AZ, 85258
www.safeguard.us

CALIFORNIA
AlarmWatch
P.O. Box 867
Merced, CA 95340
www.alarmwatch.com

American Alarm Systems, Inc.
1101 S. Grand Ave.
Suite G
Santa Ana, CA 92705
www.800amalarm.com

Bay Alarm Co.
60 Berry Dr.
Pacheco, CA 94553
www.bayalarm.com

Crime Alert Monitoring Center, Inc.
690 Lenfest Rd.
San Jose, CA 95133
www.crimealert.com

ECam Secure
436 West Walnut St.
Gardena, CA 90248
www.ecamsecure.com

First Alarm Security Services
1111 Estates Dr.
Aptos, CA 95003
www.firstalarm.com

Grand Central Station
23194 Kidder St.
Hayward, CA 94545
www.gcsmonitoring.com

Imperial Capital
2000 Avenue of the Stars,
9th Floor, South Tower
Los Angeles, CA 90067
www.imperialcapital.com

Mace CSSS
401 W. Lincoln Ave., #101
Anaheim, CA 92805
www.macecs.com

MAS
2955 Red Hill Ave.,
Suite 100
Costa Meda, CA 92626
www.utcfssecurityproducts.com

STOP THE INTRUDER™ | KNOWLEDGE IS THE BEST PROTECTION™

Matson Alarm Co., Inc
8401 N. Fresno St.
Fresno, CA 93720
www.matsonalarm.com

National Monitoring Center
26800 Aliso Viejo Parkway,
Suite 250
Aliso Viejo, CA 92556
www.nmccentral.com

Pacific Alarm Systems, Inc.
4444 S. Sepulveda Blvd.
Culver City, CA 90230
www.pacificalarms.com

Post Alarm Systems, Inc.
P.O. Box 60051,
47 East Joseph St.
Arcadia, CA 91006
www.postalarm.com

RFI Security, Inc.
360 Turtle Creek Court
San Jose, CA 95125
www.rfi.com

SDA Security
2054 State St.
San Diego, CA 92101
www.sdasecurity.com

Secure Global Solutions LLC
41 Corporate Park Drive,
Suite 200Irvine, CA 92606
www.secglobe.net

Security Monitoring Technologies
1009 S. Claremont St.
San Mateo, CA, 94402
www.calsecurity.com

Total Monitoring Service, Inc.
2440 Glendale Lane
Sacramento, CA 95825
www.tmscentral.com

Watchlight Corporation
111 S. Marshall Ave.
El Cajon, CA 92020
www.watchlight.com

COLORADO

Bold Technologies, Ltd.
421 Windchime Place
Colorado Springs, CO 80919
www.boldgroup.com

Rocky Mountain Security Services
2171 S. Grape St.
Denver, CO 80222
www.rmssi.com

Safe Systems, Inc.
421 S. Pierce Ave.
Louisville, CO 80027
www.safe, systems.com

Security Central, Inc.
7100 S. Clinton St.,
Suite 200
Centennial, CO, 80112
www.securitycentralinc.com

CONNECTICUT

Fire, Lite Alarms by Honeywell
One Fire, Lite Pl.
Northford, CT, 06472
acscorp.honeywell.com

Security Solutions Inc.
12 Oakwood Ave.
Norwalk, CT, 06850
www.securitysolutionsinc.com

STOP THE INTRUDER™ | KNOWLEDGE IS THE BEST PROTECTION™

Visonic, Inc.
65 West Dudley Town Rd.
Bloomfield, CT, 06002
www.visonic.com

FLORIDA
ADT Security Services, Inc.
One Town Center Rd.
Boca Raton, FL 33486
www.adt.com

All American Monitoring
1375 N. East Ave.
Sarasota, FL 34237
www.allamericanmonitoring.com

Devcon Security Services Corp.
3880 N 28th Terrace
Hollywood, FL 33020
www.devconsecurity.com

DigiCom, Inc.
P.O. Box 17172
Tampa, FL 33682
www.digicom.us

Interlogix
8985 Town Center Parkway
Bradenton, FL 34202
www.interlogix.com

Micro Key Solutions
1631 East Vine Street,
2nd Floor
Kissimmee, FL 34744
www.microkey.com

Panhandle Alarm & Telephone Co.
10 Industrial Blvd.
Pensacola, FL 32503
www.panhandlesystems.com

Redwire
1136 Thomasville Rd.
Tallahassee, FL 32303
www.redwireus.com

Security Alarm Corporation
17776 Toledo Blade Blvd.
Port Charlotte, FL, 33948
www.securityalarmcorp.com

Security Networks Monitoring Center
3223 Commerce Place,
Suite 101
West Palm Beach, FL 33407
www.securitynetworks.net

SentryNet
517 N. Baylen St.
Pensacola, FL 32501
www.sentrynet.com

Sourcetek
1181 S. Rogers Circle,
Suite 21
Boca Raton, FL 33487
www.sotekusa.com

Sureview Systems
400 North Ashley Drive,
Suite 2600
Tampa, FL 33602
www.sureviewsystems.com

SVI Systems, Inc.
290 Florida St.
Stuart, FL 34994
www.svisystems.com

Universal Security Monitoring, LLC
4701 SW 34th St.
Gainesville, FL 32608
www.universalmonitoring.net

GEORGIA
Ackerman Security Systems
1346 Oakbrook Drive,
Suite 175
Atlanta, GA 30093
www.ackermansecurity.com

ComSouth Monitoring Services
108 South Lumpkin St.
Hawkinsville, GA 31036
www.comsouth.net

Ellijay Telephone Co./ETC Communications
224 Dalton Street
Ellijay, GA 30540
www.northganow.com

Telguard
2727 Paces Ferry Rd., SE,
Suite 1, 800
Atlanta, GA 30339
www.telguard.com

United Monitoring Services, Inc.
7521 Veterans Parkway
Columbus, GA 31909
www.unitedmonitoring.com

Uplink, Inc.
1600 Parkwood Circle,
Suite 500 Atlanta, GA 30339
www.uplink.com

HAWAII
Alert Holdings Group, Inc.
2668 Waiwai Loop
Honolulu, HI 96819
www.alertalarmhawaii.com

Central Security and Communications
6831 E. 32nd St.,
Suite 100
Indianapolis, IA 46226
www.centralsecurity.net

Per Mar Security Service
Per Mar Centre;
1910 E. Kimberly Rd.;
P.O. Box 4227
Davenport, IA 52808
www.permarsecurity.com

IDAHO
Alarmco, Inc., Boise
1675 N. Mitchell
Boise, ID, 83704
www.alarmcoinc.com

ILLINOIS
Alarm Detection Systems, Inc.
1111 Church Rd.
Aurora, IL 60505
www.adsalarm.com

Barcom, Inc.
923 North Belt West
Swansea, IL 62226
www.barcominc.com

DMC Security Services, Inc.
4455 W. 147th St.
Midlothian, IL 60445
www.dmcsecurity.com

EMERgency
24999 East Touhy,
Suite 500
Des Plaines, IL 60018
www.emergency24.com

STOP THE INTRUDER™ | KNOWLEDGE IS THE BEST PROTECTION™

F.E. Moran, Inc. Alarm and
Monitoring Services
201 W. University Ave.,
Suite 1
Champaign, IL 61820
www.femoranalarm.com

Protection One Security Solutions
1267 Windham Parkway
Romeoville, IL 60446
www.protection1.com

SMG Security Systems Inc
120 King Street
Elk Grove, IL 60007
www.smgsecurity.com

Stanley Convergent Security
Solutions
55 Shuman Boulevard,
Suite 900
Naperville, IL 60563
www.stanleysecuritysolutions.com

System Sensor
3825 Ohio Ave.St.
Charles, IL 60174
www.systemsensor.com

INDIANA
General Alarm
8227 Northwest Blvd., #270
Indianapolis, IN 46278
www.genalarm.com

KENTUCKY
The CMOOR Group
209 Townepark Circle,
Suite 200
Louisville, KY 40243
www.cmoor.com

LOUISIANA
Acadian Monitoring Services, LLC
P.O. Box 93088
Lafayette, LA 70509
www.acadian.com

Alarm Monitoring Services
1401 Royal Ave.
Monroe, LA 71201
www.monitor1.com

CenturyLink Security Systems, Inc.
504 Washington St.
Monroe, LA 71201
www.centurylink.com

Custom Security Systems
690 Oak Villa Blvd.
Baton Rouge, LA 70815
customsecuritysystems.com

MASSACHUSETTS
AES- IntelliNet
285 Newbury St.
Peabody, MA 01960
www.aesintellinet.com

Alarm Central, Inc.
680 Hancock St.
Quincy, MA, 02170
www.alarmcentral.com

American Alarm &
Communications, Inc.
297 Broadway
Arlington, MA, 02474
www.americanalarm.com

Cape Cod Alarm Co. Inc.
204 Old Townhouse Rd.
West Yarmouth, MA, 02673
www.capecodalarm.com

Fleenor Security Systems
21 North Ave.
Burlington, MA, 01803
www.fleenorss.com

G4S Monitoring & Data Center Inc.
21 North Ave.
Burlington, MA, 01803
www.g4s.us

RBS Citizens
NA28 State Street,
15th Floor, MS 1510
Boston, MA, 02109
www.citizensbank.com

Wayne Alarm Systems, Inc.
424 Essex St.Lynn, MA, 01902
www.waynealarm.com

Xtralis, Inc
700 Longwater Drive
Norwell, MA, 02601
xtralis.com

MARYLAND
Alarm Security Group LLC
12301 Kiln Ct. Suite A
Beltsville, MD 20705
www.asgsecurity.com

Dunbar Alarm Systems, Inc.
7675 Canton Center Dr.
Baltimore, MD 21224
www.dunbaralarm.com

Dynamark Monitoring
525 Northern Avenue
Hagerstown, MD 21742
www.dynamarkmonitoring.com

MAINE
Seacoast Security Inc.
290 West,
P.O. Box A
West Rockport, ME, 04865
www.seacoastsecurity.com

MICHIGAN
Comtronics One Comtronics Place
315 Water Street
Jackson, MI 49203
www.comtronics.com

CoverX Corporation
26600 Telegraph Road
Southfield, MI 48033
www.coverx.com

DICE Corporation
1410 S. Valley Center Dr.
Bay City, MI 48706
www.dicecorp.com

Engineered Protection Systems
750 Front Ave. NW
Grand Rapids, MI 49504
www.epssecurity.com

Guardian Alarm Co. of Michigan
20800 Southfield Rd.
Southfield, MI 48075
www.guardianalarm.com

Midstate Security Company, LLC
3495 Viaduct SW
Grandville, MI 49418
www.midstatesecurity.com

Safety Systems, Inc.
P.O. Box 1079
Jackson, MI 49204
www.safetysystemsinc.net

STOP THE INTRUDER™ | KNOWLEDGE IS THE BEST PROTECTION™

Vigilante Security, Inc./
Michigan Monitoring Service
2681 Industrial Row Drive
Troy, MI 48084
www.michmon.com

VirSec
1300 Combermere Drive
Troy, MI 48083
www.huffmaster.com

MINNESOTA
Checkpoint Systems, Inc.
8180 Upland Circle
Chanhassen, MN 55317
www.checkpointsystems.com

Cooperative Response Center, Inc.
2000 8th St. NW
Austin, MN 55912
www.crc.coop

Custom Alarm/Custom
Communications, Inc.
1661 Greenview Drive SW
Rochester, MN 55902
www.customalarm.com

RSI Video Technologies
1375 Willow Lake Blvd., #103
Vadnais Heights, MN 55110
www.videofied.com

Security Response Services, Inc.
9036 Grand Ave. South
Bloomington, MN 55420
www.floydtotalsecurity.com

Silent Knight
7550 Meridian Circle, North,
Suite 100
Maple Grove, MN 55369
www.silentknight.com

Trans, Alarm, Inc.
500 East Travelers Trail
Burnsville, MN 55337
www.transalarm.com

WH International Response Center
P.O. Box 330,
6800 Electric Dr.
Rockford, MN 55373
www.whirc.com

MISSOURI
Alarm Central LLC
5510 E 31st St.
Kansas City, MO 64128
www.alarmcentral.net

American Burglary & Fire Inc.
507 Rudder Rd.
Fenton, MO 63026
www.abfsecurity.com

Atlas Security Service, Inc./Alarm
Control Center
1309 E Republic Rd., Suite B
Springfield, MO 65804
atlassecurity.com

Centerpoint Technologies LLC
2001 S. Hanley Rd.,
Suite 530
St.Louis, MO 63144
www.centerpointtech.com

Central District Alarm, Inc.
6450 Clayton Ave.
St.Louis, MO 63139
www.mycda.net

DMP
2500 N. Partnership Blvd.
Springfield, MO 65803
www.dmp.com
www.securecomwireless.com

STOP THE INTRUDER™ | KNOWLEDGE IS THE BEST PROTECTION™

Federal Response Center2
500 North Airport Commerce Dr.
Springfield, MO 65803
www.federalprotection.com

Interface Security Systems, LLC
3773 Corporate Center Dr.
Earth City, MO 63045
www.interfacesystems.com

Potter Electric Signal Co.
5757 Phantom Drive,
Suite 125
St.Louis, MO 63042
www.pottersignal.com

NORTH CAROLINA
Comporium Security
P.O. Box 306,
245 E. Main Street
Rock Hill, NC 29730
www.comporium.com

CPI Security Systems
4200 Sandy Porter Rd.
Charlotte, NC 28273
www.cpisecurity.com

DIY Alarm Forum
63 Pondview Dr.
Clyde, NC 28721
www.diyalarmforum.com

Holmes Electric Security Systems
127 Hay St.
Fayetteville, NC 28302
www.holmeselectricsecurity.com

Loss Prevention Services, Inc.
2511 Neudork Rd., Suite E
Clemmons, NC 27012
lpssecurity.com

Security Central, North Carolina
316 Security Dr.
Statesville, NC, 28677
www.security, central.com

Security Network of America
714 S. Bennett Street
Southern Pines, NC 28387
www.snaonline.com

Sentry Watch, Inc.
1705 Holbrook St.
Greensboro, NC 27403
www.sentrywatch.com

Universal Monitoring
1330 Sharon Road, West
Charlotte, NC 28210
www.universalmonitoring.com

NEBRASKA
Security Equipment, Inc.
13505 C St.
Omaha, NE 68144
www.sei, security.com

NEW HAMPSHIRE
Centra, Larm Monitoring, Inc.
994 Candia Rd.
Manchester, NH, 03109
www.centralarm.com

NEW JERSEY
Atlantic Coast Alarm, Inc.
5100 Harding Highway,
Suite 203
Mays Landing, NJ, 08330
atlanticcoastalarm.com

C.O.P.S. Monitoring
P.O. Box 836
Williamstown, NJ, 08094
www.copsmonitoring.com

STOP THE INTRUDER™ | KNOWLEDGE IS THE BEST PROTECTION™

Intertek Testing Services, Inc./ETL
41 Plymouth Street
Fairfield, NJ, 07004
www.intertek.com

Merchants Alarm Systems, Inc.
203 Paterson Ave.
Wallington, NJ, 07057
merchantsalarm.com

Securall Monitoring Corp.
206 Washington Dr.
Brick, NJ 8724
www.securall.com

Supreme Security Systems, Inc.
1565 Union Ave.
Union Avenue, NJ, 07083
www.supremealarm.com

NEVADA
Alarmco, Inc. , Las Vegas
2007 Las Vegas Blvd., South
Las Vegas, NV 89104
www.alarmco.com

I, View Now
1421 E Sunset Rd, #2
Las Vegas, NV 89119
www.i, viewnow.com

NEW YORK
ADI
263 Old Country Rd.
Melville Road, NY 11747
www.adiglobal.com,

Affiliated Central, Inc
354 Neptune Ave.
Sheepshead, NY 11235
www.affiliated.com

Alarm Lock Systems, Inc.
345 Bayview Ave.
Amityville, NY 11701
www.alarmlock.com

Alarm Tech Central Service Inc.
56 Enter Lane
Islandia, NY 11749
www.alarm.tc

Altronix Corp.
140 58th St., Bldg. A, 3
WestBrooklyn, NY 11220
www.altronix.com

Amherst Alarm Inc.
435 Lawrence Bell Dr.
Amherst, NY 14221
www.amherstalarm.com

Bosch Security Systems, Inc.
130 Perinton Parkway
Fairport, NY 14450
www.boschsecurity.us

CASCO Systems
40 Rutter Street
Rochester, NY 14606
www.cascosecurity.com

CMS Monitoring
2211 Route 112
Medford, NY 11763
www.cmsmonitoring.com

Commercial Instruments and Alarm Systems, Inc.
2 Summit Ct.
Fishkill, NY 12524
www.ciasecurity.com

Continental Access
355 Bayview Avenue
Amityville, NY 11701
www.cicaccess.com

STOP THE INTRUDER™ | KNOWLEDGE IS THE BEST PROTECTION™

DGA Security Systems, Inc.
580 5th Ave.
New York, NY 10036
www.dgasecurity.com

Doyle Security Systems, Inc.
792 Calkins Rd.
Rochester, NY 14623
https://www.godoyle.com

Electronix Systems Central Station Alarms, Inc.
1555 New York Ave.
Huntingdon Station, NY 11746
www.electronixsystems.com

Honeywell Security Group
2 Corporate Center Drive,
Suite 100, P.O. Box 9040
Melville, NY 11747
www.security.honeywell.com

Honeywell Security Products Americas
2 Corporate Center Drive,
Suite 100, P.O. Box 9040
Melville, NY 11747
www.security.honeywell.com

Lowitt Alarms & Security Systems, Inc.
25 Bethpage Rd.
Hicksville, NY 11801
www.lowittalarms.com

MARKS USA
365 Bayview Avenue
Amityville, NY 11701
www.marksusa.com

Napco Security Technologies, Inc.
333 Bayview Ave.
Amityville, NY 11701
www.napcosecurity.com

Nationwide Central Station Monitoring Corp.
P.O. Box 7297
Freeport, NY 11520
www.nationwidedigital.com

Rapid Response Monitoring Services, Inc.
400 West Division St.
Syracuse, NY 13204
www.rrms.com/#home,

Speco Technologies
200 New Hwy.
Amityville, NY 11701
www.specotech.com

Statewide Central Station
2047 Victory Boulevard
Staten Island, NY 10314
www.statewidecs.com

Time Warner Cable Security
6400 Fly Rd.
Syracuse, NY 13057
www.timewarnercable.com

Tri, Ed Distribution
135 Crossways Park Drive,
Suite 101 Woodbury, NY 11797
www.tried.com

United D&W Central Station Alarm, Inc.
205 W. Houston Street
New York, NY 10014
www.weprotect.com

USA Central Station Alarm
28 Willett Ave. Port Chester, NY 10573
www.usacentralstation.com

Vision Monitoring/World Wide Security
One Commercial Avenue
Garden City, NY 11530
www.visionmonitoring.com

OHIO
Bass Security Services Inc.
26701 Richmond Rd.
Cleveland, OH 44146
www.basssecurity.com

Buckeye Protective Service, Inc.
2215 Sixth Street, SW
Canton, OH 44706
www.buckeyeprotective.com

Diebold, Inc.
3800 Tabs Dr.,
Dept. 8317, S
Uniontown, OH 44685
www.diebold.com

Excel Central Inc.
2820 May Street
Cincinnati, OH 4520
6www.U2canxl.fuse.net

Gillmore Security Systems
26165 Broadway Ave.
Cleveland, OH 44146
www.gillmoresecurity.com

Quick Response Monitoring Alarm Center
4734 Spring Rd.
Cleveland, OH 44131
www.quickresponse.net

Sedona Office
549 E. Washington Street
Chagrin Falls, OH 44022
www.sedonaoffice.com

VRI (The Care Center)
1400 Commerce Center Drive
Franklin, OH 45005
www.monitoringcare.com

OKLAHOMA
Communication Service Solutions (CSS)
301 Maine Street,
Suite 301
Enid, OK 73701
www.comservicesolutions.com

OREGAN
Alarm Central Station, Inc.
15050 SW Koll Pkwy.,
Suite 1A
Beaverton, OR 97006
www.alceste.com

Central Station Monitoring
303 SW Zobrist
Estacada, OR 97023
www.csmul.com

iWatch Communications, Inc.
4970 SW Griffith Dr., #100
Beaverton, OR 97005
www.iwatchcomm.com

PENNSYLVANIA
Buchanan Ingersoll & Rooney PC
301 Grant St., 20th Floor
Pittsburgh, PA 15219
www.bipc.com

Guardian Protection Services
174 Thorn Hill Rd.
Warrendale, PA 15086
www.guardianprotection.com

Intertech Security, LLC
1501 Preble Ave.
Pittsburgh, PA 15233
www.intertechsecurity.com

STOP THE INTRUDER™ | KNOWLEDGE IS THE BEST PROTECTION™

Kleinbard Bell & Brecker LLP
One Liberty Place,
46th Floor,
1650 Market Street
Philadelphia, PA 19103
www.kleinbard.com

Security Alarm Monitoring, Inc.
254 Fairview Rd.
Woodlyn, PA 19094
www.electronicsecuritycorp.com

Security Partners LLC
241 N Plum St.
Lancaster, PA, 17602
www.securitypartners.com

Security Service Company
110 West Arch Street,
Suite 200
Fleetwood, PA 19522
www.sscsince73.com

The Protection Bureau
197 Philips Dr.
Exton, PA 19341
www.protectionbureau.com

Towne Monitoring Service, LP
208 N. Main St.
Souderton, PA 18964
www.towneanswering.com

Universal Atlantic Systems, Inc.
(UAS)
700 Abbott Dr.
Broomall, PA 19008
www.uas.com

Vector Security
3400 McKnight East Dr.
Pittsburgh, PA 15237
www.vectorsecurity.com

RHODE ISLAND
NEXgeneration Central
400 Reservoir Ave.,
Suite LL, GH
Providence, RI, 02907
www.nexgenerationcentral.com

SOUTH DAKOTA
Midwest Alarm Co., Inc.
2300 South Dakota Ave.
Sioux Falls, SD 57105
www.midwestalarm.com

TENNESSEE
ADS Security, LP
3001 Armory Dr.,
Suite 100
Nashville, TN 37204
www.adssecurity.com/index.aspx,

Miller Protective Service, Inc.
1203 Ridgeway Blvd.,
Suite 202
Memphis, TN 38119
www.millerprotective.com

TEXAS
Allstate Security Industries, Inc.
3433 Plains Blvd.
Amarillo, TX 79102
www.allstatesecurity.com

Counterforce USA
7700 Gulf Freeway
Houston, TX 77017
www.counterforceusa.com

Dispatch Center, Ltd.
101 Galleria Fair
San Antonio, TX 78232
www.dispatchcenter.net

STOP THE INTRUDER™ | KNOWLEDGE IS THE BEST PROTECTION™

Innovative Business Software (IBS)
1320 Greenway Dr.,
Suite 850
Irving, TX 75038
www.ibsoft, us.com

Kings III of America Inc.
751 Canyon Drive, Suite 100
Coppell, TX 75019
www.kingsiii.com

Monitronics International, Inc.
P.O. Box 814530
Dallas, TX 75381
www.monitronics.com

Response Center USA
11235 Gordon Rd.,
Suite 102
San Antonio, TX 78216
rc, usa.com

Siemens Industry Inc.
8600 N. Royal Lane,
Suite 100
Irving, TX, 75063
www.siemens.com/entry/cc/en

Superior Central Station, Inc.
604 Ash Ave.,
P.O. Box 3097
McAllen, TX 78501
www.superiorcentral.com

United Central Control
8415 Datapoint Dr.,
Suite 500
San Antonio, TX 78229
www.teamucc.com

Westec Intelligent Surveillance, Inc.
6340 International Parkway,
Suite 100
Plano, TX 75093
www.westec.net

WM Security Services
17340 Chanute Rd.
Houston, TX 77032
www.wm.com/index.jsp,

UTAH
AvantGuard Monitoring Centers
4699 Harrison Blvd.,
Suite 100
Ogden, UT 84403
www.agmonitoring.com

OneTel
343 West 400 South,
Suite 110
Salt Lake City, UT 84101
onetelone.com

Peak Alarm Co., Inc.
1534 S. Gladiola St.
Salt Lake City, UT, 84104
www.peakalarm.com

Vivint
4931 North 300 West
Provo, UT 84604
www.vivint.com

VIRGINIA
1Time, Inc.
949 Empire Mesa Way
Henderson, VA 89011

Alarm.com
8150 Leesburg Pike,
Suite 1400
Vienna, VA 22182
www.alarm.com

CheckVideo
1925 Isaac Newton Square,
3rd FloorReston, VA, 20190
www.checkvideo.net

LogicMark
8625 Hampton Way
Fairfax Station, VA 22039
www.logicmarksecurity.com

Richmond Alarm
14121 Justice Road
Midlothian, VA 23113
www.richmondalarm.com

Williams and Hannon, PLLC
493 McLaws Circle,
Suite, 2
Williamsburg, VA 23185
www.williamshannonlaw.com

Alarm Center, Inc.
PO Box 3401
Lacey, WA 98509
www.acimonitoring.com

Moon Security Services, Inc.
515 W. Clark
Pasco, WA 99301
www.moonsecurity.com

Northwest Alarm Monitoring, LLC
1743 1st St, Ave., South, Suite 201
Seattle, WA 98134
nwalarm.discware.org

Washington Alarm, Inc.
1253 S. Jackson
Seattle, WA 98144
www.washingtonalarm.com

Crime Analysis

Robbery Location Analysis

Robbery	Number of offenses 2010	Percent change from 2009	Percent distribution[1]	Average value
Total	300,274	-10.6	100.0	$1,239
Street/highway	129,605	-9.6	43.2	908
Commercial house	39,705	-13.4	13.2	1,858
Gas or service station	6,955	-14.6	2.3	939
Convenience store	15,687	-14.3	5.2	782
Residence	51,888	-8.8	17.3	1,491
Bank	6,536	-8.8	2.2	4,410
Miscellaneous	49,898	-11.0	16.6	1,115

Burglary Location Analysis

Burglary	Number of offenses 2010	Percent change from 2009	Percent distribution[1]	Average value
Total	1,897,963	-2.0	100.0	2,119
Residence (dwelling):	1,402,214	-0.2	73.9	2,137
Residence Night	389,910	-0.8	20.5	1,868
Residence Day	722,231	+0.2	38.1	2,158
Residence Unknown	290,073	-0.5	15.3	2,445
Nonresidence (store, office, etc.):	495,749	-6.6	26.1	2,070
Nonresidence Night	204,605	-8.8	10.8	1,765
Nonresidence Day	168,912	-4.7	8.9	2,010
Nonresidence Unknown	122,232	-5.5	6.4	2,662

STOP THE INTRUDER™ | KNOWLEDGE IS THE BEST PROTECTION™

Larceny-Theft Location Analysis

Larceny-Theft	Number of offenses 2010	Percent change from 2009	Percent distribution[1]	Average value
Total	5,391,580	-2.6	100.0	988
Pocket-picking	21,056	-8.3	0.4	526
Purse-snatching	24,450	-7.1	0.5	400
Shoplifting	925,107	-7.1	17.2	174
From motor vehicles (except accessories)	1,423,947	-5.6	26.4	704
Motor vehicle accessories	477,848	-5.5	8.9	681
Bicycles	179,595	-1.7	3.3	351
From buildings	607,927	-0.4	11.3	1,406
From coin-operated machines	17,648	-20.8	0.3	365
All others	1,714,002	+3.2	31.8	1,654

Larceny Theft by Value

	Number of offenses 2010	Percent change from 2009	Percent distribution[1]	Average value
Over $200	2,443,142	-0.9	45.3	2,089
$50 to $200	1,235,096	-1.8	22.9	111
Under $50	1,713,342	-5.5	31.8	17

STOP THE INTRUDER™ | KNOWLEDGE IS THE BEST PROTECTION™

Regional Information

Regional Crime Rates Figure

Regional Crime Rates 2010
Violent and Property Crimes per 100,000 Inhabitants

Region	Property Crime	Violent Crime
Northeast	2,115.8	357.0
Midwest	2,833.6	362.5
South	3,438.8	452.0
West	2,886.5	400.8

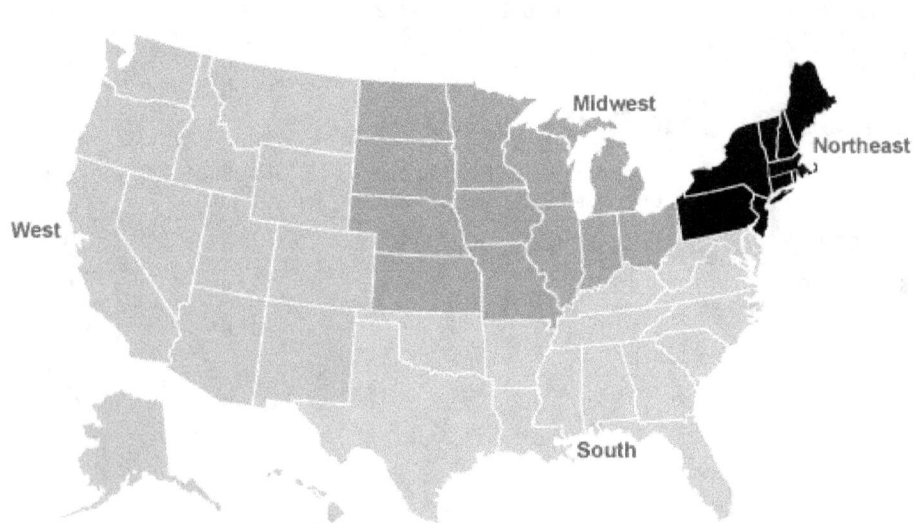

Interview with a Killer

STOP THE INTRUDER™ | KNOWLEDGE IS THE BEST PROTECTION™

CONNECTICUT STATE POLICE
DEPARTMENT OF PUBLIC SAFETY
CENTRAL DISTRICT MAJOR CRIME SQUAD
CFS-07-00294907
CHESIDRE TRIPLE HOMICIDE INTERVIEW WITH KOMISARJEVSKY

Det. Vitello: Statement of Joshua Komisarjevsky

Det. Vitello: Today's date is July 23, 2007, and the time is 4:55pm.

Det. Vitello: The statement is taking place at the Cheshire Police Department Headquarters, 500 Highland Avenue, Cheshire, Connecticut.

Det. Vitello of the: Those present are, myself, which is Detective Joseph Vitello the Cheshire Police Department, Detective Rafael Medina of Central District Major Crime Squad of the Connecticut State Police and Joshua Komisarjevsky

Det. Vitello: Joshua would you please spell your first name.

Komisarjevsky: J-O-S-H-U-A

Det. Vitello: And your middle initial please.

Komisarjevsky: A

Det. Vitello: And your last name, spell it please.

Komisarjevsky: K-O- M-I-S -A-R-J - E- V - S-K- Y

Det. Vitello: Um, your birth date.

Komisarjevsky: 8 -10 - 80

Det. Vitello: Your address.

Komisarjevsky: XXXXXXXXXX

Det. Vitello: Your home phone.

Komisarjevsky: XXXXXXXXXX

Det. Vitello: And your cell phone number, if you have one.

Komisarjevsky: XXXXXXXXX

Det. Vitello: And do you know where you are at right now?

Komisarjevsky: The Cheshire Police Department.

Det. Vitello: Do you know why you are here?

Komisarjevsky: Um, for uh, home invading gone terribly wrong.

Det. Vitello: Okay, Joshua how many years education do you have?

Komisarjevsky: Um, High School and some college.

Det. Vitello: Did you get your diploma from high school?

Komisarjevsky: Yes

Det. Vitello: Okay and you have some college?

Komisarjevsky: Yes

Det. Vitello: Okay, so you understand and can read and write English?

Komisarjevsky: Yes

Det. Vitello: Okay, now Joshua, when we were with you a little while ago and we started talking to you, we read you a Notice and Waiver of Rights, which is your Constitutional Rights.

Komisarjevsky: That's correct.

Det. Vitello: You read those rights, you signed those rights, you initialed those rights, and you did it in two separate locations. One acknowledging that you were read your rights and you understood them, and the second in which you waived your rights to an attorney and you wish to speak to us. Is that correct?

Komisarjevsky: That's correct.

Det. Vitello: Now did you do that, did you do that freely and of your own will and will power?

Komisarjevsky: Yes

Det. Vitello: Okay, um do you have any questions on that?

Komisarjevsky: No

Det. Vitello: Okay, that form is in front of us and it has been signed by you, Detective Medina and myself.

Komisarjevsky: That's correct.

Det. Vitello: Okay, and we did, discussed this incident and we started to give us a written statement. And um, you got about, made it through one page and at that point we discussed if you would like to give us a taped, audio taped statement and you agreed to that, correct?

Komisarjevsky: That's correct.

Det. Vitello: And that's a decision you're comfortable with?

Komisarjevsky: That's correct.

STOP THE INTRUDER™ | KNOWLEDGE IS THE BEST PROTECTION™

Det. Vitello: Okay, now in your written statement we had you stop and we had you write that uh, you, you wanted to go from the written form to the taped form, correct?

Komisarjevsky: That's correct.

Det. Vitello: Okay, now the written form is in front of us; you, you have ended that statement and signed it. Now we are gonna begin the taped statement, we are gonna go over the uh, the entire incident from the start.

Det. Vitello: Um, we have the waiver and so forth so, lets go back to the beginning where this, this is your statement, so you stated you had spent some time in rehab, basically and you have done some jail time and that you met up with this other fellow.

Komisarjevsky: Yeah, uh, Steven Hayes, we met at a halfway house once we, I was let out of prison.

Det. Vitello: Okay, and then we discussed, yesterday you, you started around afternoon time I guess and you started telling us what transpired, that you went to Stop & Shop in Cheshire.

Komisarjevsky: That's correct.

Det. Vitello: To meet a contractor.

Komisarjevsky: To meet, up and to receive payment on a, uh, uh, from a contractor that I did work for on that day.

Det. Vitello: So let's go through and go over the whole, the whole statement that you were gonna put in writing.

Komisarjevsky: Alright, uh,

Office phone ringing in background.

STOP THE INTRUDER™ | KNOWLEDGE IS THE BEST PROTECTION™

Komisarjevsky: Uh, at that point uh, at that point I had uh,

Det. Medina: At what time?

Komisarjevsky: Um, towards 6 O'clockish or so.

Det. Medina: In the evening?

Komisarjevsky: In the evening.

Komisarjevsky: And uh, I was waiting for a contractor urn, to make payment and uh, while waiting I saw a mother and a daughter walk into a store, into uh, the Stop & Shop.

And uh, I thought they were driving a very nice vehicle. And I really didn't think much of it at that time uh, because the contractor had shown up and uh, we were discussing business and making payment. Uh, at which point, uh, about 15 minutes later the mother came back out uh, with the daughter and got in their car. Uh, as the contractor was also driving off, uh, we had completed our transaction uh, for whatever reason I chose to follow the mom and the daughter uh, to the house and started thinking it's a very nice house uh, and very nice car and uh, thought it would be nice to be their someday. Not have to worry about financial problems and stress and all that uh, and what comes with it.

Um, Throughout the day uh, uh, Mr. Hayes had been calling me uh, wanting to hook up and discuss options on how we could come up with some money fast uh, whether it be legally or illegally obtained. Uh, that evening uh, I had spent uh, the rest of the, I had spent the rest of the evening with my daughter. Uh, she had just recently come back from a one week vacation with her grandparents and I hadn't seen her in little over a week so uh, I stayed home and spent some time with, with her and I, and I put her to bed. And about ten o'clock rolled around uh, I uh, I made a decision to go out and, and meet up with uh, Mr. Steven Hayes and uh, at the Stop & Shop plaza. Uh, from there we started uh, he asked where we were going and we drove around for a while, trying to come up with, with uh, ideas for like what we could do to uh, make money and make money quick.

Det. Vitello: Did, did he drive there in uh, in a vehicle or did somebody drop him off?

Komisarjevsky: No, he, he drove in, in his bosses' truck

Det. Vitello: Which is?

Komisarjevsky: Uh, I think, a red Chevy

Det. Vitello: Okay, when you, you were at the Stop & Shop parking lot.

Komisarjevsky: We were both at the Stop & Shop parking lot.

Det. Vitello: He got into your vehicle?

Komisarjevsky: He got in mine, yeah.

Det. Vitello: Ok, go ahead.

Komisarjevsky: Uh, so from then, we went on driving around, talking about ways to score money and with different contracts and we, we tried making new material. Nothing seemed to be fast enough. Uh, we had uh, many debts and obligations. And uh, the conversation then turned to uh, the possibility of uh, maybe illegally obtaining uh, cash uh, quickly uh. One of which of the ideas was uh, was to maybe uh, to come up on, you know, people taking money out of ATM's and catching them. by surprise or uh, uh possibly some people coming out of a bar late at night. Uh, we uh, neither one of those uh, ideas panned out and we just sort of aimlessly drove around instead. Uh, at which time uh, I had recalled uh, that uh, I had seen this uh, lady driving a very nice car and knew where a very nice house was and had made mention of that to uh, Mr. Hayes and the possibility of a lot of money in the house uh, might be uh, fairly decent. Um, so we made it over uh, over to that house and parked uh, on their street, but around the corner a little ways, out of sight. Uh, we donned face masks and put on rubber gloves and, and uh, walked down the sidewalk to the house.

Det. Vitello: Can you describe those face masks to us, what they, they might have looked like?

Komisarjevsky: Uh, well consider we really did it on the fly and there was no planning involved or anything, so I used, I had no hat or anything, so I used a, my dark shirt, cut some holes in it and just uh, tied it around my face. And uh, Mr. Hayes had used uh, a work hat that he had that he just pulled down over his face and cut two holes out for eyes and the nose and just a little below his chin.

Det. Vitello: Were you carrying any weapons at that point, did you have anything on you illegal?

Komisarjevsky: I had, I did not carry a weapon at that point. Uh, Mr. Hayes had a uh, a pellet, a handgun, pellet gun, a BB gun uh, that he had purchased uh, at Wal-Mart in Southington.

Det. Vitello: What day did you purchase it at?
Komisarjevsky: Uh, I'm not sure uh, what day he purchased it at, the day prior I believe it was, to this incident.

Det. Vitello: Were you with him when he purchased it?

Komisarjevsky: Uh, I was in the store with him, yes.

Det. Vitello: At, the Wal-Mart in Southington?

Komisarjevsky: Wal-Mart in Southington.

Det. Vitello: Did you pay cash?

STOP THE INTRUDER™ | KNOWLEDGE IS THE BEST PROTECTION™

Komisarjevsky: Uh, He went to the teller and he paid uh, cash, yes

Det. Vitello: Okay, now you approach the house. No other weapons?

Komisarjevsky: No other weapons, no.

Det. Vitello: Okay

Komisarjevsky: Uh, we approached the house and uh, went around back to see who was uh, if there where any lights on or if anyone was awake. Uh, at that time , we noticed that the father was uh, sleeping downstairs uh, in the sunroom uh.

Det. Vitello: Which is where, on the front of the house, side, it's?

Komisarjevsky: It is on the back of the house.

Det. Vitello: Okay

Komisarjevsky: Uh, we continued to do a walk around the house, checking windows and doors, all of which were uh, locked. Uh, till uh, we came to the bilco door at the rear of the house uh, and went down to the basement which was unlocked. Uh, I opened it and proceeded down the steps and found out that the door into the basement itself was also unlocked. Uh.

Det. Vitello: What time do you think this is about?

Komisarjevsky: This is about uh, it's about 2:00, 2:15 uh, by the time I had uh, made access into the house.

Det. Vitello: In the morning?

Komisarjevsky: In the morning.

Det. Vitello: So, you now you are inside of the residence.

STOP THE INTRUDER™ | KNOWLEDGE IS THE BEST PROTECTION™

Komisarjevsky: Actually, it actually might have been a little bit later; it might be closer to like 2:30 or of 3:00.

Det Vitello: Okay

Komisarjevsky: (Not audible) Urn, I had uh, mentioned that I didn't think that I would be able to take on the father alone and Steve had mentioned that uh, he didn't think that he could creep into the house quietly enough to get up close to him uh, and mentioned that maybe I should find a bat or object of similar uh, weight uh, to club him with and to incapacitate him temporarily uh, so that I, we could tie him up. Uh, so I went and proceeded down into the basement and uh, happened to find a uh, a baseball bat leaning on the stairs leading up into the kitchen. Uh, I took that bat and went up the stairway, sort of made my way through the, the dinette area uh, to the doors uh, leading into uh, the sunroom where the father was sleeping. Uh, at which point I, I just stood there uh, for a good 15, 20 minutes. I was standing behind him uh, with this bat and not wanting to hit him, and not, not thinking that I, I could uh, I could see Mr. Hayes in the window uh, motioning to, to strike him and get it over with and get it done so we could move on, and uh.

Det. Vitello: Did you strike him?

Komisarjevsky: I did.

Det. Vitello: Okay, you got up close. Where and how many times did you strike this man?

Komisarjevsky: I uh, I hit him in the head with the baseball bat. He let out this, this unearthly scream. Uh, I couldn't take his screaming. Like I had never hit anybody in the head with uh, anything uh, never mind a baseball bat and I uh, just kept hitting him until he finally backed up into a comer of the couch and, and quieted down and was just staring at me with wide open eyes, just shear confusion.

STOP THE INTRUDER™ | KNOWLEDGE IS THE BEST PROTECTION™

Det. Vitello: Was he bleeding?

Komisarjevsky: Yeah, he was bleeding uh, profusely.

Det. Vitello: Okay so, now, now, he is on the couch curled up and then what happens?

Komisarjevsky: Urn, Mr. Hayes is now tapping on the, the door window to my right, um mentioning, or motioning for me to, to unlock the door for him. I uh, I gathered myself and unlocked the door and he came in. Db, we argued for a minute as to who was going to, to tie him up. At which point we, we both ended up tying him up. Mr. Hayes tied his hands and I, I tied his feet. Urn, we sat him on the couch.

Det. Vitello: And what did you use to tie him up with?

Komisarjevsky: Uh, I had seen a uh, a cotton rope uh, similar to uh, one you would use a, clothes for a clothes line, urn sitting at the top of the stairs, leading into the kitchen and retrieved that and cut it into two foot lengths, roughly uh, to bind hands and feet with.

Uh, I tied his hands and feet, or 1, I tied his feet and Hayes tied his hands and, and we sat him on the furniture. Uh, when I say furniture, the couch and he asked us uh, quietly uh, who we, what our intentions were, and who we, who we wanted. And I replied that we were simply here for money. Uh once, once we have everything we came up here for, then we, we would be out of there, you know we'd, we'd be gone.

Um, I had asked if there's anybody in, else, in the house now and how many and uh, the homeowner uh, mentioned that there are, that the three women were upstairs. At which point Mr. Hayes and I um, proceeded up he stairway. Um, he with the BB gun and me with the bat, and both of us with rope, many different pieces of rope. Urn, we passed the first daughters room on the left hand side and uh, went down the hallway uh, to the master bedroom. Urn where, were, we would just do the mother first and then the two children uh, only to find out that uh, one of the youngest daughters was, had actually, had fallen asleep with mom watching TV in the master bedroom.

Um, Mr. Hayes and uh, I walked into the room and um, I to the uh, daughter's uh, side of the bed and Mr. Hayes to the mothers side of the bed. Uh, at which point Mr. Hayes put his hand over mom's mouth and shook her uh, gently awake and I did, I followed suit with the youngest uh, daughters. Uh, they both had woken up uh, they were very confused as to what was going on, but very compliant uh, when told to, to roll over onto their stomachs and put their hands behind their backs, so we tied their hands and feet. Uh, we then left the room and proceeded back towards uh, the daughter's room that we had passed, uh and walked in. And um, Mr. Hayes stood over her, um the oldest daughter, I went to the headboard and I, I shook, I shook her gently awake. Uh, she was a little sup, uh, more than a little surprised uh, by what was going on. Uh, asked what we wanted and please don't hurt her. Uh, at which point I explained to her that we weren't there to hurt her. We were just looking for money and then we would be on our way. Uh, when she didn't say anything else, I asked her to roll over on her stomach and put her hands behind her back, she did so I tied up her hands. Uh, then tied her feet and Mr. Hayes tied her hands. After which uh, Mr. Hayes and I proceeded to, to empty the house of valuables and now we are both in the uh, mother's room and uh, she we was telling uh, Mr. Haynes where the different, where different locations were of her jewelry and what not. Um, things in which I wasn't interested in. Um uh, I had, it was my understanding that Mr. Hayes and I were there strictly for cash and I was getting a little frustrated with him planning to do other than that.

STOP THE INTRUDER™ | KNOWLEDGE IS THE BEST PROTECTION™

Det. Vitello: You were strictly looking for cash?

Komisarjevsky: Just cash.

Det. Vitello: And where is the father at this time?

Komismjevsky: The father was still down stairs, um in the sunroom, on the couch. We'd periodically um, go down stairs to check on him. Uh, at one point, um on one of my trips down there, he was still, still bleeding uh, profusely. So I found a towel in the kitchen and put it on his head uh, so, so it would uh, stop the bleeding.

Det. Medina: When you tied up the daughters, did you tie them to anything?

Komisarjevsky: Um, no, not at first uh. They were, they were tied up, they weren't restrained to like the bed or, or anything like that, they're just.

Det. Vitello: You mean that their hands and feet were tied but they weren't tied to anything at that time.

Komisarjevsky: That's right.

Det. Vitello: Okay

Komisarjevsky: Uh, so uh, Steve and I uh, continued doing uh, poking around for money and realizing that, there was no money there. Uh, the uh, mother had mentioned that there was no safe and Steve had uh, found a uh, check register um, with the uh, the amount of forty something thousand dollars in it. Um, and we discussed the possibility of possibly sending um, the mother down to the bank to retrieve a uh, sum amount of $15,000.00 dollars. Um, we didn't want to withdraw the full amount of $40,000.00 dollars in fear of raising some kind of red flag at the bank. Um, the mother agreed. Um, and we reassured her that if she complied that

	you know, there wouldn't be any problems. You know, we were simply here for money and we would be on our way.
Det. Vitello:	What time do you think it was now?
Komisarjevsky:	Um, getting um, around 3, 3:30 or 4:00 0' clock or around that time.
Det. Vitello:	Okay, aside from them being tied up and the father being injured, no one else at this point was injured?
Komisarjevsky:	That's correct.
Det. Vitello:	Okay
Komisarjevsky:	Uh.
Det. Vitello:	Go ahead.
Komisarjevsky:	Mr. Hayes has continued to uh, to rifle around the uh, bedroom for some time to come, he was getting on my nerves with the amount of noise that he was making. Um, I had locked eyes with the, the youngest daughter um, I was kind of taken back by how calm she was being um, and she had this look on her face that she understood, like you know that, yeah we were here, and we were invading her home and that she understood, like she seemed to have his look on her, you know that, she understood that we, we wouldn't hurt them you know, we'd just be on our way, and uh, that sort of caught me off guard.
	Um, we um, going, we kept going back and forth between downstairs you know, checking on the dad and then I realized that it was starting to get uh, a little light outside and realized that we were going to have to make a decision on what we were going to do with my car because it was still parked out on the street, around the comer, and we knew uh, I knew that I couldn't leave it there, um. Steve and I got into

an argument about, um how we were going, where and how we were going to um, to uh, to move it, and where to bring it, uh.

Det. Vitello: Why hadn't you left the house at this point?

Komisarjevsky: Where urn, to park the vehicle?

Det. Vitello: No, why didn't you just leave the house then?

Komisarjevsky: Um the money.

Det. Vitello: Okay

Komisarjevsky: Uh, uh.

Det. Vitello: So you had no intent on leaving the house at that point, you were just concerned about the car and where you were going to put it?

Komisarjevsky: Yeah,

Det. Vitello: Okay

Komisarjevsky: Um, because we had sort of set upon, um, on having the mom go to the bank and, and withdraw money for us once the banks opened at 9 o'clock.

Det. Vitello: Okay

Komisarjevsky: Uh, the mother seemed uh, compliant about it.

Det. Vitello: Okay, so you were going wait it out until, until it was time to do that, okay?

Komisarjevsky: Yeah, we were going to sit it out.

Det. Vitello: Okay

STOP THE INTRUDER™ | KNOWLEDGE IS THE BEST PROTECTION™

Komisarjevsky: Um, so we um, had to make arrangements to move the car, um, but nobody in the house was um, restrained to anything and um, Steve was worried that, you know, once we left to move the vehicle somewhere, that they would just scatter and we would come back to a house full of cops.

Det. Vitello: So they were tied but not restrained?

Komisarjevsky: That's correct.

Det. Vitello: Okay

Komisarjevsky: Um, so at which point we went back upstairs, um, Steve and I, and went into the mom's bedroom where the youngest daughter and uh, the mom were. Um, I untied the feet of the youngest daughter and moved her um, into her own room. Uh, where I tied her um, to the, the rope that was tying her hands and looped it under, untied one of her hands and looped it underneath the bed frame and then reattached the other end of the rope to her other wrist.

Det. Vitello: In her own bedroom?

Komisarjevsky: In, in her own bedroom yeah.

Det. Vitello: Okay

Komisarjevsky: In her own bed and then urn, and then uh, I did the same with her ankles uh, tied one ankle and then looped the rope hrough the bed frame and then tied the other ankle with the other end. Uh, so it was not too tight because I had noticed that she had eczema and I, I suffer from that myself.

Um, so um, I walked out of the youngest daughter's bedroom and um, Mr. Hayes had tied the mother uh, to the master bed um, on her stomach uh, sprawled out. Um, I thought it was a little uncomfortable for mom. Um, but uh, time was sort of, of the essence and went down the hall and uh, entered the other daughters bedroom uh, and untied her restraints and reattached them to uh, the bed, in a similar fashion, in a similar fashion that I did uh, for the youngest daughter. Uh, untying one wrist and looping it. Um, the only problem with hers, is where her top head board, was she didn't have a cross bar so we had to tie um, her wrists together and then loop it onto the bed posts and the, then her legs um, headboard we um, we looped it around the lower bed posts.

Det. Vitello: So she was tied differently than, than the younger daughter?

Komisarjevsky: She, She was laying; she was lying in the same position, just uh, modified a different knot.

Det. Vitello: A different knot?

Komisarjevsky: Yeah

Det. Vitello: Okay

Komisarjevsky: Um, and went downstairs um, and asked the father for his keys to his vehicle. Um, we couldn't find them because stuff was scattered all over the place. Um, so Steve went back upstairs and asked the mother where her keys where. Um, he found them and uh, came back downstairs and um, he went out on the uh, sunroom back door and uh, got into the mom's vehicle and I went down into the basement and out the uh, basement Bilco hatch door urn, and walked in the opposite direction to uh, where my van was parked.

Det. Vitello: Your van is a what?

Komisarjevsky: Um, a white Chevy uh, Venture.

Det. Vitello: And that was parked out on the street?

STOP THE INTRUDER™ | KNOWLEDGE IS THE BEST PROTECTION™

Komisarjevsky: Yeah, it was parked out on the street, around the comer.

Det. Vitello: Okay, did you do anything with the telephones before you left?

Komisarjevsky: I had uh, I had uh, Steve and I had uh, taken all of the uh, the cell phones location and all the um, portable phones and had uh, put them in a central so we could keep track of where the phones were.

Det. Vitello: You had taken the families phones then?

Komisarjevsky: Yeah, the families phones.

Det. Vitello: Okay and you did that for what purpose?

Komisarjevsky: Um, so, so that nobody would make any phones calls, you know, without us knowing about it.

Det. Vitello: Okay

Komisarjevsky: Uh,

Det. Vitello: Now is everyone in the house is restrained at this point or just, just clarify that for us. You have mom and the younger daughter tied and restrained to their beds?

Komisarjevsky: That's correct.

Det. Vitello: And what about the other daughter?

Komisarjevsky: Um, well the other daughter was also restrained to, to her bed.

Det. Vitello: To her bed, in her own bed?

Komisarjevsky: In her own bedroom.

STOP THE INTRUDER™ | KNOWLEDGE IS THE BEST PROTECTION™

Det. Vitello: And the father is still downstairs in the sunroom,

Komisarjevsky: He's

Det. Vitello: Sitting on the couch?

Komisarjevsky: He's, he's, he's tied but not restrained to the couch.

Det. Vitello: Okay, so go ahead.

Komisarjevsky: So far whatever reason uh, we, we didn't.

Det. Vitello: You didn't restrain him?

Komisarjevsky: We didn't restrain him.

Det. Vitello: Okay

Komisarjevsky: So um, he uh, we left. Steven in mom's car and me in my car. Um, we drove down um, Mountain Road.

Det. Vitello: Did you leave the father in that sunroom?

Komisarjevsky: Yes

Det. Vitello: Okay, so your driving, you go get with your car, Steven takes mom's 4- wheel drive?

Komisarjevsky: Uh, It's, it's a sport utility uh, but much sportier, uh.

Det. Vitello: Like an SUV?

Komisarjevsky: Kind of except, it was a crossbreed between a car and a SUV.

Det. Vitello: Okay, do you remember the color?

Komisarjevsky: Urn, not off the top of my head, uh.

Det. Vitello: Okay, so Steve drives, you drive, where did you go?

Komisarjevsky: Um, we drove down Mountain Road. Um, we the, the original plan was to park my van at Stop & Shop. Um, but Steve felt that it was to far away, so I noticed that um, I passed Steve um, on Mountain Road and pulled into uh, a condo complex across the street um, from West Main Street, at the end of Mountain.

Det. Vitello: Any particular reason you picked that?

Komisarjevsky: No, I just figured that I, I could park in one of the visitor parking spots and it, it wouldn't,

Det. Vitello: It wouldn't be noticed,

Komisarjevsky: No, no we'd be hiding in plain site.

Det. Vitello: Okay

Komisarjevsky: Um, I got out of my vehicle, I locked it and um, as uh, Steve turned around and came back and I got into mom's car with Steve uh, and drove back to the house. Um, we had gotten into an argument on the way back to the house about um, his speed uh, because I knew that Cheshire Police patrolled Mountain Road for speeders on a regular.

Det. Vitello: So you didn't want to get stopped?

Komisarjevsky: Yeah we didn't want to get stopped on the way back to the house in a vehicle that wasn't ours.

Det. Vitello: Okay, so now you are back at the house, you came in, in the home owner's vehicle.

Komisarjevsky: Yes

Det. Vitello: You, you go back into the house.

Komisarjevsky: We enter from uh, we enter into the house from the uh, sunroom backdoor. Um, and the father is still sitting on the couch.

Det. Vitello: Okay

Komisarjevsky: Uh, he had asked if the uh, the uh, if the women were alright and our, I responded by saying uh, reassuring him that they were fine. They were behaving themselves and um, that everything would be fine.

Det. Vitello: Okay

Komisarjevsky: Um so Steve uh, was jumping around the house and looking through stuff and what not. I went upstairs. So I stopped at the youngest daughter. Um, I noticed that she was, since being separated from her mom um, earlier um, she was a lot more uh, she, she was a lot more stressed out than, than she was earlier.

Det. Vitello: Okay

Komisarjevsky: Um, and um, was sweating profusely on her bed. Uh, I went back downstairs and got her a glass of water. Brought that back up to her. Um, I untied her hands and um uh I asked if she wanted something to drink. Um, the sleeping bag that she used as a bedspread and the top sheet, I uh, took off and threw it off to the side because um, they were soaking wet.

Det. Vitello: Okay

Komisarjevsky: And then when she was done with the glass of water, I uh, I let her lay back down without tying her hands uh, so that, she was a little more comfortable.

Det. Vitello: Okay

Komisarjevsky: Uh, I felt comfortable not tying her up as she was very well behaved. Um, very compliant.

Det. Vitello: Do you do anything to her during your time together?

Komisarjevsky: No, we just um, talked about things. About her music and like what not, and we periodically, you know, we checked on the older sister and uh, the mother and the father.

Det. Vitello: Okay

Komisarjevsky: Uh,

Det. Vitello: So things are pretty status quo at this point in the house. You guys are still.

Komisarjevsky: Yeah

Det. Vitello: Buying time.

Komisarjevsky: Yeah we were buying time. Um, Steve and I uh, were nipping at each other a little bit because the stress level was very high and um, I never done anything uh, like this. Anyway I was very uncomfortable uh, with the situation and um, I, I just felt very out of control in the whole thing.

Det. Vitello: Okay

Komisarjevsky: And something happens, the stress was starting to build between Steve and I.

Det. Vitello: Okay, so where are we, time wise, what time do you think we are at?

Komisarjevsky: Uh, this probably about ob, 5 0' clockish, 5 :30ish.

STOP THE INTRUDER™ | KNOWLEDGE IS THE BEST PROTECTION™

Det. Vitello: 5 O'clock in the morning?

Komisarjevsky: Yeah

Det. Vitello: Okay

Komisarjevsky: And there is definitely light outside, it's starting to,

Det. Vitello: Starting to get light out, okay.

Komisarjevsky: At that point we realized that we had to get the father out of the sunroom, uh, because it was getting so light and um, the potential of the high visi uh, high visibility that would um, we didn't want anybody to, to see him um, tied up in, with a towel on his head.

Det. Vitello: Now, you were afraid that someone could see him through the house,

Komisarjevsky: Yeah

Det. Vitello: And see that he was hurt and whatever?

Komisarjevsky: Yeah, so we uh, untied his feet and um, and asked him if he uh, was able to, to walk down to the basement. Um, he said he, he was able to um, and I helped him, you know, get up and, he was a little dizzy. Um, but he, he walked over to the basement stairs and he made his way down the steps and down into the basement.

Det. Vitello: Okay

Komisarjevsky: Um, we, were gonna have him lean up uh, sit down in the middle area of the basement and lean up against one of the uh, concrete lolly columns.

Det. Vitello: Uh, uh.

STOP THE INTRUDER™ | KNOWLEDGE IS THE BEST PROTECTION™

Komisarjevsky: Um, he was a little shaky from uh, probably the issues of shock and losing blood. Uh, he wasn't making, he wasn't bleeding as bad as he was when I, we had started the towel.

Det. Vitello: Okay

Komisarjevsky: So I went upstairs and grabbed him the big uh, cushions off the couch and slid his head on that instead of the cold concrete floor and I got another pillow for his back against the lolly column.

Det. Vitello: Did you tie him back up?

Komisarjevsky: Yeah, we, I, we, we tied his feet and as Steve uh, stood over the two of us, uh, with the fake gun.

Det. Vitello: Was he assaulted again?

Komisarjevsky: He was not, no he was not assaulted again, he was, he just, that, that one time.

Det. Vitello: Just that one time? Okay, so he was back downstairs, he's estrained, is he tied to the lolly column?

Komisarjevsky: No, he wasn't uh, tied to the lolly column, he was just sitting there.

Det. Vitello: Okay, go ahead.

Komisarjevsky: Uh, so we went up, back upstairs and urn, we had just, Steve was just rummaging around. He did do some clean-up in the sunroom, Steve did.

Det. Vitello: Okay

Komisarjevsky: The table was knocked over and there was some blood on he tile floor. So we threw a blanket over it Uh, we threw a

	spread, like a throw spread over the couch. Over the back of the couch.
Det. Vitello:	Okay.
Komisarjevsky:	So somebody looking wouldn't notice.
Det. Vitello:	Wouldn 't notice.
Komisarjevsky:	Because there was blood all over the place.
Det. Vitello:	Okay
Komisarjevsky:	I went back upstairs and, to check on the two daughters, um.
Det. Vitello:	So you came downstairs with dad, with Steve, you re-tied him, you moved him because you were worried about daylight, so then you came up, you took care of some blood in the sunroom, you went back upstairs you said, you went back upstairs to check on the other, other females that were restrained. Their still restrained in the same spot that they were before you went and moved the cars and what not?
Komisarjevsky:	Yeah, yeah we had them still in their beds urn, we had also or Steve had brought up the point that um, about what they did for work and whether or not they needed to be, someone needed to call in sick for them.
Det Vitello:	Yup
Komisarjevsky:	Um, so Steve went in, down to the basement and asked the father um, when he needed, what time he needed to be into work, and who needed to be called. Um, he then informed, you know, that he was going to be late.
Det. Vitello:	Uh, uh

STOP THE INTRUDER™ | KNOWLEDGE IS THE BEST PROTECTION™

Komisarjevsky: Urn, I went to the mother and asked her um, what, what time she needed to be into work and she uh, advised me that she was a uh, teacher and that she uh, was off for the summer so it was a non issue. Uh, the father on the other hand is a doctor apparently and needed to make, he didn't have to be in the office until 8:30, but he needed to make rounds at the hospital around 7:00 so he was expected to be somewhere at 7:00. Um, he had made mention that um, of a supervisors name um, that he um, that he had contact and he said, saying that he wasn't feeling well and that he would not be on time.

Det. Vitello: Okay, was that call made?

Komisarjevsky: No, that call wasn't made, urn, Steve and I went up stairs and untied the mother from her bed, um, we had her come, um, on the way down um, downstairs, um, she had asked if she uh, could uh, peek into um, both children's um, rooms and um, just to make sure that, you know both daughters are fine and I was fine with that and it sort of helped reassure um, KK as well, uh.

Det. Vitello: Now who's KK.?

Komisarjevsky: Uh, KK is the youngest daughter. The one that, that I was spending time talking to.

Det. Vitello: Okay

Komisarjevsky: Uh, we head downstairs ah, with the mother and have her sit on the love seat in the living room. Um, where I um, retied her, her feet. um, then her hands and uh, Steve went to uh, up the uh, the other phone, the house phone uh, which was in the kitchen.

Det. Vitello: Okay

STOP THE INTRUDER™ | KNOWLEDGE IS THE BEST PROTECTION™

Komisarjevsky: Uh, he got back, came back over and uh, gave the phone to her uh, but she couldn't dial it so, it just reenergized while I untied her hands again um, and so she made the phone call. I was sort of, I had then gone in. I, posted up in the kitchen just uh, you know, looking around uh, looking out, out the windows and, just you know, overseeing different entry points in the house while Steve uh, was uh, went to the door to make the necessary phone calls.

Det. Vitello: Okay

Komisarjevsky: To call the father out.

Det. Vitello: Okay

Komisarjevsky: When that was done Steve had uh, called me over to tie her hands back up uh, he put the phone back in the kitchen and uh, he uh, had thanked her, that she did a good job, for doing that.

Det. Vitello: Okay

Komisarjevsky: Um, at that point Steve was feeling a lot more comfortable with um, the mother going into the bank and withdrawing urn, the $15,000.00. Um, that we had originally come to.

Det. Vitello: Okay, and what bank where you planning on doing this at?

Komisarjevsky: Um, the original plan was that we were going to the Bank of America in Waterbury.

Det. Vitello: In Waterbury?

Komisarjevsky: That was my understanding.

Det. Vitello: Okay

Komisarjevsky: Um, I felt that it would be better that uh; we had then, a bank that's not familiar with her,

Det. Vitello: Okay

Komisarjevsky: and would notice that she was in distress.

Det. Vitello: Okay, at this point now uh, you check and you allow the mom to check the bedroom and those children, the two female daughters were tied but not, not harmed?

Komisarjevsky: No

Det. Vitello: Fully clothed?

Komisarjevsky: Yeah, they were.

Det. Vitello: No, no issues?

Komisarjevsky: No, no, no issues at all.

Det. Vitello: Okay, go on.

Komisarjevsky: Um, at this point uh, several hours to kill. It's only about uh, 6:30, of ½ of 7 at that point. Um.

Det. Vitello: It's daylight?

Komisarjevsky: Yeah it's definitely daylight outside. Um, I was getting with Steve again because um, there weren't that many shades downstairs and he was constantly walking back and forth across windows. Um, I got to the point where I was getting so frustrated, that I just went back upstairs again to check on the daughters and began uh, struck up a uh, conversation with KK. Um, got her some more water. Uh, she had needed to go to the bathroom so I untied her and uh, allowed her to use the bathroom in the master bedroom.

STOP THE INTRUDER™ | KNOWLEDGE IS THE BEST PROTECTION™

Det. Vitello: Okay

Komisarjevsky: Um, when she was done, um, she came back into her room. Um, where I then restrained her feet, but you know, let her, her hands be where they were previously. Um, I also went to go give some water to the oldest daughter but she uh, wasn't really that thirsty. Um, which was fine, you know um. Um, I was, we were starting to get, get down to crunch time and, um.

Det. Vitello: Crunch time meaning?

Komisarjevsky: The um, um we were getting.

Det. Vitello's cellular ringing in the background

Komisarjevsky: We had uh, we were thinking of uh, Steve leaving with the mom at about 8:45. The bank closed at 9:00. And um, so about 8:45 would be a good time to leave. The bank was in Waterbury and it takes about 20 minutes to get there.

Det. Vitello: Okay, so how it looks still where we are, okay, as far as one no ones injured, but other, other than the father?

Komisarjevsky: Yeah

Det. Vitello: You were buying time until 9 0' clock uh, when you think you should go to the bank?

Komisarjevsky: Yeah

Det. Vitello: Mom had already called dad in uh, you were going to call the mom.

Komisarjevsky: Um, there were the times that uh, I was sitting in the bedroom with KK um, Steve had come in and um, and motioned for me to, to follow him into the office um, where the occupants of the house couldn't over hear us talking, and said that uh, we were going to need gasoline. Um, and I was surprised um, that gasoline was even a factor in what was going on here. We were just supposed to get the money and get out and he was going on and on and on about DNA and, and even a drop of sweat, or uh, a hair falling of your head um, is enough to, to put us back in jail because we were both convicted felons and they have our DNA on record.

Um, he had first mentioned that uh, that we would take the occupants of the home with us, um in their vehicles um, and leave the house burning uh, in their wake. Um, I'm a little stunned and perplexed about the whole situation and he went back downstairs um, and I went back into um, KK.'s room. Um, about 15 minutes later Steve came back and he motioned to me to go back into the office with him, and he began ranting and raving about DNA, and he was mad at me because I had on several occasions accidentally used his name in front of um, the occupants in the house um, and I, all of a sudden you know we gotta kill them

Det. Vitello: We gotta what?

Komisarjevsky: We gotta kill them.

Det. Vitello: Kill them?

Komisarjevsky: Yeah kill the, the family and then burn the house down on top of them.

Um, that was, that was not in, that was not the plan. I'm, I'm not killing anyone. You know that's it, that's not how it's going down. Like, we were here simply for the money, get in and get out, you know it's almost 9 O'clock and why, why you bugging out now, you know. Plus, then I had gotten on his case, if he was so worried about DNA why was he walking around without his gloves on now.

Det. Vitello: He removed his gloves?

STOP THE INTRUDER™ | KNOWLEDGE IS THE BEST PROTECTION™

Komisarjevsky: Yeah, yeah, yeah, he had removed his gloves. And I was like, you know - what, what are you doing?

Det. Vitello: Why did he remove them?

Komisarjevsky: I don't know, I'm not sure.

Det. Vitello: At this point he no longer had his gloves on?

Komisarjevsky: He had no longer had his gloves on

Det. Vitello: And you still did?

Komisarjevsky: And I had, I had gloves on the entire time

Det. Vitello: Are your masks still on your heads?

Komisarjevsky: Um, sometimes, um, we'd sometimes; we'd pull it up um, so that we could pull it down at a moments notice. Um, we had put um, pillowcases over the occupant's heads

Det. Vitello: You did?

Komisarjevsky: Yeah so that they couldn't see us, um

Det. Vitello: When did you do that?

Komisarjevsky: When um, we had done that, um, after um, after we had split them up and, they come, came back from the car ride um, because um, it was getting a little, vision was difficult uh, more difficult to be walking around the house with uh, these very awkward um, the face shields that we'd come up with on the fly.

Det. Vitello: So you covered their faces because you wanted to uncover your face?

Komisarjevsky: Yes, correct

STOP THE INTRUDER™ | KNOWLEDGE IS THE BEST PROTECTION™

Det. Vitello: Okay, were you trying to suffocate them at that time?

Komisarjevsky: No, not at all

Det. Vitello: You're just trying to prevent them from seeing you?

Komisarjevsky: Exactly

Det. Vitello: But at this point other than you slipping with using Steve's real name.

Komisarjevsky: Uh, um

Det. Vitello: They really couldn't identify you, facially because you were pretty much concealed.

Komisarjevsky: Yeah.

Det. Vitello: Okay

Komisarjevsky: I was very confident that they wouldn't be able to, to be able to um, you know recognize us.

Det. Vitello: Okay, so go ahead.

Komisarjevsky: As far as like the suffocation part um, the suffocation thing, with the pillowcases um, like when we put it over, like I made a point to like roll up, to roll it back up, like put it over their head, but then roll the back up.

Det. Vitello: Did you just cover their eyes?

Komisarjevsky: So it would just cover their eyes not their nose and mouth

Det. Vitello: Okay

Komisarjevsky: Um, and it does get hot, especially, you know, underneath the pillowcases.

STOP THE INTRUDER™ | KNOWLEDGE IS THE BEST PROTECTION™

Det. Vitello: Sure.

Komisarjevsky: I'm sure, especially when you're stressed.

Det. Vitello: Absolutely

Komisarjevsky: Uh, so uh, so I lost my train of thought.

Det. Vitello: You were, you were up to almost up to 9 0' clock where he starts to bug out on you?

Komisarjevsky: He's starting to feel the pressure about leaving the house with the mom, and then having to lose site of the mom while she went into the bank alone. And he is sitting in the parking lot um, so, so things are getting a little tense uh, between the two of us um, uncomfortable at times.

Det. Vitello: Alright, now how did the conversation about killing the family end?

Komisarjevsky: Like he just walked away like he was, a statement, it wasn't a conversation, it was, it was a statement, and that's how it was going to be, you know and that's that.

Det. Vitello: Okay

Komisarjevsky: Um, in my mind that's, it's simply not an option,

Det. Vitello: Okay

Komisarjevsky: It just isn't, um.

Det. Medina: Did you mention that to him?

Komisarjevsky: I, I had made mention um, that you know, I'm not killing anybody, you know, that's, I don't, I'm not going to, um he didn't seem to care or whatever, he was just focused on going to his truck in the next uh, 10, 15 minutes.

STOP THE INTRUDER™ | KNOWLEDGE IS THE BEST PROTECTION™

Det Vitello: Okay

Komisarjevsky: Um, just, just to back up a little bit when he um, had first mentioned um, about burning the house down um, he had gone down to the garage, and taken a bunch of bottles of one gallon bottles, bottles of a windshield wiper fluid.

Det. Vitello: Okay

Komisarjevsky: And uh, drained those into the kitchen sink um, I had heard the chugging of something being drained in the sink. I went downstairs to see what he was up to this time and um, again he had said, you know, I'm going to go get gas. I'll be in mom's car, I'll be back.

Det. Vitello: So he, at this point, he drains the bottles and he's gonna go get gas?

Komisarjevsky: With the bottles!

Det. Vitello: Which he does in fact do, taking mom's car, leaving you home with everyone else.

Komisarjevsky: With everybody else, leaves me with everybody and just takes off.

Det. Vitello: Okay, what time do you think that was?

Komisarjevsky: Um, the drop was at 9, or the pick-up was at 9, so this is probably about 8' clockish.

Det. Vitello: Eight 0' clock in the morning, where do you think he went?

Komisarjevsky: Well, he didn't, he didn't say where he was going to get it. um, I was assuming he was just probably going to go the gas station around mountain because it's right there.

Det. Vitello: Uh, uh.

Komisarjevsky: Um, but he somehow managed to end up over on Main Street, heading towards Richard's Chevrolet and called me, asking if there was a gas station up there. I was like well where are you? He was like I just passed Richard's Chevrolet. I was like well your next gas station isn't until Southington.

Det. Vitello: Okay

Komisarjevsky: He was like, oh well I'll find one closer, and then hung up. But then called back, you know, 15, 20 minutes later and said, how do I get back to Cheshire from Waterbury?

Det. Vitello: So he's calling you, saying he's in Waterbury?

Komisarjevsky: Yeah

Det. Vitello: Did he have the gas?

Komisarjevsky: He, he apparently had the gas and was on his way back

Det. Vitello: Okay

Komisarjevsky: Um, when he had gotten back to the house um, he had um, 4 of those containers um,

Det. Vitello: Filled with gas?

Komisarjevsky: Filled with gasoline um, which he put in the garage.

Det. Vitello: Put in the garage, meaning he put them down in the garage.

Komisarjevsky: Yeah

Det. Vitello: Or he poured them out?

Komisarjevsky: No he, he put them um, down in the garage.

STOP THE INTRUDER™ | KNOWLEDGE IS THE BEST PROTECTION™

Det. Vitello: Okay

Det. Medina: Did you help him put this away?

Komisarjevsky: No, I was in the kitchen.

Det. Medina: You were in the kitchen?

Komisarjevsky: Yeah the dinette, kitchen area.

Det. Vitello: There was no one else down there with you at that time correct, everyone else is upstairs in the bedrooms or downstairs in the basement?

Komisarjevsky: No, mom, mom is downstairs.

Det. Vitello: Mom is downstairs?

Komisarjevsky: Yeah she's sitting on the uh, on the love seat.

Det. Vitello: So mom has been down there the whole time since she made that call in for dad, for her husband to be late for work.

Komisarjevsky: Yeah from that point on she's been downstairs with her (not audible).

Det. Vitello: Okay, tied but not restrained.

Komisarjevsky: Tied but not restrained.

Det. Vitello: Okay

Komisarjevsky: Um, so 9, 9, whatever the hour I had made mention before. It was originally, it was quarter to 9 um, mentioned that because he made uh, you know, detour in the plan and got back there and (not audible) her, he also wanted to make a bunch of phone calls to uh, um, the Bank of America, he called uh, 411 uh, to get their number um,

Det Vitello: Okay

Komisarjevsky: Using the home phone, um wanting, he basically wanted to get, and ask you know somebody at the branch what he needed, specifically how to withdraw a large amount sum, a large sum of money from one's own account.

Det. Vitello: Okay

Komisarjevsky: Uh, in general, he was speaking in generalities uh, how he was going to um, however, he couldn't get through cause it wasn't 9 O'clock yet. So, no one is in the bank so they kept referring him to the 1-800 number which was the automated system.

Det. Vitello: So he never actually made contact with the bank?

Komisarjevsky: No, he was very frustrated about that, um so finally he just hung up.

Det. Vitello: Okay

Komisarjevsky: And then uh, he got the mom by the hand uh, the two of them got in the car, um

Det. Vitello: Did he untie her?

Komisarjevsky: Yes

Det. Vitello: Okay, completely?

Komisarjevsky: Completely, yeah

Det. Vitello: So, her hands and feet are no longer tied?

Komisarjevsky: She's, she's untied.

Det. Vitello:	She's in the car with him, heading to the Bank of America in Waterbury?
Komisarjevsky:	That's correct
Det. Vitello:	Okay
Det. Medina:	Who is driving the car?
Komisarjevsky:	I believe she was driving the car.
Det. Vitello:	Okay
Komisarjevsky:	Uh, so, they left uh, at about nine o'clock um, I went down to check on Dad, um, he was still sitting downstairs tied um, I had gone upstairs and I checked on the older sister um, she had needed to go to the bathroom, so I untied her let her go to the bathroom and retied her in the same position that she was in. Um, asked her if she wanted water, she said no. Um, then I went into KK.'s room and uh, began, sat down and we were talking about um, just you know, shooting the shit I guess uh, you know, just to pass the time.
Det. Vitello:	And how old do you think KK is?
Komisarjevsky:	Uh, somewhere between 14 and 16 possibly.
Det. Vitello:	And the other sister you thought was how old?
Komisarjevsky:	Uh, between 18 and 19.
Det. Vitello:	Okay, so KK, obviously she told you her nickname or whatever as KK or you made that up?
Komisarjevsky:	No, that's the name that both her sister and her mother uh, referred to her as.
Det. Vitello:	Okay, you're talking to KK. about just general things?

Komisarjevsky: Yeah, things, school and summer plans and you know, stuff like that, boredom sometimes um, obviously not mine.

Det. Vitello: Right

Komisarjevsky: Um, and uh, then one thing lead to another and uh, I ended up having or performing oral sex on her, on KK.

Det. Vitello: You performed oral sex on KK.?

Komisarjevsky: On K.K, yeah

Det. Vitello: Did you do that while she was tied?

Komisarjevsky: Um, yes

Det. Vitello: Was it against her will?

Komisarjevsky: Her, her hands were tied, but her feet weren't

Det. Vitello: Was it against her will or was she, or was it something you talked her into, how did that go?

Komisarjevsky: Um, it, it started off as against her will um, and then like, she wasn't like resisting or anything, so I just kept doing it you know.

Det. Vitello: Um, did she reciprocate to you?

Komisarjevsky: Uh no um, I um, after about 5 minutes or so uh, she uh I had uh, let her get dressed again, but before she did that she had asked if she could take a shower uh, in the master bedroom shower.

Det. Vitello: Okay

Komisarjevsky: You know which it was.

STOP THE INTRUDER™ | KNOWLEDGE IS THE BEST PROTECTION™

Det. Vitello: Now when you said you let her get dressed again, how, how was it she came upon being undressed, because you originally said she was dressed?

Komisarjevsky: She, I had uh, I used a pair of scissors and like, cut her, her shirt off and her skirt off.

Det. Vitello: Was that for purpose of having sex with her or was there another reason you did it?

Komisarjevsky: For the purpose of having sex.

Det. Vitello: Okay

Komisarjevsky: Um, he, I had may, well, let me rephrase that, like I didn't, my purpose wasn't to have like, actual like, sex with her, just oral sex.

Det. Vitello: So you're saying you didn't have intercourse with her?

Komisarjevsky: That's correct

Det. Vitello: But you performed oral sex is what you said?

Komisarjevsky: Yeah

Det. Vitello: So you cut her clothes off for that purpose?

Komisarjevsky: Yes

Det. Vitello: Okay, did you take pictures of her?

Komisarjevsky: Uh, I did yes.

Det. Vitello: With?

Komisarjevsky: Uh, with my camera phone.

STOP THE INTRUDER™ | KNOWLEDGE IS THE BEST PROTECTION™

Det. Vitello: Camera phone in your cell phone.

Komisarjevsky: Yeah

Det. Vitello: Okay so, go ahead, so now, you let her take a shower in the master bedroom, you leave the door open.

Komisarjevsky: I'd (long pause)

Det Vitello: It's okay

Komisarjevsky: She had uh, she still had her uh, pillowcase on her head.

Det. Vitello: Alright, when you had oral sex upon her, her face was still covered..

Komisarjevsky: Yeah.

Det. Vitello: Okay

Komisarjevsky: Um, and I had uh, had ejaculated on her stomach, that's why she wanted to take a shower.

Det. Vitello: Okay, you ejaculated on her stomach while you were performing oral sex on her?

Komisarjevsky: No, after.

Det. Vitello: After?

Komisarjevsky: After the fact

Det. Vitello: Then, what then?

Komisarjevsky: Uh, what did I do?

Det. Vitello: With yo, you,

Komisarjevsky: Yes

Det. Vitello: She didn't, you did not force her to do that to you, you did it?

Komisarjevsky: I did it on my own.

Det. Vitello: Okay, so then that's why you allowed her to take a shower?

Komisarjevsky: Yeah

Det. Vitello: Okay

Komisarjevsky: Um, well I asked her if she wanted to shower, she was like yes please, she said yes please, um.

Det. Vitello: Okay, did you let her take a shower without the pillowcase?

Komisarjevsky: Um, yes (laughing)

Det. Vitello: Did you cover your face at that time?

Komisarjevsky: I re-covered my face.

Det. Vitello: Alright, so she still had never seen you at this point?

Komisarjevsky: That's correct

Det. Vitello: Okay

Komisarjevsky: Well, so she went and took a shower, when she was done um, she came back into the room and I stepped our of the room so that she could get dressed

Det. Vitello: Okay

Komisarjevsky: Um, I went and checked on, on her older sister and then I started to go downstairs um, to go and check on the father, realizing that he's all the way in the basement and KK wasn't

	restrained at all. Um, so I turned back and stood outside the hall until she was done, then came in and she sat back down, down on the bed and I retied her feet
Det. Vitello:	So she re-enters, her face is not covered at this point, but yours is so, so she can't see you,
Komisarjevsky:	She can't see me.
Det Vitello:	So you re-tie her.
Komisarjevsky:	I re-tie her, I left her pillowcase off as well, you know, so the only thing at that point was, that was tied, was just her feet.
Det. Vitello:	Did you restrain her back to the bed?
Komisarjevsky:	Her feet were, but not her hands.
Det. Vitello:	Her feet were tied to the bed?
Komisarjevsky:	To the bed.
Det. Vitello:	So she couldn't get up and walk out?
Komisarjevsky:	No
Det. Vitello:	Okay, go ahead.
Komisarjevsky:	I then went downstairs to check on the father um, yet he had, during this whole time uh, Steve kept calling me, giving me updates of where they were and what they were doing and.
Det Vitello:	Okay, so while you're having sex with the youngest girl, performed oral sex on her so far, Steve and the mom are still out, to the bank.
Komisarjevsky:	Yes

Det. Vitello: When you checked on the older daughter did you have any sexual relations with her?

Komisarjevsky: No I didn't.

Det. Vitello: Okay, so we still have them, be's calling you for what reasons?

Komisarjevsky: Uh, for uh, for it was, well uh, the conversation was weird because it was more like he was having a conversation with himself um, like he was, he was talking like he was talking to me; however it was, it was more a show for, or it came across as more of a show for, for the mom.

Det. Vitello: What was he saying?

Komisarjevsky: Um, he was like you know uh, so far everything, everything's going well and, and uh, she was very and like, she was very, very, she was very well aware of the fact that uh., she needs to comply or things could go very badly um.

Det. Vitello: So he was on his way to the bank, trying to convince her to?

Komisarjevsky: Yeah, convince.

Det. Vitello: The mom?

Komisarjevsky: Yeah, it seemed more like he was more trying to convince her than, than updating me about anything.

Det. Vitello: Okay, did he ask you, did he ask you at that time anything about pictures. I recall you said something about pictures.

Komisarjevsky: Um no, I, I put them on for my own personal use.

Det. Vitello: Okay, so he didn't ask you to send him that picture, you took those pictures for yourself?

Komisarjevsky: I was,

Det. Vitello: Okay, okay, so he's, he's trying to convince her that this is real and take the money and there won't be any problems, and he's calling you kind of, calling to update?

Komisarjevsky: Yeah

Det. Vitello: Okay, go ahead

Komisarjevsky: Um, they. Because I was a little curious because they made it back so quickly. I was uh, under the understanding that they were going to go all the way out to Waterbury and use the bank out there. And it wasn't the mom's primary bank.

Det. Vitello: Oh, okay, they may have, I'm, I'm not sure what bank they actually used.

Komisarjevsky: On his way, way back, they uh, put, I'm not sure which Bank of America they did actually go to.

Det. Vitello: Did he get the money?

Komisarjevsky: He did come home, back to the house with the money, um the mother, he and the mother walked in through the sunroom door in the back and uh, he had the money in his hands. Then um, um, what do you call those things, um?

Det. Vitello: Envelopes

Komisarjevsky: The envelopes, yeah money envelopes.

Det. Vitello: Bank envelopes?

Komisarjevsky: Yeah

Det. Vitello: That said Bank of America?

Komisarjevsky: Bank of America

Det. Vitello: Okay, how many of them?

Komisarjevsky: Um, 4 or 5.

Det. Vitello: 4 or 5?

Komisarjevsky: There's a stack of them.

Det. Vitello: Did you actually see the money?

Komisarjevsky: I didn't actually see the money itself, no, just the bank, the bank envelopes.

Det. Vitello: Okay

Komisarjevsky: Um, I had actually reached for them and so uh, he yanked them away from me and then this bag that he had put, put in little odds and ends, and jewelry uh.

Det. Vitello: Where did he get the bag?

Komisarjevsky: Um, from the, the mother's room. It was a uh, the mother's.

Det. Vitello: like a purse?

Komisarjevsky: Like a large purse type thing.

Det. Vitello: So he had been dumping valuables in there?

Komisarjevsky: Yeah, or some of the valuable type stuff.

Det. Vitello: Alright, so when you reached for the money, he kind of pulled it back and put it in the bag without you ever seeing it.

Komisarjevsky: Without me ever seeing it, yeah.

Det. Vitello: Okay, go ahead

Komisarjevsky: There was also a weird conversation when he had, when he had called prior to getting back to the house, he had, was calling to let me know that he was on his way and uh, I asked, did everything go alright and he sort of side stepped the question. And then uh, I asked him how much did you uh, did you get and uh, he sidestepped that, that question as well. And I thought that was really odd, like was he trying to, I guess he was pulling a fast one on me, be just take off with the mom and leave, and leave me here at the house by myself, so there was a lot of tension in the air when be did finally get to the house.

Det. Vitello: Okay, then what happens when he gets back?

Komisarjevsky: Um, when he got back to the house um, and uh, he put the money in the bag, uh, he uh, said sort of bluntly ordered me to uh, re-tie mom uh, back on the love seat, in the living room and tied her feet and her uh, her hands um, like we had always done, you know, like in the bed.

Det. Vitello: Okay

Komisarjevsky: Um, we had then, he had pulled me to the side uh, we go into the dining room which was on the other side of the house, and says uh, very matter of fact, okay you, you ready, we gotta, we gotta kill them and burn the house down. I'm like, I'm not killing anyone, there's no way. I was, I'm not, I'm not there's, we have the money, there's, there's not a problem, you know, they've done everything, don't know who we are, they can't recognize us.

Det. Vitello: Why did he want them killed?

Komisarjevsky: He was, he was upset with the fact that I had, messed up and used his first name uh, he was also going on and on about DNA um.

Det. Vitello: Why was he so concerned about DNA? Did he have any sexual relations with the mom?

Komisarjevsky: Not to my knowledge um, if anyone had anything, he would not have the most to worry about DNA, it would have been me. Um, but I wasn't worried about it because she had taken a shower.

Det. Vitello: Okay,

Komisarjevsky: Uh, so I don't know why he was so like up in arms about it.

Det Vitello: Okay

Komisarjevsky: Um, so he uh.

De.t Vitello: So you're arguing with him?

Komisarjevsky: Yeah, we're going back and forth about um, he's like, well then, you know, I'll kill the two daughters and you can kill the mom. I was like, I'm not killing anyone. I was like, I don't know how to put it more matter of fact, there's uh, no one's dying by my hand today. There, that's not going to happen. It's, it can't.

Det Vitello: You didn't want to kill anyone?

Komisarjevsky: I didn't want to kill anyone.

Det. Vitello: Okay

Komisarjevsky: Um, he even with, I'm, doing it with the, the father, like I, I couldn't keep hitting him. Like, I uh, just couldn't do it. You know, it's, that sound, it's just horrific, like I just,I

Det. Vitello: I don't know, I couldn't imagine.

STOP THE INTRUDER™ | KNOWLEDGE IS THE BEST PROTECTION™

Komisarjevsky: Like, like, it's not going to happen and we kept going back and forth about it. And finally he was like, you know what, fuck it, I'll, I'll take care of them, all three of them. And uh, he'd, he'd go, he was walking around with these stockings um, that he had, that we had run out of rope at one point.

Det. Vitello: Stocking, as in lady's stockings?

Komisarjevsky: Yeah, apparently he used those for the rope. So he was walking around with a stocking uh, talking about he was going to just strangle them, all three of the women. And uh, see we used to go into. I'm sitting in the dinning room, the formal dinning room which is on the other side of the house and he leaves to go into the living room where the mother is. And after a couple of minutes, he comes back and then over to the dining room where I am. But then he leaves again and to the other end of the house and made it back and went back and forth like, you know, 4 or 5 times.

Det. Vitello: What was he doing, was he, was he?

Komisarjevsky: It seemed like he was trying to like, psyche himself up for whatever, you know, like.

Det. Vitello: To strangle the women?

Komisarjevsky: Yeah, to do what he thought he needed to do.

Det Vitello: Okay

Komisarjevsky: Uh, and I'm sitting there and like uh, I'm like besides myself, I'm like, I don't know what to do. Like I,

Det Vitello: Where are you at this point?

Komisarjevsky: Uh, I was sitting in the, the formal dining room.

Det. Vitello: And everyone else is upstairs except for mom and dad who's in the basement and you're downstairs with mom and Steve?

Komisarjevsky: That's correct. Um, I had a, I had clear sh, a view of the stairway, the front stairway that goes upstairs. Um, then you start going around the corner uh, and you're in the kitchen.

Det. Vitello: Yup.

Komisarjevsky: Then you go through the kitchen, and then you're in the living room, where the mom was, and as far as, you know, the father was downstairs in the basement. Um, the 4th or 5th time that he had walked back into, to the room that I was in, the dining room, uh, he left me and, and then he was in there for, like, the room, like 15 minutes, like.

Det. Vitello: Alone with the mom?

Komisarjevsky: Alone with the mom yeah, and I'm assuming he's just, still trying to psyche himself up, and um, at which time I hear this noise down in the basement and, I certainly recognized it as the bilco door that led to the outside.

Det. Vitello: Which is where the dad was?

Komisarjevsky: Which is right where the dad was and I yelled, but at the same time I jumped up um, screaming to Steve that the father just took off. He just left, and uh, was racing uh, towards the room that he was in, and uh, he was then coming back towards me and as we were converging on the basement door um, I can see behind Steve that uh, the mother was uh, laying lifelessly on the floor uh, with her head on the loveseat um, and her pants were down around her ankles.

Det. Vitello: So she's, she's in your opinion, lifeless. Her pants are down by her ankles?

Komisarjevsky: That's correct,

Det. Vitello: Which they hadn't been at any time prior to this.

Komisarjevsky: Definitely no.

Det. Vitello: And did you check on her, did you ask him what he did?

Komisarjevsky: No because my priority concern at that point was the father getting out the basement door.

Det. Vitello: What made you think she was lifeless?

Komisarjevsky: Um, the color of her face was a deep, deep purple, from the neck up.

Like, blue-ish, purple-ish, like pool of blood. Um, being an EMT, I have seen plenty of lifeless bodies and I recognized the color as being quite lifeless. Uh, her tongue was also sticking out of her mouth and her eyes were very puffed up.

Det. Vitello: Her eyes were puffed up. So your EMT experience tells you what, what did you think occurred?

Komisarjevsky: Um, I was fairly confident that, that Steve had finally built up the, the uh, the nerve to, to strangle her.

Det. Vitello: So at this point you think she's strangled and dead, pants are down so you?

Komisarjevsky: So like, I make the assumption that he assault, had also, had raped her.

Det. Vitello: Okay, you didn't actually see him strangle or rape her, but that's your opinion of it?

Komisarjevsky: Right, that's my opinion.

STOP THE INTRUDER™ | KNOWLEDGE IS THE BEST PROTECTION™

Det. Vitello: She's definitely lifeless, in your opinion, dead at this time?

Komisarjevsky: Yes, that's true.

Det. Vitello: Okay, so now you both head towards the basement?

Komisarjevsky: I uh, he stops at the basement door and barks at me to run down there and check, to make sure that he did in fact go out uh, which I did. I went down there and uh, sure enough he had definitely uh, taken off, out the back bilco door.

Det. Vitello: So the father basically escaped the house at this point?

Komisarjevsky: Yeah, that's correct, yes.

Det. Vitello: Did you chase him?

Komisarjevsky: No

Det. Vitello: Go ahead

Komisarjevsky: I went; I went back upstairs and told Steve that he's gone. We gotta get out of here right now, we have, we have to leave right this second.

Det. Vitello: So, on the upstairs, you mean, the first floor where mom was lying already?

Komisarjevsky: That's correct, yes.

Det. Vitello: Motionless, lifeless?

Komisarjevsky: Yeah

Det. Vitello: Okay

Komisarjevsky: Yeah, we're, we gotta get out.

STOP THE INTRUDER™ | KNOWLEDGE IS THE BEST PROTECTION™

Det. Vitello: You want out?

Komisarjevsky: Yeah, we have to go now, like, there's no option.

Det Vitello: Okay

Komisarjevsky: Um, here it's only a matter of minutes before he gets to the neighbors or seconds even before he gets to the neighbors house and the police are called.

Det Vitello: Yeah

Komisarjevsky: And Steve's taking all this time, you know, to, I don't know, I don't know what is what he was thinking. He ends up taking the bag with the money in it, and you know, shoving it in my chest and telling me to go start the car.

Det. Vitello: Okay

Komisarjevsky: And I'm like, where's the keys, where's the key, where's the keys. And he's like, I don't know, over there somewhere and we're going back and forth, like, with our heads chopped off. And you know, realized he darts into the garage.

Det. Vitello: Uh, uh

Komisarjevsky: Um, I turn around and keep looking for these keys, and um, I turn back around uh, and he's pouring a whole bunch of gasoline on the kitchen floor, and down the front hallway which leads to the stairwell.

Det. Vitello: Now mom is in the living room at this time, point?

Komisarjevsky: Yeah, which is like, where, like the kitchen floor is like, the living room where the mom is, is sort of like a, sunken living room.

Det. Vitello: Okay, so, kind of, it's connected?

Komisarjevsky: Yes

Det. Vitello: In a way?

Komisarjevsky: Yes, that's correct.

Det. Vitello: Did he pour gasoline in there where mom is?

Komisarjevsky: Yeah he'd, I maybe did. I didn't see him pour gasoline on her, but uh, he uh, there was certainly gasoline there, because it definitely reeked.

Det. Vitello: You could smell it?

Komisarjevsky: Oh yeah, it smelled like, you know, you light a cigarette and the place would blow apart.

Det. Vitello: Okay, well he goes up the stairs?

Komisarjevsky: He then went up the stairs uh, with two bottles um and.

Det Vitello: Did you follow him upstairs?

Komisarjevsky: I, I did. I followed him up the stairs, cause I, I couldn't understand like, I was like, you can't seriously be, be contemplating, burning these, these two girls alive.

Det. Vitello: um,

Komisarjevsky: I just like, that's unconscionable. Like,

Det. Vitello: Yes

Komisarjevsky: It is unreal.

Det. Vitello: It' bizarre.

STOP THE INTRUDER™ | KNOWLEDGE IS THE BEST PROTECTION™

Komisarjevsky: This is, it's really unreal. It's just not what, you can't do that. It's, you just can't. And um, I was a little relieved, well not relieved but, that he had not poured it in the bedrooms but, he had poured it up the stairway, down the hallway, and into the master bedroom.

Det. Vitello: How do you know that?

Komisarjevsky: Um, cause he was walking out of the master bedroom and you could see the uh, the gasoline on the uh, carpet.

Det. Vitello: Leading back to which bedroom?

Komisarjevsky: The master bedroom, which is in the back.

Det. Vitello: (Not audible)

Komisarjevsky: I, he, he walked out of the master bedroom, walked past me, back to the stairs, I went to KK.'s room um, there was no gasoline in there, she was still in her bed, I.

Det. Vitello: She's still alive?

Komisarjevsky: Oh yeah, absolutely.

Del. Medina: Okay

Det. Vitello: Her face is covered?

Komisarjevsky: Uh, yes, the pillow case was kept over her face.

Det. Vitello: Okay

Komisarjevsky: But, but, up enough so that, so she, she could breath. Um, then I closed the door and then I went down to the back towards the stairway, then past the oldest daughter's room. Uh, she too was sitting in her room um, tied to her bed uh,

	like she was previously, and I closed that door and I went downstairs.
Det. Medina:	Is she still alive?
Komisarjevsky:	Absolutely.
Det. Vitello:	Why did you close the doors?
Komisarjevsky:	I, I, I, I can't imagine, anyone being burned alive. You know, so I, I thought, I, I, I fucked up. You know I uh, I got myself in this horrible position, but, you know they did every, they did, they did what they were supposed to do. There was no reason for them to die. You know, they were compliant the entire way, both you know, very bright young ladies. Uh, and even the mother shouldn't have died, she didn't, she went out of her way to, to be, you know.
Det. Vitello:	Compliant?
Komisarjevsky:	Compliant to the tee, like you know, no talk back, no, no nothing and why is this happening. Like I, I don't understand, this, this isn't the plan; we were supposed to just get the money and get out, like hey. They haven't seen our faces, so what, I fucked up you know. I used your name, there's a million Steve's in this world.
Det. Vitello:	Okay
Komisarjevsky:	You know,
Det. Medina:	So he is trying to fill-up, boss you?
Komisarjevsky:	I'm trying to buy some time, you know and.
Det. Medina:	But, they're tied up, why didn't you untie them?

STOP THE INTRUDER™ | KNOWLEDGE IS THE BEST PROTECTION™

Komisarjevsky: I didn't even think about untying them, like for, for, for whatever stupid reason, like, it just didn't cross my mind, like when,

Det. Vitello: You didn't untie them, but you closed the doors, and

Det. Medina: To buy them time!

Det. Vitello: Just to, in the hopes of buying them time?

Komisarjevsky: Yeah

Det. Vitello: But you didn't untie them, why?

Komisarjevsky: I, I didn't untie them. Well, I just, you know, I shouldn't of, but I knew that, like I shouldn't have even fucking been there in the first place.

Det. Vitello: I know, go on.

Komisarjevsky: But, I, I, I get downstairs, and you know I was, and I'm like yelling at Steve, we gotta, it's already been 5 minutes now and you know, I'm confident, you know there's like, any of police officers right outside the door waiting to open fire on me as I open the door.

Det. Vitello: You could imagine.

Komisarjevsky: And uh, so we went straight for the back door and Steve was like, right behind me um, and I get out the back door and I'm going towards the back part of the house, which leads to the garage. The front side of the garage where the cars parked, and I turn around and Steve's not behind me anymore. So now, I'm back tracking back into the house and as I'm doing that, I'm looking, through the sunroom, and I can see in the neighbor's yard, that there is somebody plainly sitting there in the bushes watching us. I'm like; I was like, this isn't happening.

Det. Vitello: You can see outside?

Komisarjevsky: Yeah, once again Steve's racing upstairs.

Det. Vitello: He's racing up the stairs?

Komisarjevsky: Up the stairs again.

Det. Vitello: And you can see in the yard, outside?

Komisarjevsky: No, I'm, I'm walking into, into the house.

Det. Vitello: Oh, you're coming back in to see where he went?

Komisarjevsky: Yeah, I was like well, where the hell did he go?

Det. Vitello: What is he doing?

Komisarjevsky: He's racing up the stairs, and uh, I wasn't sure what he had at first, until he comes racing back down the stairs, and he throws one of the empty bottles into the kitchen.

Det. Vitello: Empty bottles of?

Komisarjevsky: Of, of, gasoline.

Det. Vitello: Of gasoline, so he went back up with another bottle of gas?

Komisarjevsky: With another bottle of gas.

Det. Vitello: So how many's that, 3 or 4?

Komisarjevsky: 4 all together.

Det. Vitello: Okay, so there's 4, he got, he went back up with the last bottle?

Komisarjevsky: That's correct.

STOP THE INTRUDER™ | KNOWLEDGE IS THE BEST PROTECTION™

Det. Vitello: And what did he do with it?

Komisarjevsky: I wasn't up there, and uh, I'm assuming, I was hoping that he was just pouring it into the office because, we didn't pour any gasoline, or he didn't pour any gasoline in, in the office. You know and, we had spent a lot of time sitting in the chairs in there.

Det. Vitello: (Not audible) into rooms unless you were either, correct?

Komisarjevsky: That's correct.

Det. Vitello: So you have no idea what he did with the gasoline?

Komisarjevsky: No, I can't say for sure what he did with it, um.

Det. Vitello: He didn't tell you?

Komisarjevsky: He did not say anything at all and I'm, I'm screaming at this point, we gotta get out of here um, this is madness. We finally uh, race out, race out the door, out back. Um, I have the key. I get, I get into the car and I start it up, and as I'm starting it up, Steve is just coming around the corner, (not audible) um, he poured the rest of the house. Um, he's stumbling with this oversized pack of matches, trying to light one.

Det. Vitello: Okay

Komisarjevsky: And he gets through two of them, and none of them are lighting, and I keep telling him we gotta go, we gotta go, we gotta go. And I can still see this person in the grass, watching us.

Det. Vitello: Okay

Komisarjevsky: And um, he barely gets one lit and like, like, flicks it.

STOP THE INTRUDER™ | KNOWLEDGE IS THE BEST PROTECTION™

Det Vitello: Yup.

Komisarjevsky: And I, I see it sailing, I see the puddle of gasoline that was sitting on the tile floor in the kitchen, and the entire kitchen just erupts.

Det. Vitello: Ignites

Komisarjevsky: Yeah, there was like a sea of flames.

Det. Vitello: One match, just one match lit?

Komisarjevsky: One yeah, uh, uh the, the third one that he tried,

Det. Vitello: Okay, he was pretty unsuccessful, the third one lights, ignites?

Komisarjevsky: The third one lights, ignites the pool of gasoline in the kitchen and it travels like, through, you can see it travel down the front hallway.

Det. Vitello: Towards, towards where the mother would be or?

Komisarjevsky: No, towards where the stairway would be. .

Det. Vitello: Okay

Komisarjevsky: Um, I was, I had already, had my back turned and I'm running to the door because I knew that the couch that the mom was um, dead against uh, was doused. And I'm thinking, my mind its, its confined space, confined space with gas vapors everywhere. I'm thinking like, one of those action movies, like blowouts the windows.

Det. Vitello: Windows?

Komisarjevsky: Yeah, so, I'm racing out the door and uh, I reach around the corner and jump into a car. Put the key into the ignition, and I start it up. And uh, just as I start it up, Steve comes running out. And uh, jumps into the passenger side, and then I throw it in reverse. The vehicle is in reverse, and I hear uh, a cop's siren and then I look in my rear view and there's an unmarked car, just pulling up and blocking the, the driveway.

Det. Vitello: Okay

Komisarjevsky: Um, which I proceeded to hit and um, and.

Det. Vitello: The unmarked car?

Komisarjevsky: The unmarked car and, was, when I hit it, it sort of jerked me, in which, I turned the wheel in, in sort of, in this crazy arc, up into, and I uh, backwards, driving backwards into the curve, and I went fast into the bushes.

Det. Vitello: Now, at this point, is the house fully on fire? Can you tell if the house is on fire?

Komisarjevsky: I, I wasn't even looking.

Det. Vitello: You didn't know at this time?

Komisarjevsky: So, so I could hear the fire alarm going off,

Det. Vitello: Okay

Komisarjevsky: Or a smoke detector uh, going off.

Det. Vitello: Okay

Komisarjevsky: I figured that was going to happen anyway, because the kitchen was fully in flames.

Det. Vitello: On fire. When you left, the kitchen was actually in flames?

Komisarjevsky: Yes

STOP THE INTRUDER™ | KNOWLEDGE IS THE BEST PROTECTION™

Det. Vitello: Okay

Komisarjevsky: The whole hallway and kitchen was in flames.

Det. Vitello: So you back up, you hit the cruiser, you hit the unmarked, you try and go forward?

Komisarjevsky: Um, I got caught up in some bushes and I was trying to put it in drive, and for whatever reason I just, it wasn't happening. I couldn't figure out how to drive anymore. Like, I was just panic stricken, and I didn't know how to drive. I literally forgot how to drive. And Steve grabs the uh, the shifter and throws it in drive and yells gas it. And uh, which I did. And uh, took off, off the curve and onto the street. And uh, you know, looking around at this, this is what happens in like, slow mo.

And I'm looking around, there was cops everywhere, and every single gun was like, trained like, right at my head. And uh, I was like, I'm gonna die today. Either their going or I'm going away for the rest of my life, or I'm going to die.

Det. Vitello: Okay, now, now you're, you're going down the street, in the car, you're driving the, the homeowner's vehicle.

Komisarjevsky: That's correct.

Det. Vitello: You already hit the unmarked, you drove through the front lawn, headed up the street and.

Komisarjevsky: Like uh, towards like, this little bend uh, in the road and there's two um, Cheshire police cars uh, parked you know, barricading the road.

Det. Vitello: Yep

Komisarjevsky: Uh, and then suddenly that an uh, officer uh, with a rifle uh, trained right on me, some other officers off to the side.

STOP THE INTRUDER™ | KNOWLEDGE IS THE BEST PROTECTION™

Det Vitello: Did you try to run him over?

Komisarjevsky: Um, I wasn't trying to specifically run him over, but I was trying to get away.

Det. Vitello: You weren't stopping?

Komisarjevsky: No, I wasn't stopping. I was, I, I had to get through those police cars, there's no other way out.

Det. Vitello: Did you hit the officer?

Komisarjevsky: I sure hope not.

Det. Vitello: Okay, you don't know if you did or not? Okay, did you hit the cruisers?

Komisarjevsky: I certainly hit the cruisers.

Det. Vitello: And then what?

Komisarjevsky: Um, the air bags deployed, I then uh. It got really blurry for a little bit and all I can hear in, like the distance, echo, was my hands out of the car uh, get out of the car, hands out of the car, come out slowly um, then it sort of, it felt like an eternity uh. I sort of, slowly complied and got out of the car and laid down, face, face down on the pavement.

Det. Vitello: Did you say anything to the police officers at that time?

Komisarjevsky: Um, there were a lot of questions being thrown at me uh, and I was still like uh, you know, what do I do, what do I do, what do I do. um, finally um, one of the officers had finally gotten close enough for he was up uh, putting the handcuffs on, then he asked me, how many people uh, were in the house and who, was there, is there any other accomplices? I said there's absolutely no other accomplices. There's just me and him. And that there's uh, three people in the house uh, one of which I thought was dead um.

Det. Vitello: Referring to the mother?

Komisarjevsky: Referring to the mother, that's correct. Um, he again asked uh, how many people were in the house or something to that effect? And I said uh, two girls in the upstairs bedroom uh, front facing bedrooms uh, and that they were still alive. Um, and then he got on the radio or called or radioed it in.

Del. Medina: Did you tell him the house was on fire?

Komisarjevsky: Um, I didn't because I, I knew that he already knew, because he was just, just talking to a civilian or somebody was mentioning that to him on the radio. Um, and that's why I said to him, the, the two front bedrooms, there, there right there, there's two windows for each room, the, the only two front bedrooms there.

Det. Vitello: So at that point, you were, you were, you were basically caught and you were detained.

Komisarjevsky: That's correct.

Det Vitello: Arrested here but, you were transported here, uh, once you got here, I just want to reiterate the fact that I asked you early on, and when I mentioned this at the beginning of the tape, I asked you if you had any allergies, illnesses or were under the influence of drugs or alcohol. And you said, you were not; you were not allergic to anything, correct?

Komisarjevsky: No, no, I'm allergic to uh, aspirin.

Det. Vitello: Oh, you said aspirin, correct.

Komisarjevsky: Right

STOP THE INTRUDER™ | KNOWLEDGE IS THE BEST PROTECTION™

Det Vitello: We provided you with lunch and that was part of the reason I had asked you, McDonald's, you had soda, coffee, uh

Det. Medina: Cheeseburgers.

Det. Vitello: Cheeseburgers and you were provided use of the bathroom, correct. And this statement, and the other statement, other written statement, all of that was voluntary and un-coerced by us. This is, your doing this of your own free will?

Komisarjevsky: Yes

Det. Vitello: Correct?

Komisarjevsky: Yeah, and I feel they deserved it, you know. They earned this and uh, I fucked up.

Det. Vitello: Absolutely, you're absolutely right. Alright, what's going to happen Josh is, having said all that um, this statement has been recorded as you know. It will be transcribed into a typewritten form. Um, after this you will be asked to read and sign the typewritten statement which is your statement. Is that agreeable to you?

Komisarjevsky: Yes

Det. Vitello: Okay, Is there anything you want to add? You kind of just said it, that you, you screwed up and the family was,

Komisarjevsky: It wasn't supposed to be like this, it was strictly, strictly go to the bank and leave.

Det. Vitello: As far, as far as your statement, your statement's been truthful that, it's, you're not saying that you strangled anybody and you're not saying you, you lit the match, you're not saying that you poured the gas.

Komisarjevsky: Right

STOP THE INTRUDER™ | KNOWLEDGE IS THE BEST PROTECTION™

Det. Vitello: But, obviously you were there, you did all the other things that you, you admit to assaulting the father?

Komisarjevsky: I, I, I did assault the father um.

Det. Vitello: And you had sexual uh, contact with the daughter?

Komisarjevsky: Yes

Det. Vitello: Okay.

Komisarjevsky: So, um I, it's, I, I adamantly deny that any kind of, of strangulation or any, any of that.

Det. Medina: Did you helped bind them up, tying them up, tie them up?

Komisarjevsky: Yes, I admit that I did.

Det. Vitello: You admitted freely to that.

Komisarjevsky: Yeah.

Det. Vitello: O kay,

Det. Medina: And shutting the doors?

Komisarjevsky: When I go back in to shut the doors, I was hoping to buy them time, you know, obviously.

Det. Medina: You know they're alive in the house!

Komisarjevsky: Obviously, I should have done better.

Det. Vitello: Okay, Thank you Joshua. And the time is now 6:28 or 1828 in military time. This concludes the taped statement of Joshua Komisarjevsky.

Komisarjevky and Hayes were convicted and are on death row.

STOP THE INTRUDER™ | KNOWLEDGE IS THE BEST PROTECTION™

Resource List - Alphabetical

1st Choice Locksmith LLC - (L)
17117 Westheimer
Suite: 31
Houston TX 77082
www.houston1stchoicelocksmith.com

1Time Inc. - (A)
949 Empire Mesa Way
Henderson VA 89011

24 Hr Lock & Key - (L)
P.O. Box 38222
Houston TX 77091
https://24hrlocksmith.net

A -1 Locksmith & Security Ctr - (L)
1707 E. Weber Drive
Suite 1 Tempe AZ 85281
www.a1locksmith.com

A & A Lock Service - (L)
633 S 3rd Ave
Wausau WI 54401
www.a-a-lock.com

A & E Lock and Key - (L)
dba GLS Locksmith
www.glslocksmith.net

A & E Locksmith - (L)
Albuquerque NM 87111
www.aelocksmith.com

A Absolute Security Tech - (L)
www.aasecuritytech.com

A Act Fast Locksmith - (L)
16621 SE 82nd Drive
Clackamas OR 97015
www.aactfastlocksmith.com

A All-Safe Safe & Lock Inc - (L)
1141 East Blue Heron
Riviera Beach FL 33404
www.yoursecurityexperts.com

A American Key & Safe / A Top
Notch Locksmith - (L)
6055 E Southern Ave #103
Mesa AZ 85206
www.americankeyandsafe.com

A B Bonded Locksmiths Co Inc - (L)
4344 Montgomery Road
Cincinnati OH 45212
www.ablocks.com/ index.php

A Dave's Lock & Safe - (L)
2019 Emerson Ave. No.
Minneapolis MN 55411
www.adaveslock.com

A Professional Locks - (L)
940 N Alma School Rd
Chandler AZ 85224
www.aprofessionallocks.com

A W Gifford Inc (Since 1866) - (L)
11 Lyman Street
Springfield MA 1103
www.giffordlock.com

A-1 Key & Lock LLC - (L)
2289 Louisville Ave
Monroe LA 71201
www.a1keyandlock.net/index.htm

A-1 Lock & Key Inc - (L)
1933 Dawson Road
Albany GA 31707
www.keyedup.com

STOP THE INTRUDER™ | KNOWLEDGE IS THE BEST PROTECTION™

A-1 Locksmith Inc - (L)
3005 Nolensville Pike
Nashville TN 37211
www.a1locksmith247.com

A-1 Mobile Lock & Key - (L)
1956 South Burlington Blvd.
Burlington WA 98233
www.a1mobilelock.com

A-A Bowman Lock Safe & Key - (L)
36036 Airport Drive
Lebanon OR 97355
www.aabowmanlock.com

A-Max Security Solutions Inc - (L)
9050 SW Barbur Blvd.
Portland OR 97219
www.amaxsecurity.com

A-Paul's Lock Service - (L)
9S020 Frontage Rd.
Willowbrook IL 60527
www.paulslocksmithservice.com

A1 Security Center - (L)
13 Coffman Avenue
Malvern PA 19355
www.a1securitycenter.com

AA Lock & Key Inc - (L)
1055 Colonel Ledyard Hwy.
Ledyard CT 6339
www.aalockkey.com

AAA Locksmith Solutions - (L)
3219 columbia pike
Arlington VA 22204
www.servicelocksmith.com

AAA Systems - (L)
1101 Shive Lane
Bowling Green KY 42103
www.aaasystems.com

AAA-1 Lock & Key - (L)
1507 N. Midland Blvd
Nampa ID 83651
www.aaa1lock.com

Aable Locksmith - (L)
47 Marlboro Drive
Milford CT 6461
www.aablelocksmiths.com

Aames Lock & Safe Co - (L)
818 W Chapman Ave
Orange CA 92868
www.aameslock.com

Aaron Neil's Locksmith Service - (L)
253 Russell Rd
Fulton NY 13069
www.aaronneilslocksmithservice.com

Aaron's Lock Service - (L)
3757 Gulf Shores Pkwy Ste E
Gulf Shores AL 36542
www.aaronslockservice.com

Abbey Locksmiths Inc - (L)
1558 2nd Ave
New York NY 10028
www.abbeylock.com

ABC Lock & Key Inc - (L)
2424 Nolensville Pike
Nashville TN 37211
www.456lock.com

Able Locksmiths - (L)
511 E. Northern Lights
Anchorage AK 99503
www.ablelocksmith.net

About Town Lock & Safe Co - (L)
2404 N. Dixie Hwy.
Fort Lauderdale FL 33305
www.abouttownlockandsafe.liveonatt.com

STOP THE INTRUDER™ | KNOWLEDGE IS THE BEST PROTECTION™

Acadian Monitoring Services - (A)
P.O. Box 93088
Lafayette LA 70509
www.acadian.com/site486.php

Access Safe & Lock Co - (L)
5532 US HWY 98 North
Lakeland FL 33809
www.accesssafeandlock.com

Accurate Security Pro's Inc. - (L)
9919 Hibert St Suite D
San Diego CA 92131
www.accuratesecuritypros.com

Ace & Fathers Lock & Safe - (L)
7303 Timmons Street
Pittsville MD 21850
www.locksmithmdde.com

Ace Locksmithing - (L)
680 Island Ford RD.
Statesville NC 28625
www.ace-locksmithing.com

Ackerman Security Systems - (A)
1346 Oakbrook Drive
Suite 175 Atlanta GA 30093
www.ackermansecurity.com

ACME Locksmith - (L)
2735 E Main St STE 10
Mesa AZ 85213
www.acmelocksmith.com

Acme Locksmith Service - (L)
261B East Main Street
Oceanport NH 7757
www.acmelocksmithnj.com

Acme SecuritySolutions - (L)
P.O. Box 17944
Tampa FL 33682
www.affordablelock.com

Acoma Locksmith Service - (L)
421 Perry St
Castle Rock CO 80104
www.acomalocksmithservice.com

Acorn Safe & Lock - (L)
409 Lake Avenue
Lake Worth FL 33460
www.acornlock.com

Action Locksmith - (L)
245 East 3900 South
Salt Lake City UT 84107
www.actionlocksmith.com

Action Security Inc. - (L)
243 East 5th Ave.
Anchorage AK 99501
www.actionsecurity.com

ADI - (A)
263 Old Country Rd.
Melville Road NY 11747
www.adiglobal.com

ADS Security LP - (A)
3001 Armory Dr.
Suite 100
Nashville TN 37204
www.adssecurity.com/index.aspx

ADT Security Services Inc. - (A)
One Town Center Rd.
Boca Raton FL 33486
www.adt.com

Advanced Lock & Safe - (L)
PO Box 10532
Fort Mohave AZ 86427
www.advancedlocknsafe.com

Advanced Lock and Key LLC - (L)
10966 W Highlander Rd
Boise ID 83709
www.unlockidaho.com

STOP THE INTRUDER™ | KNOWLEDGE IS THE BEST PROTECTION™

AES-IntelliNet - (A)
285 Newbury St.
Peabody MA 1960
www.aes-intellinet.com

Affiliated Central Inc - (A)
354 Neptune Ave.
Sheepshead NY 11235
www.affiliated.com

Affordable Lock Express - (L)
15118 E Sprague Avenue
Spokane WA 99037
www.affordablelockexpress.com

Affordable Locksmith & Son - (L)
1018 Lunalilo St
Honolulu HI 96822
www.affordablelocksmithandsons.com

Agoura Lock Technologies Inc - (L)
29134 Roadside Drive Unit #108
Agoura Hills CA 91301
www.agouralock.com

AGP Lock & Security LLC - (L)
3481 Dixie Highway
Suite 109
Franklin OH 45005
www.agplock.com

AHC Safe &Lock/Ormond Hdwe - (L)
54 W. Granada Blvd.
Ormond Beach FL 32174
www.ahcsafe.com

Alabama Lock & Key - (L)
1800 Green Springs Highway South
Birmingham AL 35205
www.alabamalock.com

Alarm Center Inc. - (A)
PO Box 3401
Lacey WA 98509
www.acimonitoring.com

Alarm Central LLC - (A)
5510 E 31st St.
Kansas City MO 64128
www.alarmcentral.net

Alarm Central Station Inc. - (A)
15050 SW Koll Pkwy.
Suite 1A
Beaverton OR 97006
www.alceste.com

Alarm Central Inc. - (A)
680 Hancock St.
Quincy MA 2170
www.alarmcentral.com

Alarm Detection Systems Inc. - (A)
1111 Church Rd.
Aurora IL 60505
www.adsalarm.com

Alarm Lock Systems Inc. - (A)
345 Bayview Ave.
Amityville NY 11701
www.alarmlock.com

Alarm Monitoring Services - (A)
1401 Royal Ave.
Monroe LA 71201
www.monitor1.com

Alarm Security Group LLC - (A)
12301 Kiln Ct. Suite A
Beltsville MD 20705
www.asgsecurity.com

Alarm Tech Central Service - (A)
56 Enter Lane
Islandia, NY 11749
www.alarm.tc

STOP THE INTRUDER™ | KNOWLEDGE IS THE BEST PROTECTION™

Alarm.com - (A)
8150 Leesburg Pike
Suite 1400
Vienna VA 22182
www.alarm.com

Alarmco Inc. - Boise - (A)
1675 N. Mitchell
Boise ID 83704
www.alarmcoinc.com

Alarmco Inc. - Las Vegas - (A)
2007 Las Vegas Blvd. South
Las Vegas NV 89104
www.alarmco.com

AlarmWatch - (A)
P.O. Box 867
Merced CA 95340
www.alarmwatch.com

Alcatraz Locksmith - (L)
610 E Bell Rd Ste 2-372
Phoenix AZ 85022
www.alcatrazlock.com

Alden Lock & Security Inc - (L)
48 Lantern Rd
Belmont MA 2178
www.aldenlockandsecurity.com

Alert Holdings Group Inc. - (A)
2668 Waiwai Loop
Honolulu HI 96819
www.alertalarmhawaii.com

All Access Lock And Security - (L)
4F Adrian Court Cortlandt
Manor NY 10567
www.allaccesslock.com

All Alert Alarm & Locksmiths- (L)
P.O. Box 5 Putnam
Valley NY 10579
www.allalertalarm.com

All American Monitoring - (A)
1375 N. East Ave.
Sarasota FL 34237
www.allamericanmonitoring.com

All City Locksmith - (L)
161 Del Vale Avenue
San Francisco CA 94127
www.allcitylocksmith.com

All Pro Alarm LLC - (L)
P.O. Box 33
Tiger GA 30576
www.allproalarm.com

All Secure Inc. - (L)
107 Independence Drive
Warner Robins GA 31088
www.allsecuresafe.com

Allied Lock Safe - (L)
709 N Shipley St
Wilmington DE 19801
www.allied-lock.com

Allsafe & Lock Inc - (L)
399 So. Main St.
Manchester NH 3102
www.allsafenh.com

Allstate Security Industries Inc. - (A)
3433 Plains Blvd.
Amarillo TX 79102
www.allstatesecurity.com

AlS Locksmith Service - (L)
1911 West Broadway Rd.
Mesa AZ 85202
www.locksmith-mesa.com

Altronix Corp. - (A)
140 58th St. Bldg. A 3 West
Brooklyn NY 11220
www.altronix.com

Always Secure Locksmithing - (L)
12621 N 39Th Way
Phoenix AZ 85032
www.alwayssecurelocksmithing.com

American Alarm & Communications Inc. - (A)
297 Broadway
Arlington MA 2474
www.americanalarm.com

American Alarm Systems Inc. - (A)
1101 S. Grand Ave.
Suite G
Santa Ana CA 92705
www.800amalarm.com

American Atlas Locksmith - (L)
51105 Washington Oakland Macomb and St.
Cl MI 48047
www.atlaslocksmith.com

American Burglary & Fire Inc. - (A)
507 Rudder Rd.
Fenton MO 63026
www.abfsecurity.com

American Lock & Key Inc. - (L)
1974 Mall Boulevard
Auburn AL 36830
www.american-lockandkey.com

American Locksmiths - (L)
8619 Manchester Rd
St.Louis MO 63144
www.fixmylock.com

American Locksmiths LLC - (L)
2120 E. Moreland Blvd
Waukesha WI 53186
www.autolocksmithing.com

American Pride Services Inc - (L)
501 Wisconsin St Eau
Claire WI 54702
www.changemylocks.com

AMERIKEYS - (L)
16274 San Pedro Ave (Hwy 281 N.)
San Antonio TX 78232
www.amerikeys.com

Amherst Alarm Inc. - (A)
435 Lawrence Bell Dr.
Amherst NY 14221
www.amherstalarm.com/web

Amherst Lockworks - (L)
64 Montague Rd
Amherst MA 1002
www.amherstlockworks.net

Amity Safe & Lock Co - (L)
1336 Whalley Ave
New Haven CT 6515
www.amitysafeandlock.com

Anderson Lock & Safe LLC - (L)
6146 N. 35th Ave. #101
Phoenix AZ 85017
www.andersonlockandsafe.com

Anderson Lock Company - (L)
850 Oakton Street
Des Plaines IL 60018
www.andersonlock.com

Angel Fire Lock & Key Inc. - (L)
PO Box 411
Angel Fire NM 87710
www.angelfirelockandkey.com

Anytime Lock & Key - (L)
6216 Fairview Avenue
Boise ID 83704
www.anytimelockandkey.com

STOP THE INTRUDER™ | KNOWLEDGE IS THE BEST PROTECTION™

Anytime Lock & Safe - (L)
5050 State Hwy 303 #109
Bremerton WA 98311
www.anytimelock.com

Anytime Lock & Safe Inc - (L)
PO Box 911
LaMarque TX 77568
www.anytimelockandsafe.com

Anytime Lock and Safe - (L)
306 N Evergreen St
Chandler AZ 85225
www.anytimelock.net

Apex Lock & Key - (L)
PO Box 1041
Apex NC 27502
www.apexlockandkey.com

Apex Lock & Safe Service - (L)
4697 Tote Road
Comins MI 48619
www.apexlock.com

Archway Locksmith - (L)
1218 North 17th Street
Swansea IL 62226
www.archwaylocksmith.com

Area Safe & Lock - (L)
3301 Mt Vernon Ave
Alexandria VA 22305
www.areasafe.com/index.htm

Areawide Lock & Key - (L)
106 Arrow Head
Hilton Head SC 29928
www.areawidedecorativehardware.com

ARG Locks - (L)
Bowling Green KY 42104
www.arglocks.com

Arizona School Of Locksmith - (L)
3832 West Davidson Lane
Phoenix AZ 85051
www.azschooloflocksmithing.org

ARK Security & Electronics - (L)
47 East Main Street
Rexburg ID 83440
www.arksecurity.com

Armor Lock & Key - (L)
www.alexlocks.com

Arnold's Safe & Lock Co. Inc. - (L)
3615 Haddonfield Rd.
Pennsauken NJ 8109
www.arnoldslock.com

Arrowhead Lock & Safe Inc. - (L)
2211 Marietta Blvd. NW
Atlanta GA 30318
www.arrowheadlockandsafe.com

Assa Technical Services Inc - (L)
6174 State Route 88
Finleyville PA 15332
www.assatechnicalservicesinc.com

Assured Security Inc. - (L)
6144 Olson Memorial Highway
Golden Valley MN 55422
www.assuredsecurityinc.com

Atlantic Coast Alarm Inc. - (A)
5100 Harding Highway
Suite 203
Mays Landing NJ 8330
www.atlanticcoastalarm.com

Atlantic Locksmiths - (L)
549 Killingly St.
Johnston RI 2919
www.locksmithri.com/about.htm

STOP THE INTRUDER™ | KNOWLEDGE IS THE BEST PROTECTION™

Atlas Security Service Inc./Alarm Control Center - (A)
1309 E Republic Rd. Suite B
Springfield MO 65804
www.atlassecurity.com

AvantGuard Monitoring - (A)
4699 Harrison Blvd. Suite 100
Ogden UT 84403
www.agmonitoring.com

Aviation Lock & Key - (L)
1316 Aviation Blvd
Redondo Beach CA 90278
www.aviationlock.com

Avid Locksmith LLC - (L)
P.O. Box 965
Gilbert AZ 85299
www.avidlocksmith.com

Axis Communications - (A)
9910 N. 47 Pl.
Phoenix AZ 85028
www.axis.com

AZ REO Locksmith - (L)
34315 N 81st St
Scottsdale AZ 85266
www.azreolocksmith.com

Baker T Lock & Key - (L)
3-2600 KAUMUALII HWY 1300
Lihue HI 96766
www.bakertlockandkey.net

Baldino's Lock & Key - (L)
111 Chinquapin Round Rd
Ste 105
Annapolis MD 21401
www.baldinos.com

Baldino's Lock & Key - (L)
1001-B N. Fillmore St
Arlington VA 22201
www.baldinos.com

Bankers Service Co Inc - (L)
604 Suzanne Avenue
St. Paul MN 55126
www.site.bankersserviceco.com

Barcom Inc. - (A)
923 North Belt West
Swansea IL 62226
www.barcominc.com

Barrys City Lock & Safe Co - (L)
1657 Hannington Avenue
Wantagh NY 11793
www.barrylockandsafe.com

Bass Security Services Inc. - (A)
26701 Richmond Rd.
Cleveland OH 44146
www.bass-security.com

Bates Security Lock & Safe - (L)
213 Walton Ave
Lexington KY 40502
www.batessecurity.com

Bay Alarm Co. - (A)
60 Berry Dr.
Pacheco CA 94553
www.bayalarm.com

Bay Cities Lock & Safe Co - (L)
1155 Chess Drive Unit 117
Foster City CA 94404
www.baycitieslock.com

BC Lock & Key Inc - (L)
1537 Brookdale Ave
Charlotte NC 28210
www.bclockandkey.com

STOP THE INTRUDER™ | KNOWLEDGE IS THE BEST PROTECTION™

Bear Lock & Safe Service - (L)
205 Cleveland Ave
Baltimore MD 21222
www.bearlock.com/ALOA_Link.html

Beishir Lock & Security Inc. - (L)
5423 S Lindbergh Blvd
St.Louis MO 63123
www.stlsecurity.com

Benny's Security Solutions - (L)
3245 W Bay to Bay Blvd
Tampa FL 33629
www.bennykey.com

Big Red Locksmiths Inc - (L)
629 N 46th St
Omaha NE 68132
www.bigredlocksmiths.com

Bill Lorenz Locksmith - (L)
437 Westside Blvd
Catonville MD 21228
www.lorenzlocks.com

Bill's Key & Lock Service Inc - (L)
148 W. Orion Street Suite C2
Tempe AZ 85283
www.billskey.com

Bill's Lock & Safe Inc - (L)
1001 Pike Avenue North
Little Rock AR 72114
www.billslockandsafe.com

Bill's Locksmith Service Inc. - (L)
W1598 Lee Road
Lee Road WI 54843
www.billslocksmithinc.com

Billy's Lock & Alarm Co. Inc. - (L)
8 Bedford Ave
Brooklyn NY 11222
www.billyslocksmith.com

Birmingham Lock & Key - (L)
P O Box 1289
Meridian MS 39302
www.oddlocks.com

Blackhawk Products - (L)
25913 Road T.5
Dolores CO 81323
www.blackhawk7.com

Blue Knight Lock & Key - (L)
7102 N 11th Ave
Phoenix AZ 85021
www.blueknightlock.com

Blue Ridge Locksmithing - (L)
P.O. Box 272
Charles Town WV 25414
www.blueridgelocksmithing.com

Bob Fraser Security Center - (L)
129 Watchung Ave.
Montclair NJ 7043
www.bob-fraser.com

Bob's Lock n Key - (L)
1166 Hwy 178 W
Midway AR 72651
www.bobslock-n-key.com

Bob's Lock Safe & Key - (L)
3112 W. 3500 So.
West Valley City UT 84119
www.bobslockshop.com

Bold Technologies Ltd. - (A)
421 Windchime Place
Colorado Springs CO 80919
www.boldgroup.com

Bonded Lock & Key - (L)
1321 Bemidji Avenue
Bemidji MN 56601
www.bondedlock.com

Bosch Security Systems Inc. - (A)
130 Perinton Parkway
Fairport NY 14450
www.boschsecurity.us/en-us

Boston Car Keys Inc. - (L)
P.O.Box 489
East Boston MA 2128
www.bostoncarkeys.com/index.html

Bozeman Safe & Lock - (L)
2304 North 7th Ave
Bozeman MT 59715
www.bozemansafeandlock.com

Brad's Safe & Lock Service Inc - (L)
PO Box 675
Reisterstown MD 21136
www.bradssafeandlock.com

Bradford Lock & Key - (L)
PO Box 1702
Denham Springs LA 70727
www.bradfordlockandkey.com

Bradfords Ace Hardware - (L)
231 Main St P.O. Box 760
Hyannis MA 2601
www.bradfordsace.com

Brock Lock & Key - (L)
8014 Elkhart Ave
Lubbock TX 79424
www.brocklockkey.com

Brooks Lock & Key - (L)
411 6th St SE
Decatur AL 35601
www.brookslock.com

Buchanan Ingersoll & Rooney - (A)
301 Grant St.
20th Floor
Pittsburgh PA 15219
www.bipc.com

Buckeye Lock Service - (L)
130 Carter Cir
Boardman OH 44512
www.buckeyelockservice.com

Buckeye Protective Service - (A)
2215 Sixth Street SW
Canton OH 44706
www.buckeyeprotective.com

Buckley's SecuritySmiths - (L)
124 W Tabb St
Petersburg VA 23803
www.securitysmiths.com

Bullet Lock & Safe Co Inc - (L)
181 Broadway
Long Branch NJ 7740
www.bulletlock.com

Burts Security Center Inc - (L)
49 Water Street
Hallowell ME 4347
www.burtsinc.com

C & E Lock & Safe Inc. - (L)
2337 N. College
Fayetteville AR 72703
www.candelockandsafe.com

C.O.P.S. Monitoring - (A)
P.O. Box 836
Williamstown NJ 8094
www.copsmonitoring.com

Calvert Safe & Lock Ltd - (L)
40 Caroline Street
Derby CT 6418
www.calvertsafeandlock.com

Cape Cod Alarm Co. Inc. - (A)
204 Old Townhouse Rd.
West Yarmouth MA 2673
www.capecodalarm.com

STOP THE INTRUDER™ | KNOWLEDGE IS THE BEST PROTECTION™

Captains Lock & Key LLC - (L)
P.O. Box 796 St.
Amant LA 70774
www.captlocknkey.com

CASCO Systems - (A)
40 Rutter Street
Rochester NY 14606
www.cascosecurity.com

Casey Lock & Key Inc - (L)
1117 Southeast 33rd Street
Bentonville AR 72712
www.caseylockandkey.com

Centerpoint Technologies LLC - (A)
2001 S. Hanley Rd. Suite 530
St.Louis MO 63144
www.centerpointtech.com

Centra-Larm Monitoring Inc. - (A)
994 Candia Rd.
Manchester NH 3109
www.centra-larm.com

Central District Alarm Inc. - (A)
6450 Clayton Ave.
St.Louis MO 63139
www.mycda.net

Central Key & Safe Co Inc - (L)
305 N. Market
Wichita KS 67202
www.centralkeyandsafe.com

Central Security and
Communications - (A)
6831 E. 32nd St. Suite 100
Indianapolis IA 46226
www.central-security.net

Central Station Monitoring - (A)
P.O. Box 1005 303 SW Zobrist
Estacada OR 97023
www.csmul.com

CenturyLink Security Systems - (A)
504 Washington St.
Monroe LA 71201
www.centurylink.com

Certified Lock & Access - (L)
3 Germay Drive
Suite 7
Wilmington DE 19804
www.certifiedlockandaccess.com

Charles Stuttig Locksmith Inc - (L)
158 Greenwich Ave
Greenwich CT 6830
www.stuttiglocksmith.com

Charleys Southside Lock/Safe - (L)
5123 S. Peoria
Tulsa OK 74105
www.charleyslock.com

Checkpoint Systems Inc. - (A)
8180 Upland Circle
Chanhassen MN 55317
www.checkpointsystems.com

CheckVideo - (A)
1925 Isaac Newton Square
3rd Floor
Reston VA 20190
www.checkvideo.net

CLC Locksmiths - (L)
2103 Branch Pike Unit 5
Cinnaminson NJ 8077
www.clclocksmiths.com

ClearStar Security Network - (L)
4454 Lopez Ave Port
Townsend WA 98368
www.clearstar.com

STOP THE INTRUDER™ | KNOWLEDGE IS THE BEST PROTECTION™

Cleveland Lock Service Ltd - (L)
2410 Brookview Blvd
Cleveland OH 44134
www.clevelandlockservice.com

Clifton Lock & Key - (L)
8935 Holt Springer Road
Athens AL 35611
www.shoalslocksmith.com

CMS Monitoring - (A)
2211 Route 112
Medford NY 11763
www.cmsmonitoring.com

Coast Safe & Lock Company - (L)
P.O. Box 66257
457 Dauphin Island Parkway
Mobile AL 36606
www.coastsafelock.com

Commercial Door & Hardware - (L)
708 W. 22nd St.
Tempe AZ 85282
www.cdhsecurity.com/index.htm

Commercial Instruments/Alarm Systems Inc. - (A)
2 Summit Ct.
Fishkill NY 12524
www.ciasecurity.com

Communication Service Solutions (CSS) - (A)
301 Maine Street
Suite 301
Enid OK 73701
www.comservicesolutions.com

Comporium Security - (A)
P.O. Box 306
245 E. Main Street
Rock Hill NC 29730
www.comporium.com

CompuKey Lock And Safe - (L)
PO Box 330849
Nashville TN 37203
www.compukeylocksmith.com

ComSouth Monitoring Services - (A)
108 South Lumpkin St.
Hawkinsville GA 31036
www.comsouth.net

Comtronics - (A)
One Comtronics Place
315 Water Street
Jackson MI 49203
www.comtronics.com

Consolidated Security Systems - (L)
510 W Macarthur Blvd.
Oakland CA 94609
www.css510.com

Continental Access - (A)
355 Bayview Avenue
Amityville NY 11701
www.cicaccess.com

Cooperative Response Center - (A)
2000 8th St. NW
Austin MN 55912
www.crc.coop

Counterforce USA - (A)
7700 Gulf Freeway
Houston TX 77017
www.counterforceusa.com

CoverX Corporation - (A)
26600 Telegraph Road
Southfield MI 48033
www.coverx.com

CPI Security Systems - (A)
4200 Sandy Porter Rd.
Charlotte NC 28273
www.cpisecurity.com

STOP THE INTRUDER™ | KNOWLEDGE IS THE BEST PROTECTION™

Crime Alert Monitoring Center - (A)
690 Lenfest Rd.
San Jose CA 95133
www.crimealert.com

Critical Locksmith - (L)
3149 S Larkspur St
Gilbert AZ 85295
www.criticallocksmithaz.com

Cullman Locksmith & Safe Co - (L)
301 3rd Ave. SW.
Cullman AL 35055
www.cullmanlocksmith.com

Curt's Lock & Key Svc Inc - (L)
1102 Main Ave
Fargo ND 58103
www.curtslock.com

Custom Alarm Communications (A)
1661 Greenview Drive SW
Rochester MN 55902
www.custom-alarm.com

Custom Security Systems - (A)
690 Oak Villa Blvd.
Baton Rouge LA 70815
www.customsecuritysystems.com

Cypress Lock And Safe - (L)
5663 Lincoln Ave.
Suite A
Cypress CA 90630
www.cypresslockandsafe.com

Dan's Lock & Key Co - (L)
1639 Greenland Park
Shelbyville KY 40065
www.danslock.com

Dave's Lock & Key - (L)
4314 Dover Dr
Frederick MD 21703
www.daveslockandkey.net

Daves Lock Shop - (L)
111 3rd St South
Nampa ID 83651
www.daveslockshop.com

David's Lock & Key - (L)
106 Kent Street
Montgomery AL 36109
www.davidslocknkey.com

Davis Lock & Safe - (L)
PO Box 6507
Beaverton OR 97007
www.davislock.com

Dayton Lock Co - (L)
324 West Lancaster Avenue (Rt. 30)
Wayne PA 19087
www.daytonlock.com

Dean's Village Locksmith Inc - (L)
4225 N. Scottsdale Road
Scottsdale AZ 85251
www.locksmithaz.com

Desert Locksmiths - (L)
836 W. 5th St.
Reno NV 89503
www.desertlock.com

Devcon Security Services - (A)
3880 N 28th Terrace
Hollywood FL 33020
www.devconsecurity.com

DGA Security Systems Inc. - (A)
580 5th Ave.
New York NY 10036
www.dgasecurity.com

DICE Corporation - (A)
1410 S. Valley Center Dr.
Bay City MI 48706
www.dicecorp.com

STOP THE INTRUDER™ | KNOWLEDGE IS THE BEST PROTECTION™

Diebold Inc. - (A)
3800 Tabs Dr. Dept. 8317-S
Uniontown OH 44685
www.diebold.com/dnpssec

DigiCom Inc. - (A)
P.O. Box 17172
Tampa FL 33682
www.digicom.us

Dispatch Center Ltd. - (A)
101 Galleria Fair
San Antonio TX 78232
www.dispatchcenter.net

DIY Alarm Forum - (A)
63 Pondview Dr.
Clyde NC 28721
www.diyalarmforum.com

DMC Security Services Inc. - (A)
4455 W. 147th St.
Midlothian IL 60445
www.dmcsecurity.com

DMP - (A)
2500 N. Partnership Blvd.
Springfield MO 65803
www.dmp.com
www.securecomwireless.com/

Doaks Lock & Key - (L)
8800 Glacier Hwy #119
Juneau AK 99801
www.doaks.com

Don's Mobil Lock Shop - (L)
323 E Daws
Norman OK 73069
www.donsmobillockshop.com

Door Systems Inc. - (L)
9434 Chesapeake Drive
Suite 1210
San Diego CA 92123
www.doorsystemsinc.net

Doorway Solutions - (L)
3333 East 52nd Ave.
Denver CO 80216
www.doorwaysolutions.com

Douglas Lock & Safe - (L)
PO Box 90571
Nashville TN 37209
www.douglaslockandsafe.com

Doyle Security Systems Inc. - (A)
792 Calkins Rd.
Rochester NY 14623
https://www.godoyle.com

Duman's Lock & Safe Inc. - (L)
6779 Engle Road Suite L
Middleburg Heights OH 44130
www.dumanslock.com

Dunbar Alarm Systems Inc. - (A)
7675 Canton Center Dr.
Baltimore MD 21224
www.dunbaralarm.com

Dunlap Locksmith Inc - (L)
60 White St
Red Bank NJ 7701
www.dunlaplocksmith.com

Dynamark Monitoring - (A)
525 Northern Avenue
Hagerstown MD 21742
www.dynamarkmonitoring.com

E-Z Key Locksmith Inc - (L)
811 S. Montesano Street
Westport WA 98595
www.ezkeylocksmith.com

STOP THE INTRUDER™ | KNOWLEDGE IS THE BEST PROTECTION™

Eagle Locksmith LLC - (L)
1827 E. Indian School Rd
Phoenix AZ 85016
www.eaglelocksmithaz.com

East Point Cycle & Key Inc - (L)
2834 Church Street
East Point GA 30344
www.cycleandkey.com

Easter Lock & Access Systems - (L)
1713 E Joppa Rd
Baltimore MD 21234
www.easterslock.com

Eastern Safe & Lock Co Inc - (L)
6826 Hill Park Drive
Lorton VA 22079
www.easternsafe.com

ECam Secure - (A)
436 West Walnut St.
Gardena CA 90248
www.ecamsecure.com

Electronix Systems Central Station Alarms Inc. - (A)
1555 New York Ave.
Huntingdon Station NY 11746
www.electronixsystems.com

Ellijay Telephone Co./ETC Communications - (A)
224 Dalton Street
Ellijay GA 30540
www.northganow.com

Emerald City Locksmith - (L)
1229 W 7th Ave
Eugene OR 97402
https://sites.google.com/site/ecleugene

Emerald City Locksmith - (L)
1229 7th Avenue
Eugene OR 97402
www.emeraldlock.com

EMERgency 24 - (A)
999 East Touhy Suite 500
Des Plaines IL 60018
www.emergency24.com

Emergency Lock & Key Service - (L)
8407 Tachbrook Rd
Baltimore MD 21236
www.elkssafeservice.com

Engineered Protection Systems- (A)
750 Front Ave. NW
Grand Rapids MI 49504
www.epssecurity.com

Englewood Lock and Safe - (L)
4310 S Broadway
Englewood CO 80113
www.englewoodlock.com/compact

ESC Central Inc. - (A)
3050 Guess Park Dr.
Birmingham AL 35215
www.esccentral.com

Estridge Lock & Key Co - (L)
209 N. Rutherford Street
Wadesboro NC 28170
www.estridgelockandkey.com

Excel Central Inc. - (A)
2820 May Street
Cincinnati OH 45206
www.U2canxl.fuse.net

F.E. Moran Inc. Alarm and Monitoring Services - (A)
201 W. University Ave.
Champaign IL 61820
www.femoranalarm.com

Federal Lock & Safe Inc - (L)
5130 Wilson Boulevard
Arlington VA 22205
www.flslock.com

Federal Response Center - (A)
2500 North Airport Commerce Dr.
Springfield MO 65803
www.federalprotection.com

Fenton Lock & Safe - (L)
17195 Silver Parkway #305
Fenton MI 48430
www.fentonlockandsafe.com

Finger Lakes Lock & Security - (L)
512 East Ave
Newark NY 14513
www.fingerlakeslock.com

Fire-Lite Alarms by Honeywell - (A)
One Fire-Lite Pl.
Northford CT 6472
www.acscorp.honeywell.com

First Alarm Security Services - (A)
1111 Estates Dr.
Aptos CA 95003
www.firstalarm.com

Fleenor Security Systems - (A)
21 North Ave.
Burlington MA 1803
www.fleenorss.com

Florence Lock & Key - (L)
51 East St
Easthampton MA 1027
www.florencelock.com/index

Floyd Total Security - (L)
9036 Grand Ave S
Bloomington MN 55420
www.floydtotalsecurity.com

Foothill Locksmiths Inc - (L)
595 East Lewelling Blvd.
Hayward CA 94541
www.foothilllocksmithsinc.com

Foster Brothers Security Systems - (L)
555 South Murphy Ave.
Sunnyvale CA 94086
www.fosterbrothers.com

Foty Lock & Safe - (L)
619 E. Blue Earth Avenue
P.O. Box 464
Fairmont MN 56031
www.fotylock.com

Fred's Lock and Key - (L)
1005 3rd Ave SW Suite B
Cedar Rapids IA 52404
www.fredslockandkey.com

G4S Monitoring & Data Center Inc. - (A)
21 North Ave.
Burlington MA 1803
www.g4s.us/en-us

General Alarm - (A)
8227 Northwest Blvd. #270
Indianapolis IN 46278
www.genalarm.com

George's Locks & Security - (L)
884 Old Hollow Rd
N Ferrisburg VT 5473
www.georgeslocks.com

Gillmore Security Systems - (A)
26165 Broadway Ave.
Cleveland OH 44146
www.gillmoresecurity.com

STOP THE INTRUDER™ | KNOWLEDGE IS THE BEST PROTECTION™

Gladd Security Inc - (L)
5390 South Bay Rd
Syracuse NY 13212
www.gladdsecurity.com

Glens Keys Inc - (L)
1147 South State Street
Salt Lake City UT 84111
www.glenskey.com

Golden Bear Lock & Safe Inc - (L)
7445 Daron Court
Plain City OH 43064
www.goldenbearlock.com

Grah Safe & Lock Inc - (L)
939 University Ave
San Diego CA 92103
www.grahsecurity.com

Grand Central Station - (A)
23194 Kidder St.
Hayward CA 94545
www.gcsmonitoring.com

Grott Locksmith Center Inc - (L)
1112 Winchester Road
Lexington KY 40505
www.grottsecurity.com

Guardian Alarm Co. of Michigan Inc. - (A)
20800 Southfield Rd.
Southfield MI 48075
www.guardianalarm.com

Guardian Lock And Key - (L)
N/A Starkville MS 39759
www.guardianlockandkeyms.com

Guardian Protection Services - (A)
174 Thorn Hill Rd.
Warrendale PA 15086
www.guardianprotection.com

Guardian Security Group Inc - (L)
5424 South Tacoma Way
Tacoma WA 98409
www.securityrus.com

Hansen Locksmithing - (L)
300 W 4th St
Yankton SD 57078
www.hansenlocksmithing.com

Harbison Lock & Key Inc. - (L)
1704 28th Ave S
Homewood AL 35209
www.harbisonlock.com/ct.asp

Hartford Safe & Lock - (L)
36 Silas Deane Highway
Wethersfield CT 6109
www.locksmithhartfordct.com

Hartley Lock & Key - (L)
26 Edrow Rd
Bristol CT 6010
www.hartleylockandkey.com

Havens For Total Security - (L)
459 N. Blackstone Ave
Fresno CA 93701
www.havenslock.com

Heights Key Lock & Safe Inc - (L)
920 San Mateo NE
Albuquerque NM 87108
www.heightskey.com

Henley's Key Service Inc - (L)
117 E Boulder St
Colorado Springs CO 80903
www.henleyskeyservice.com

Holder's Inc - (L)
7027 E 40th St.
Tulsa OK 74145
www.holdersecurity.com

Holmes Electric Security - (A)
127 Hay St.
Fayetteville NC 28302
www.holmeselectricsecurity.com

Honeywell Security Group - (A)
2 Corporate Center Drive Suite 100
P.O. Box 9040
Melville NY 11747
www.security.honeywell.com

Honeywell Security Products - (A)
2 Corporate Center Drive
Suite 100 P.O. Box 9040
Melville NY 11747
www.security.honeywell.com

Hood's Locksmith Service LLC - (L)
176 West Logan St. Box #217
Noblesville IN 46060
www.hoodslock.com

Hoover Lock & Key - (L)
3229 Lorna Road
Hoover AL 35216
www.hooverlockandkeyinc.com

Huizen's Locksmith Ser Inc - (L)
5389 School Avenue
Hudsonville MI 49426
www.huizenslock.com

Hunter Security Inc. - (A)
28228 N. Main St.
Daphne AL 36526
www.huntersecurity.net

I Spinello Locksmiths - (L)
225 S 6th St # B
Rockford IL 61104
www.spinello.com

I-View Now - (A)
1421 E Sunset Rd #2
Las Vegas NV 89119
www.i-viewnow.com

Ingersoll-Rand Security
Technologies - (L)
5417 E. Ebell St.
Long Beach CA 90808
www.integratedsystems.ingersollrand.com

Innovative Business Software - (A)
1320 Greenway Dr.
Suite 850
Irving TX 75038
www.ibsoft-us.com

Integrated Security Inc - (L)
369 Central St Unit 9
Foxboro MA 2035
www.isi-security.com

Interface Security Systems LLC - (A)
3773 Corporate Center Dr.
Earth City MO 63045
www.interfacesystems.com

Interlogix - (A)
8985 Town Center Parkway
Bradenton FL 34202
www.interlogix.com

Intertech Security LLC - (A)
1501 Preble Ave.
Pittsburgh PA 15233
www.intertechsecurity.com

Intertek Testing Services Inc./ETL - (A)
41 Plymouth Street
Fairfield NJ 7004
www.intertek.com

STOP THE INTRUDER™ | KNOWLEDGE IS THE BEST PROTECTION™

247 Interactive Video Security - (A)
2101 Highland Ave. South
Suite 100
Birmingham AL 35205
www.ion247.com

iWatch Communications Inc. - (A)
4970 SW Griffith Dr. #100
Beaverton OR 97005
www.iwatchcomm.com

J & K Security Solutions - (L)
1605 S Park St
Madison WI 53715
www.jksecurity.com

J P Locks Inc. - (L)
1843 Saint Lucia Way
Vista CA 92081
www.jplocks.com

J Webb Lock & Key Svc - (L)
8003 Blue Lick Rd
Louisville KY 40219
www.jwebblockandkey.com

Jack's Security Depot - (L)
6848 East Genesee Street
Fayetteville NY 13066
https://safes-lo.accountsupport.com

JBL Hawaii Ltd - (L)
905 Kokea St
Honolulu HI 96817
www.jblhawaii.com

JK Locksmith Co - (L)
47705 West Rd #B101
Wixom MI 48393
www.jklocksmith.com

John DeCosta Jr Inc - (L)
447 North Main Street
West Bridgewater MA 2379
www.jdecosta.biz

Johnny's Locksmiths - (L)
615 E Andrew Johnson Hwy
1800 Cox Hill Rd
Greensville TN 37745
www.johnnyslocksmith.com/main.html?src=%2F

Johnson Controls - (A)
507 E. Michigan Street M-14A
Milwaukee WI 53201
www.johnsoncontrols.com

JP's Lock & Key - (L)
PO Box 712
Roseville MI 48066
www.jpslockandkey.com

K & L Locksmith - (L)
9540 Hwy 196
Collierville TN 38017
www.kandllocksmith.com

Karpilow Safe & Lock Co - (L)
4490 Main Street
Bridgeport CT 6606
www.karpilowlock.com

KEEDEX Inc - (L)
510 Cameron St
Placentia CA 92870
www.keedex.com

Kenton Brothers Inc - (L)
1718 Baltimore Avenue
Kansas City MO 64108
www.kentonbrothers.com

Kevin Wilson Master Locksmith - (L)
4155 Lawrenceville Highway #8181
Lilburn GA 30047
www.kevinwilsonlocksmith.com

STOP THE INTRUDER™ | KNOWLEDGE IS THE BEST PROTECTION™

Key Concepts Locksmith and Master SafeCracker - (L)
P.O. Box 4774
Salem OR 97302
www.keyconceptslock.com

Keystone Lock & Key Service - (L)
PO Box 270
Clarks Summit PA 18411
www.keystonelockandkey.com

Keyway Lock & Security Company - (L)
3820 W 79th Street
Chicago IL 60652
www.keywaylockandsecurityinc.com

King's Total Security - (L)
3585 E Keswick Rd
Redding CA 96003
www.locksmithredding.com

Kings III of America Inc. - (A)
751 Canyon Drive Suite 100
Coppell TX 75019
www.kingsiii.com

Kleinbard Bell & Brecker LLP - (A)
One Liberty Place 46th Floor
1650 Market Street
Philadelphia PA 19103
www.kleinbard.com

La Jolla Lock & Safe - (L)
1122 Wall Street
La Jolla CA 92037
www.lajollalock.com

Lafayette Locksmith Service Inc - (L)
411 Kaliste Saloom Rd
Lafayette LA 70508
www.lafayettelocksmith.com

Lamar's Lock & Key - (L)
Dothan AL
www.lamarslockandkey.com

Larson's Locksmith & Security Inc - (L)
1249 Noble Street
Fairbanks AK 99701
www.larsonslocksmith.com

Leak's Lock & Key - (L) \
1140 North Brindlee Parkway
Arab AL 35016
www.leakslockandkey.com

Lee's Lock And Safe - (L)
386 N El Camino Real
Encinitas CA 92024
www.leeslock.com

Lents Lock & Safe Inc. - (L)
PO Box 108/ 11 W Main St
Washington IN 47501
www.lentslock.com

Liberty Lock Shop - (L)
4002 Nasa Parkway
Seabrook TX 77586
www.libertylockshop.com

Lightning Lock & Key LLC - (L)
P.O. Box 10803
Truckee CA 96162
www.lightninglockandkey.com

Livonia Lock & Key - (L)
33861 Five Mile Road
Livonia MI 48154
www.livonialock.com

LKMAN Inc DBA Chucks Lock & Safe - (L)
3851 8th Ave.
Wisconsin Dells WI 53965
www.chuckslockandsafe.com

STOP THE INTRUDER™ | KNOWLEDGE IS THE BEST PROTECTION™

Local Locksmith - (L)
995 W. 4th Street Suite G
Benson AZ 85602
www.locallocksmithaz.com

Lock Doc Inc - (L)
3506 W Loop 281 Ste. 101
Longview TX 75604
www.locksmithlongview.com/index.htm

Lock Doc LLC - (L)
P.O. BOX 654
Kalamazoo MI 49004
www.mylockdoc.com

Lock Doctor Inc - (L)
95 Peachtree Industrial Blvd
Sugar Hill GA 30518
www.lockdoctorinc.com

Lock Specialties - (L)
1914 Highland Ave
Las Vegas NV 89102
www.lasvegascarkeys.com

Lock Specialty - (L)
1780 E. Poplar Road
Columbia City IN 46725
www.lockspecialty.com

Lock Stock & Barrel Inc - (L)
PO Box 939
Portland ME 4104
www.lockstock.net

Lockaid USA LLC - (L)
4350 East Palm Lane
Phoenix AZ 85008
www.locksmith-lockaid.com

Lockguard - (L)
4512 Williston Rd
Minneapolis MN 55345
www.lockguard.com

Lockmaster Key & Safe - (L)
1355 Logan Ave
Youngstown OH 44505
www.lockmasterkeyandsafe.com

LOCKMASTER SECURITY SERVICES INC. - (L)
1435 N. Jones Blvd.
Las Vegas NV 89108
www.lockmasterlv.com

Lockout Express LLC - (L)
748 U.S. Highway 41 Unit A
Schererville IN 46375
www.lockoutexpress.net/index.htm

Lockout Specialists of Hawaii - (L)
2110 Kamehameha Ave
Honolulu HI 96822
www.lockoutspec.com

LockPro Locksmith LLC - (L)
2973 River Road
Elberton GA 30635
www.lockprolocksmith.com

Locks and Unlocks Inc - (L)
PO Box 59
Stoughton WI 53589
www.locksandunlocks.com

LockSafe Systems - (L)
326 Walnut St
Fort Collins CO 80524
www.locksafesystems.com

Locksmith Charley - (L)
4024 N. 84Th Lane
Phoenix AZ 85037
www.locksmithcharley.com

Locksmith Services - (L)
Duluth MN 55810
www.keys4locks.com

STOP THE INTRUDER™ | KNOWLEDGE IS THE BEST PROTECTION™

Locksmith Services of Tyler - (L)
241 S. Broadway Ave
Tyler TX 75702
www.locksmithservicesoftyler.com

Locksmith-USA - (L)
8941 Atlanta Ave # 155
Huntingdon Beach CA 92646
www.locksmith-usa.com

Lockworks Unlimited - (L)
2671 El Camino Real
Redwood City CA 94061
www.lockworksunlimited.com

LogicMark - (A)
8625 Hampton Way
Fairfax Station VA 22039
www.logicmarksecurity.com

Loss Prevention Services Inc. - (A)
2511 Neudork Rd. Suite E
Clemmons NC 27012
www.lpssecurity.com

Lowitt Alarms & Security Systems Inc. - (A)
25 Bethpage Rd.
Hicksville NY 11801
www.lowittalarms.com

Lubbock Lock & Key Inc - (L)
2434 34Th St
Lubbock TX 79411
www.lubbocklockandkey.com

Mace CSSS - (A)
401 W. Lincoln Ave. #101
Anaheim CA 92805
www.macecs.com

Maffey's Security Group - (L)
1172 E Grand St
Elizabeth NJ 7201
www.maffeys.com

Mainline Security - (L)
617 7Th Street
San Francisco CA 94103
www.mainline-security.com

Marie's Lock & Safe Inc - (L)
9608 Rogers Avenue
Fort Smith AR 72903
www.marieslockandsafe.com

Mark's Locksmith - (L)
13470 SW Allen Blvd
Beaverton OR 97005
www.markslocksmith.com

MARKS USA - (A)
365 Bayview Avenue
Amityville NY 11701
www.marksusa.com

Marshall Locksmith Svc Inc - (L)
4205 Poole Road
Poole Road NC 27610
www.marshallslocks.com

Martin Lock & Safe Co - (L)
26072 Merit Circle Suite 108
Laguna Hills CA 92653
www.martinlock.com

Marx Locksmith Service Inc. - (L)
12821 S. Saginaw St D-17
Grand Blanc MI 48439
www.marxlocksmith.com

Maryon's Locksmiths Co Inc - (L)
14800 Main Street
Upper Marlboro MD 20772
www.maryonslock.com

MAS - (A)
2955 Red Hill Ave.
Suite 100
Costa Meda CA 92626
www.utcfssecurityproducts.com

STOP THE INTRUDER™ | KNOWLEDGE IS THE BEST PROTECTION™

Matson Alarm Co. Inc - (A)
8401 N. Fresno St.
Fresno CA 93720
www.matsonalarm.com

May Hardware - (L)
809 N 3rd Street
McCall ID 83638
www.mayhardware.com

McCumber Locksmith Shop - (L)
1026 Alger Ave
Cody WY 82414
www.mccumberlocksmith.com

McGuire Lock & Safe - (L)
4800 NE Vivion Rd
PO Box 25373
Kansas City MO 64119
www.mcguirelock.com

Merchants Alarm Systems Inc. - (A)
203 Paterson Ave.
Wallington NJ 7057
www.merchantsalarm.com

Mercury Lock & Safe - (L)
10893 N Scottsdale Rd
Scottsdale AZ 85254
www.mercurylock.com

Metro Lock Service Inc - (L)
10209 North 35th Avenue
Phoenix AZ 85051
www.metrolockandsafe.com

Michiana Lock & Key Inc - (L)
621 East Jefferson Blvd.
South Bend IN 46617
www.michianalock.com

Micro Key Solutions - (A)
1631 East Vine Street
Kissimmee FL 34744
www.microkey.com/microkey

MID AMERICA LOCKSMITH - (L)
9421 Pflumm Rd. #100
Lenexa KS 66215
www.midamlockkc.com

Mid Valley Lock & Key - (L)
26873 Sierra Hwy #245
Santa Clarita CA 91321
www.midvalleylocknkey.com

Mid-State Lock & Key - (L)
104 Teelia Dr.
Old Hickory TN 37138
www.midstatelock.com

Midstate Security Company - (A)
3495 Viaduct SW
Grandville MI 49418
www.midstatesecurity.com

Midwest Alarm Co. Inc. - (A)
2300 South Dakota Ave.
Sioux Falls SD 57105
www.midwestalarm.com

Millbrae Lock - (L)
311 El Camino Real
Millbrae CA 94030
www.millbraelock.com

Miller Protective Service Inc. - (A)
1203 Ridgeway Blvd.
Suite 202
Memphis TN 38119
www.millerprotective.com

Monitronics International Inc. - (A)
P.O. Box 814530
Dallas TX 75381
www.monitronics.com

Montgomery Lock & Key - (L)
131 Eastdale Rd. South
Montgomery AL 36117
www.montgomerylockandkey.com

STOP THE INTRUDER™ | KNOWLEDGE IS THE BEST PROTECTION™

Moon Security Services Inc. - (A)
515 W. Clark
Pasco WA 99301
www.moonsecurity.com

Moss Lock and Key - (L)
9266 E. Lobo Ave.
Mesa AZ 85209
www.agentlocksmith.com

Muenzer's Inc - (L)
221 5th Street
Hollister CA 95023
www.muenzers.com

Murphy's Lock & Key - (L)
Greenwood IN 46143
www.murphyslockandkey.com

Napco Security Technologies - (A)
333 Bayview Ave.
Amityville NY 11701
www.napcosecurity.com

Nason's Lock & Safe Inc - (L)
2418 Saviers Rd
Oxnard CA 93033
www.nasonslock.com

National Monitoring Center - (A)
26800 Aliso Viejo Parkway
Suite 250
Aliso Viejo CA 92556
www.nmccentral.com

Nationwide Central Station Monitoring Corp. - (A)
P.O. Box 7297
Freeport NY 11520
www.nationwidedigital.com

Neff's Safe Lock & Security Inc - (L)
1039 N Christian St
Lancaster PA 17602
www.askyourlocksmith.com

New Hampshire Safe & Lock - (L)
78 Northeastern Blvd. #3
Nashua NH 3062
www.nhsafeandlock.com

NEXgeneration Central - (A)
400 Reservoir Ave.
Suite LL-GH
Providence RI 2907
www.nexgenerationcentral.com

North Carolina Locksmith Inc - (L)
8107 Keating Ct.
Oak Ridge NC 27310
www.nclocksmithinc.com

Northwest Alarm Monitoring - (A)
1743 1st St Ave. South Suite 201
Seattle WA 98134
www.nwalarm.discware.org/services.html

Omega Locksmith - (L)
4329 WEST 26TH STREET
Chicago IL 60623
www.omegalocksmith.com

OneTel - (A)
343 West 400 South Suite 110
Salt Lake City UT 84101
www.onetelone.com

Pacific Alarm Systems Inc. - (A)
4444 S. Sepulveda Blvd.
Culver City CA 90230
www.pacificalarms.com

Pacific Lock & Safe - (L)
2290 Alahao Pl. #201
Honolulu HI 96819
www.pacificlock.net

STOP THE INTRUDER™ | KNOWLEDGE IS THE BEST PROTECTION™

Panhandle Alarm & Telephone - (A)
10 Industrial Blvd.
Pensacola FL 32503
www.panhandlesystems.com

Paul's Lock Service - (L)
4009 East 17th Street
Tucson AZ 85711
www.paulslockservice.com/index.htm

Peak Alarm Co. Inc. - (A)
1534 S. Gladiola St.
Salt Lake City UT 84104
www.peakalarm.com

Peifer Safe & Lock - (L)
5287 Knight Arnold Rd
Memphis TN 38118
www.peiferlock.com

Per Mar Security Service - (A) Per Mar Centre;
1910 E. Kimberly Rd.;
P.O. Box 4227
Davenport IA 52808
www.permarsecurity.com

Peterson Lock & Key - (L)
608 Frisco St
Monett MO 65708
www.petersonlockandkey.com

Pinnacle Lock and Safe - (L)
7755 E Redfield Rd.
Scottsdale AZ 85260
www.pinnaclelock.com

Plainfield Lock Techs - (L)
14730 S Naperville Rd
Plainfield IL 60544
www.plainfieldlocktechs.com

Plant City Lock & Key - (L)
1002 South Collins Street
Plant City FL 33566
www.plantcitylock.com

Pop A Lock of Las Vegas - (L)
6280 S Valley View Ste 102
Las Vegas NV 89118
www.popalocklv.com

Pop A Lock of New Orleans - (L)
4300 South I-10 Service Rd Suite P
Metarie LA 70001
www.popalock.com

Pop-A-Lock - (L)
4142 Stanton-Ogletown Rd
Newark DE 19713
www.popalock.com/franchise/wilmington_de_locksmith.php

Pop-a-Lock - (L)
425 N Claiborne Ave
New Orleans LA 70112
www.popalocknola.com

Pop-A-Lock / Northshore Inc. - (L)
P.O. Box 2887 Sidell LA 70459
www.popalock.com/franchise/slidell_la_locksmith.php

Pop-A-Lock Of Honolulu - (L)
3133 Waialae Avenue #3721
Honolulu HI 96816
www.popalock.com/franchise/honolulu_hi_locksmith.php

Pop-A-Lock Of Milwaukee - (L)
544 E. Ogden Ave
Suite 700-382
Milwaukee WI 53202
www.popalock.com/franchise/milwaukee_wi_locksmith.php

Pop-a-Lock Of Phoenix - (L)
5115 N. Dysart Rd Ste 202 #609
Litchfield Park AZ 85340
www.popalock.com/franchise/
maricopa_county_az_locksmith.php

Pop-A-Lock Of Portland - (L)
2848 NE Everett St
Portland OR 97232
www.popalockportlandor.com

Pop-A-Lock Of Tampa - (L)
405 S Dale Mabry Hwy. Ste 383
Tampa FL 33609
www.popalocktampafl.com

POP-A-LOCK of Upstate S.C. - (L)
367 S. Pine Street
Spartanburg SC 29302
www.popalock.com/franchise/
upstate_sc_locksmith.php

Pop-A-Lock Of Utah - (L)
2467 Fairview Rd
American Falls ID 83211
www.popalock.com/franchise/
idaho_falls_id_locksmith.php

Post Alarm Systems Inc. - (A)
P.O. Box 60051
47 East Joseph St.
Arcadia CA 91006
www.postalarm.com

Potter Electric Signal Co. - (A)
5757 Phantom Drive
Suite 125 St.Louis MO 63042
www.pottersignal.com

Precision Lock & Key - (L)
15 Golf Tee Lane
Maryville MO 4468
www.precisionlockandkey.com

Precision Locksmith - (L)
25 Syracuse Lane
Covington GA 30016
www.precision-locksmith.com

Precision Locksmith Co. LLC. - (L)
3211 Peoples Drive Suite 120
Harrisonburg VA 22801
www.precisionlocksmithco.com

Precision Locksmith Service - (L)
10345 SW Canyon Rd
Beaverton OR 97005
www.precisionlocksmith.com

Premier Lock and Security - (L)
Grand Blanc MI 48439
www.premierlockandsecurity.com

Premier Security Svcs - (L)
7931 S Broadway 323
Littleton CO 80122
www.premiersecuritysvcs.com

Prestige Locksmith - (L)
1287 N. Fairfield Road
Beavercreek OH 45432
www.prestigelocksmith.com

Pride Locksmith - (L)
321 Chestnut Street North
Attleboro MA 2760
https://www.pridelocksmith.com

Protec U Corp - (L)
200 South Main Street
Waynesville NC 28786
www.protec-u.com

Protection One Security Solutions - (A)
1267 Windham Parkway
Romeoville IL 60446
www.protection1.com

STOP THE INTRUDER™ | KNOWLEDGE IS THE BEST PROTECTION™

Quick Response Monitoring Alarm Center - (A)
4734 Spring Rd.
Cleveland OH 44131
www.quickresponse.net

RAC Locksmith Services LLC - (L)
PO Box 3015
Vancouver WA 98668
www.raclocksmithservices.com

Racine's Locksmithing & Security - (L)
408 N. Santa Fe Ave.
Peublo CO 81003
www.keyalarms.com

Rackliffe Lock & Safe - (L)
P. O. Box 331
Trumbull CT 6611
www.rackliffelock.com

Rapid Response Monitoring Services Inc. - (A)
400 West Division St.
Syracuse NY 13204
www.rrms.com/#home

Ray's Lock & Key Service Inc - (L)
85-791 Farrington Highway
Waianae HI 96792
www.rayslockandkey.com

RBS Citizens NA - (A)
28 State Street
15th Floor - MS 1510
Boston MA 2109
www.citizensbank.com

Red Rock Lock - (L)
PO Box 2931
Sedone AZ 86339
www.redrocklock.net

Redwire - (A)
1136 Thomasville Rd.
Tallahassee FL 32303
www.redwireus.com

Reed's Lock & Access Control Systems Inc - (L)
700 E. Main St.
Annville PA 17003
www.reedslock.com

Response Center USA - (A)
11235 Gordon Rd.
Suite 102
San Antonio TX 78216
www.rc-usa.com

RFI Security Inc. - (A)
360 Turtle Creek Court
San Jose CA 95125
www.rfi.com

Rhode's Lock & Glass Inc. - (L)
39 NE 77th Ave
Fridley MN 55432
www.rhodeslockandglass.com

Richmond Alarm - (A)
14121 Justice Road
Midlothian VA 23113
www.richmondalarm.com

Rick's Locksmithing - (L)
394 N Main St
Youngstown OH 44514
www.rickslock.com

Rite Lock & Safe - (L)
3508 Dempster
Skokie IL 60076
www.ritelocksmith.com

STOP THE INTRUDER™ | KNOWLEDGE IS THE BEST PROTECTION™

Roadrunner Lock & Safe - (L)
4444 E Grant Rd.
Tucson AZ 85712
www.roadrunnerlock.com

Robblee's Total Security Inc. - (L)
751 Tacoma Ave S.
Tacoma WA 98402
www.robblees.com

Robert's Lock - (L)
424 Main Street
Malvern AR 72104
www.robertslocks.com

Rocky Mountain Security Services Inc. - (A)
2171 S. Grape St.
Denver CO 80222
www.rmssi.com

Romans Lock Service - (L)
www.romanslock.com

RSI Video Technologies - (A)
1375 Willow Lake Blvd. #103
Vadnais Heights MN 55110
www.videofied.com

Safe Systems Inc. - (A)
421 S. Pierce Ave.
Louisville CO 80027
www.safe-systems.com

Safeco Security Inc - (L)
2636 W. Townley Avenue
Phoenix AZ 85021
www.safecosecurity.com/services.html

Safeguard Security and Communications Inc. - (A)
8454 N. 90th Street
Scottsdale AZ 85258
www.safeguard.us

Safety Systems Inc. - (A)
P.O. Box 1079
Jackson MI 49204
www.safetysystemsinc.net

Salz Lock & Safe - (L)
3012 Waialae Ave #3
Honolulu HI 96816
www.salzlock.com

Saylor Safe & Lock Inc - (L)
11035 Cypress N Houston
Houston TX 77065
www.saylorsafe.com

Schoell's Lock & Safe Service - (L)
PO Box 175
Confluence PA 15424
www.schoellslockandsafe.com

SDA Security - (A)
2054 State St.
San Diego CA 92101
www.sdasecurity.com

Seacoast Security Inc. - (A)
290 West
West Rockport ME 4865
www.seacoastsecurity.com

Securall Monitoring Corp. - (A)
206 Washington Dr.
Brick NJ 8724
www.securall.com

Secure Global Solutions LLC - (A)
41 Corporate Park Drive
Suite 200
Irvine CA 92606
www.secglobe.net/wiki

Security Alarm Corporation - (A)
17776 Toledo Blade Blvd.
Port Charlotte FL 33948
www.securityalarmcorp.com

STOP THE INTRUDER™ | KNOWLEDGE IS THE BEST PROTECTION™

Security Alarm Monitoring Inc. - (A)
254 Fairview Rd.
Woodlyn PA 19094
www.electronicsecuritycorp.com

Security Central-North Carolina - (A)
316 Security Dr.
Statesville NC 28677
www.security-central.com

Security Central Inc. - (A)
7100 S. Clinton St.
Suite 200
Centennial CO 80112
www.securitycentralinc.com

Security Concepts Inc - (L)
3478 E. Jamison Ave.
Centennial CO 80122
www.keycuff.com

Security Equipment Inc. - (A)
13505 C St.
Omaha NE 68144
www.sei-security.com

Security Monitoring Technologies - (A)
1009 S. Claremont St.
San Mateo CA 94402
www.calsecurity.com/index.html

Security Network of America - (A)
714 S. Bennett Street
Southern Pines NC 28387
www.snaonline.com

Security Networks Monitoring Center - (A)
3223 Commerce Place Suite 101
West Palm Beach FL 33407
www.securitynetworks.net/index.html

Security Partners LLC - (A)
241 N Plum St.
Lancaster PA 17602
www.securitypartners.com

Security Response Services - (A)
9036 Grand Ave. South
Bloomington MN 55420
www.floydtotalsecurity.com

Security Service Company - (A)
110 West Arch Street
Suite 200
Fleetwood PA 19522
www.sscsince73.com

Security Shop - (L)
1605 E. 55th St.
Chicago IL 60615
www.securityshopinc.com

Security Solutions Inc. - (A)
12 Oakwood Ave.
Norwalk CT 6850
www.securitysolutionsinc.com

SedonaOffice - (A)
549 E. Washington Street
Chagrin Falls OH 44022
www.sedonaoffice.com

Sellers Lock & Key - (L)
303 5th Place NW
Austin MN 55912
www.sellerslock.com

Sentry Watch Inc. - (A)
1705 Holbrook St.
Greensboro NC 27403
www.sentrywatch.com

SentryNet - (A)
517 N. Baylen St.
Pensacola FL 32501
www.sentrynet.com

STOP THE INTRUDER™ | KNOWLEDGE IS THE BEST PROTECTION™

Shamrock Brothers Lock & Safe - (L)
PO Box 6045
Goodyear AZ 85338
www.shamrockbros.com

Shearer Locksmith - (L)
5450 Derry Street
Harrisburg PA 17111
www.shearerlocksmith.com

Shorty Wallin Lock & Security - (L)
1971 E. Pembroke Ave.
Hampton VA 23663
www.shortywallin.com

Siemens Industry Inc. - (A)
8600 N. Royal Lane
Suite 100
Irving TX 75063
www.siemens.com/entry/cc/en

Silent Knight - (A)
7550 Meridian Circle North
Suite 100
Maple Grove MN 55369
www.silentknight.com

Silverton Lock & Key LLC - (L)
PO Box 1024
Bedford Park IL 60499
www.silvertonlock.com

SMG Security Systems Inc - (A)
120 King Street
Elk Grove IL 60007
www.smgsecurity.com

Sourcetek - (A)
1181 S. Rogers Circle
Suite 21
Boca Raton FL 33487
www.sotekusa.com

South Penn Lock & Safe Co - (L)
936 N Providence Rd
Media PA 19063
www.southpennlock.com

South Side Lock & Key - (L)
5818 Wilmington Pike #188
Dayton OH 45459
www.southsidelockandkey.com

Southington Security Services - (L)
2211 Meriden-Waterbury Turnpike
Marion CT 6444
www.southingtonsecurity.com

Speco Technologies - (A)
200 New Hwy.
Amityville NY 11701
www.specotech.com

Stanley Convergent Security Solutions - (A)
55 Shuman Boulevard
Suite 900
Naperville IL 60563
www.stanleysecuritysolutions.com

Stanley Security Solutions - (L)
www.stanleysecuritysolutions.com

State-Wide Lock & Safe - (L)
7500 E Colfax Ave
Denver CO 80220
www.wemovesafes.com

Statewide Central Station - (A)
2047 Victory Boulevard
Staten Island NY 10314
www.statewidecs.com

Sterling Investigative Service - (L)
84 Moorage Ave
Bayville NJ 8721
www.sterlingis.com

STOP THE INTRUDER™ | KNOWLEDGE IS THE BEST PROTECTION™

Steve's Lock Out - (L)
1806 Main Street
Parsons KS 67357
www.steveslockout.com

Strauss Security Solutions - (L)
4663 121st Street
Urbandale IA 50323
www.strausslock.com

Superior Central Station Inc. - (A)
604 Ash Ave.
McAllen TX 78501
www.superiorcentral.com

Supreme Security Systems - (A)
1565 Union Ave.
Union Avenue NJ 7083
www.supremealarm.com

Sure Lock And Key - (L)
11019 Manchester Rd
St. Louis MO 63122
www.surelockandkey.net

Sure-Fit Security - (L)
8213 Fenton St.
Silver Spring MD 20910
www.surefitsecurity.com

Sureview Systems - (A)
400 North Ashley Drive
Suite 2600
Tampa FL 33602
www.sureviewsystems.com

SVI Systems Inc. - (A)
290 Florida St.
Stuart FL 34994
www.svi-systems.com

System Sensor - (A)
3825 Ohio Ave. St.
Charles IL 60174
www.systemsensor.com

TCB Locksmith Inc. - (L)
712 South US Hwy 27
Minneola FL 34715
www.locks-locksmith.com

Tebarco Door & Metal Services Inc - (L)
1905 Grassland Parkway
Alpharetta GA 30004
www.tebarcodoor.com

Telguard - (A)
2727 Paces Ferry Rd. SE
Suite 1-800
Atlanta GA 30339
www.telguard.com

Territorial Key Lock & Safe Inc - (L)
1005 St. Francis Suite 109
Santa Fe NM 87501
www.territorialsafe.com

The CMOOR Group - (A)
209 Townepark Circle
Suite 200
Louisville KY 40243
www.cmoor.com

The Flying Locksmiths Inc - (L)
1115 N Main St
Randolph MA 2368
www.flyinglocksmiths.com

The Key Guy - (L)
1684 Ala Moana Blvd 253
Honolulu HI 96815
www.keyguyhawaii.com

The Key Shop Inc - (L)
1000 Taylor St
Columbia SC 29201
www.keyshopinc.com

STOP THE INTRUDER™ | KNOWLEDGE IS THE BEST PROTECTION™

The Lock Doctor Inc - (L)
433 S Main St
Phillipsburg NJ 8865
www.thelockdoctor.com

The Locke Shoppe LLC - (L)
2062 E. Southern Ave.
Tempe AZ 85282
www.thelockeshoppe.com

The Locksmith Express - (L)
450 Central Ave
Dubuque IA 52001
www.locksmithexpress.com

The LockWorks - (L)
3619 Rocky Glade Rd
Eagleville TN 37060
www.thelockworks-tn.com

The Protection Bureau - (A)
197 Philips Dr.
Exton PA 19341
www.protectionbureau.com

The Safe House - (L)
6224 N. Park Meadow Way #305
Boise ID 83713
www.thesafehouse.info

Time Warner Cable Security - (A)
6400 Fly Rd.
Syracuse NY 13057
www.timewarnercable.com/east/learn/intelligenthome

Tom's Lock Service - (L)
215 E 3rd St
Winona MN 55987
www.tomslockservice.com

Top Security Locksmiths Inc. - (L)
2401 Bridge Ave.
Point Pleasant NJ 8742
www.topsecuritylocksmiths.com

Total Monitoring Service Inc. - (A)
2440 Glendale Lane
Sacramento CA 95825
www.tmscentral.com

Total Security Locksmith - (L)
300 Yoakum pkwy
Alexandria VA 22304
www.total-security-va.com

Towne Monitoring Service LP - (A)
208 N. Main St.
Souderton PA 18964
www.towneanswering.com

Trans-Alarm Inc. - (A)
500 East Travelers Trail
Burnsville MN 55337
www.transalarm.com

Tri-Ed Distribution - (A)
135 Crossways Park Drive Suite 101
Woodbury NY 11797
www.tri-ed.com

Tri-State Lock - (L)
8347 Dixie Highway
Florence KY 41042
www.tri-statelock.com

Troy's Lockshop - (L)
5220 W Troy AVE
Indianapolis IN 46241
www.123locksmith.com

Tru-Lock & Security Inc - (L)
2080 Traux Blvd Eau Claire WI 54703
www.tru-lock.com

Tucson Mobile Lock & Key - (L)
5425 E. Broadway # 314
Tucson AZ 85747
www.tucsonmobilelocksmith.com

STOP THE INTRUDER™ | KNOWLEDGE IS THE BEST PROTECTION™

Tullahoma Lock & Key Service - (L)
P.O Box 1898
Tullahoma TN 37388
www.tullahomalock.com

United Central Control - (A)
8415 Datapoint Dr. Suite 500
San Antonio TX 78229
www.teamucc.com

United D&W Central Station (A)
205 W. Houston Street
New York NY 10014
www.weprotect.com

United Monitoring Services - (A)
7521 Veterans Parkway
Columbus GA 31909
www.unitedmonitoring.com

Universal Atlantic Systems Inc. (UAS) - (A)
700 Abbott Dr.
Broomall PA 19008
www.uas.com

Universal Monitoring - (A)
1330 Sharon Road West
Charlotte NC 28210
www.universalmonitoring.com

Universal Security Monitoring - (A)
4701 SW 34th St.
Gainesville FL 32608
www.universalmonitoring.net

University Lock Co Inc - (L)
1031 W University Dr
Tempe AZ 85281
www.ulssecurity.com

Uplink Inc. - (A)
1600 Parkwood Circle Suite 500
Atlanta GA 30339
www.uplink.com

Urich Lock 360 Security - (L)
16540 W. Rogers Dr
New Berlin WI 53151
www.urichlock.com

USA Central Station Alarm - (A)
28 Willett Ave.
Port Chester NY 10573
www.usacentralstation.com

Valley Lock & Safe - (L)
68100 Ramon Rd Suite C-11
Cathedral City CA 92234
www.valleylock.com

Vector Security - (A)
3400 McKnight East Dr.
Pittsburgh PA 15237
www.vectorsecurity.com

Verifier Capital - (A)
7280 W. Palmetto Park Rd.
Suite 306
Boca Raton FL 33433
www.verifiercapital.com

Vigilante Security Inc./Michigan Monitoring Service - (A)
2681 Industrial Row Drive
Troy MI 48084
www.michmon.com

VirSec - (A)
1300 Combermere Drive Dr.
Troy MI 48083
www.huffmaster.com

Vision Monitoring/World Wide Security - (A)
One Commercial Avenue
Garden City NY 11530
www.visionmonitoring.com

STOP THE INTRUDER™ | KNOWLEDGE IS THE BEST PROTECTION™

Visonic Inc. - (A)
65 West Dudley Town Rd.
Bloomfield CT 6002
www.visonic.com

Vivint - (A)
4931 North 300 West
Provo UT 84604
www.vivint.com

VRI (The Care Center) - (A)
1400 Commerce Center Drive
Franklin OH 45005
www.monitoringcare.com

W C & D Locksmith - (L)
71 Nunn Blvd
Cadiz KY 42211
www.wcdlocksmith.com

Washington Alarm Inc. - (A)
1253 S. Jackson
Seattle WA 98144
www.washingtonalarm.com

Watchlight Corporation - (A)
111 S. Marshall Ave.
El Cajon CA 92020
www.watchlight.com

Watson Security - (L)
2106 3rd Avenue
Seattle WA 98121
www.watsonsecurity.com

Wayne Alarm Systems Inc. - (A)
424 Essex St.
Lynn MA 1902
www.waynealarm.com

Westec Intelligent Surveillance - (A)
6340 International Parkway
Suite 100
Plano TX 75093
www.westec.net

WH International Response - (A)
6800 Electric Dr.
Rockford MN 55373
www.whirc.com

Williams and Hannon - (A)
493 McLaws Circle Suite 2
Williamsburg VA 23185
www.williamshannonlaw.com

Wise Locksmith - (L)
7018 NE Bothwell Way Ste A
Kenmore WA 98028
www.wiselocks.com

Wizard Lock & Safe Co - (L)
218 North Prince St.
Lancaster PA 17603
www.wizardlock.com

WM Security Services - (A)
17340 Chanute Rd.
Houston TX 77032
www.wm.com/index.jsp

Woodstock Lock And Safe Inc. - (L)
1440-1 Rt 28 PO Box 243
West Hurley NY 12491
www.woodstocklock.com

Xtralis Inc - (A)
700 Longwater Drive
Norwell MA 2601
www.xtralis.com

Zizza Lock & Safe LLC - (L)
8 Frontier Way
Colebrook NH 3576
www.zizzalock.com

STOP THE INTRUDER™ | KNOWLEDGE IS THE BEST PROTECTION™

References

National Rifle Association - www.nra.org

Georgia Carry - www.georgiacarry.org

www.ingramcontent.com/pod-product-compliance
Lightning Source LLC
Chambersburg PA
CBHW052054230426
43671CB00011B/1899